# Financial Statements

Felix I. Lessambo

# Financial Statements

## Analysis and Reporting

Felix I. Lessambo
Central Connecticut State University
New Britain, CT, USA

ISBN 978-3-319-99983-8      ISBN 978-3-319-99984-5   (eBook)
https://doi.org/10.1007/978-3-319-99984-5

Library of Congress Control Number: 2018957071

Cover credit: MirageC/Getty Images
Cover design by Ran Shauli

This Palgrave Macmillan imprint is published by the registered company Springer Nature
Switzerland AG
The registered company address is: Gewerbestrasse 11, 6330 Cham, Switzerland

# ACKNOWLEDGEMENTS

Writing a book is always a challenge. But writing a book on *Financial Statements: Analysis and Reporting*, geared to M.B.A. students, a more daring intellectual exercise for twofold reasons: (i) because of the hard choice of topics to cover, and (ii) financial analysis is part science and part art.

I would like to express my gratitude to those who motivated me all along the project, knowing my dedication to the subject, and thought I am more than able to complete this project: Dr. Gordon Marsha, Dr. Linda Sama, Fouad Sayegh, Esq., Jerry Izouele.

Several good friends provided me with needed guidance and materials to complete this book, while others took from their busiest time to review and comb the manuscript: Reverend Pastor Roland Dalo, Aline Kabongo.

# CONTENTS

**Part I    Overview of Financial Statements and the Statement of Financial Position**

1    Overview of Financial Statements                                        3
    1.1    General                                                          3
    1.2    The International Accounting Standard Board: IFRS                4
    1.3    European Financial Reporting Advisory Group
           (EFRAG)                                                          4
    1.4    The USA: The FASB                                                5
    1.5    The UK: Financial Reporting Council (FRC)                        9
    1.6    Japan: The Accounting Standard Board of Japan                   11
    1.7    Australia: The Australian Accounting Standard
           Board                                                          13
    1.8    New Zealand: The New Zealand Accounting
           Standards Board (NZASB)                                        15
    1.9    India: The Council of the Institute of Chartered
           Accountants of India (ICAI)                                    15
    1.10   China: Accounting Standard for Business Enterprises            16
    1.11   The Financial Statement Materials                              16
           1.11.1    The Proxy Statement                                  17
           1.11.2    The Management Discussion & Analysis
                     (MD&A)                                               17

1.12    Interim Statements and Subsequent & Adjusting
        Events                                              18
        1.12.1    Interim Financial Statements              18
        1.12.2    Subsequent Events                         18
        1.12.3    Adjusting Events                          18
1.13    Users of Financial Statements                       21

2  Cash and Cash Equivalents                                23
   2.1    General                                           23
   2.2    Cash and Cash Equivalents                         24
          2.2.1    Bank Reconciliation                      25
          2.2.2    Bank Overdraft                           27
          2.2.3    Petty Cash                               29
   2.3    Marketable Equity Securities and Fair Value
          Measurement                                       30
   2.4    Accounting for Financial Instruments              32
   2.5    Accounting for Derivatives                        35
   2.6    Accounting for Hedging                            37

3  Short-Term Assets: Inventories                           41
   3.1    General                                           41
   3.2    Inventory Methods                                 42
          3.2.1    The Perpetual Inventory System           42
          3.2.2    The Periodic Inventory System            43
   3.3    Ownership Issues                                  46
   3.4    Valuation of Inventory                            46
   3.5    The LIFO Reserve                                  47
   3.6    LIFO Liquidation                                  48
   3.7    Comprehensive Example                             49
   3.8    Restrictions on the Use of LIFO                   51

4  Account Receivables                                      53
   4.1    General                                           53
   4.2    Cash Discount on Sales                            54
          4.2.1    The Gross Method                         54
          4.2.2    The Net Method                           54
   4.3    Bad Debts Concept                                 55
          4.3.1    Rebates                                  55

| | | |
|---|---|---|
| 4.3.2 | Doubtful Accounts | 56 |
| 4.3.3 | Accounting for Bad Debts | 56 |
| 4.4 | Accounts Receivable Aging Method | 57 |
| 4.5 | Assignment of Accounts Receivable | 58 |
| 4.6 | Factoring of Accounts Receivable | 60 |
| 4.6.1 | Recourse vs Non-recourse Factoring | 60 |
| 4.6.2 | Factoring vs Loan | 60 |
| 4.6.3 | Factoring vs Assignment of Receivables | 62 |
| 4.7 | Securitization of Receivables | 63 |
| 4.7.1 | Sale Accounting Criteria | 63 |
| 4.7.2 | Secured Borrowing | 66 |
| 4.8 | Receivables—Troubled Debt Restructurings by Creditors | 66 |

**5  Prepaid Expenses, Unearned Income, and Other Current Assets** — 69
| | | |
|---|---|---|
| 5.1 | General | 69 |
| 5.2 | Prepaid Expenses | 69 |
| 5.3 | Unearned Income | 72 |
| 5.4 | Other Current Assets | 73 |

**6  Short-Term Liabilities and Working Capital** — 75
| | | |
|---|---|---|
| 6.1 | General | 75 |
| 6.2 | Accounts Payable | 75 |
| 6.3 | Notes Payable | 76 |
| 6.4 | Current Maturities of Long-Term Debt | 77 |
| 6.5 | Other Current Liabilities | 77 |
| 6.6 | Working Capital | 77 |
| 6.6.1 | Determinants of Working Capital | 78 |
| 6.6.2 | Financing of Working Capital | 78 |
| 6.6.3 | Computation of Working Capital: Example | 79 |

**7  Long-Term Assets: Plant, Property, and Equipment** — 81
| | | |
|---|---|---|
| 7.1 | General | 81 |
| 7.2 | Property, Plant, and Equipment | 81 |
| 7.2.1 | Acquisition of Property, Plant, and Equipment | 82 |
| 7.2.2 | Cost of Land | 83 |

| | | |
|---|---|---|
| 7.2.3 | Cost of Buildings | 84 |
| 7.2.4 | Cost of Equipment | 84 |
| 7.3 | Valuation of Property, Plant, and Equipment | 84 |
| 7.4 | Amortization, Depreciation, and Depletion | 85 |
| 7.4.1 | Straight-Line Method of Depreciation | 85 |
| 7.4.2 | Declining Balance Method of Depreciation | 86 |
| 7.4.3 | Double Declining Balance Depreciation Method | 87 |
| 7.4.4 | Units of Production Method of Depreciation | 88 |
| 7.4.5 | Sum of the Years' Digits Method of Depreciation | 89 |
| 7.5 | Disposition of Property, Plant, and Equipment | 91 |
| 7.5.1 | Sale of Plant Assets | 91 |
| 7.5.2 | Involuntary Conversion | 91 |
| 7.5.3 | Miscellaneous Problems | 92 |

| | | |
|---|---|---|
| **8** | **Long-Term Assets: Intangibles** | **95** |
| 8.1 | General | 95 |
| 8.2 | The Goodwill | 96 |
| 8.2.1 | Goodwill Impairment | 97 |
| 8.3 | Computer Software | 101 |
| 8.3.1 | Research and Development Costs of Computer Software | 101 |
| 8.3.2 | Production Costs of Computer Software | 101 |
| 8.3.3 | Purchased Computer Software | 102 |
| 8.3.4 | Amortization of Capitalized Software Costs | 102 |
| 8.3.5 | Presentation and Disclosure of Software Costs | 103 |
| 8.3.6 | Software Purchased Before Technological Feasibility Established | 103 |
| 8.3.7 | Disclosure of Risks and Uncertainties Related to Capitalized Software Costs | 104 |

| | | |
|---|---|---|
| **9** | **Long-Term Liabilities: Leases** | **105** |
| 9.1 | General | 105 |
| 9.2 | Lease | 105 |
| 9.2.1 | Legal Definition of a Lease | 105 |
| 9.2.2 | Advantages and Disadvantages of Leasing | 107 |

9.3     Types of Leases                                            107
        9.3.1     Finance Lease                                    107
        9.3.2     Operating Lease                                  109
9.4     Sale–Leaseback                                             110
        9.4.1     Sale–Leaseback Advantages                        111
        9.4.2     Accounting Analysis                              111
9.5     Short-Term Lease                                           113
9.6     Lease Disclosure                                           114
        9.6.1     In the Balance Sheet                             114
        9.6.2     In the Statement of Cash Flows                   114

10   Long-Term Liabilities: Pension and Postretirement
     Liabilities                                                   117
     10.1    General                                               117
     10.2    Types of Pension Plans                                118
             10.2.1    Defined Contribution Plan                   118
             10.2.2    Defined Benefit Plan                        120
     10.3    Net Pension Asset/Liability                           120
     10.4    Projected Benefit Obligations                         121
     10.5    Plan Assets                                           121
     10.6    Reporting Pensions Plans on Financial Statements      122
             10.6.1    In the Statement of Income                  122
             10.6.2    In the Balance Sheet                        124
     10.7    Funded Status                                         124
     10.8    Postretirement Benefits Other Than Pensions           126

11   Shareholders' Equity                                          127
     11.1    General                                               127
     11.2    Common Stock                                          129
             11.2.1    Par Value of Common Stock                   130
             11.2.2    Stated Value of a Common Stock              130
             11.2.3    Authorized Capital                          130
             11.2.4    Issued Capital                              130
             11.2.5    Outstanding Capital                         130
     11.3    Issuance of Shares of Stock                           131
             11.3.1    Issuance of Par Value Stock                 131
             11.3.2    Issuance of No Par Stock                    132

| | | |
|---|---|---|
| 11.4 | *Issuance of Shares for Non-cash Items* | 133 |
| 11.5 | *Lump-Sum Stock Issuance* | 134 |
| 11.6 | *Treasury Stock—Cost Method* | 135 |
| 11.7 | *Treasury Stock—Par Value Method* | 136 |
| 11.8 | *Stock Dividends* | 138 |
| | *11.8.1   Small Stock Dividend* | 138 |
| | *11.8.2   Large Stock Dividend* | 138 |
| 11.9 | *Employee Stock Options* | 139 |
| | *11.9.1   Legal Understanding* | 139 |
| | *11.9.2   Statement of Financial Accounting Standard No. 123* | 140 |
| | *11.9.3   Illustration* | 141 |
| 11.10 | *Stock Splits* | 142 |
| 11.11 | *Retained Earnings* | 143 |

**Part II    The Statement of Income**

| | | |
|---|---|---|
| **12** | **Analysis of the Statement of Income** | 149 |
| 12.1 | *General* | 149 |
| 12.2 | *The Single-Step Income Statement* | 149 |
| 12.3 | *Multiple-Step Income Statement* | 150 |
| | *12.3.1   Analysis of the Multiple-Step Components* | 151 |
| | *12.3.2   Format and Example* | 154 |
| 12.4 | *Holding Equity* | 155 |
| 12.5 | *Income from Discontinued Operations* | 157 |

| | | |
|---|---|---|
| **13** | **Other Comprehensive Income** | 159 |
| 13.1 | *General* | 159 |
| 13.2 | *Presentation of the OCI* | 160 |
| 13.3 | *Accumulated OCI* | 161 |
| | *13.3.1   Foreign Currency Accounting* | 161 |
| | *13.3.2   Discontinued Operations* | 162 |
| 13.4 | *Reclassification Out of Accumulated Other Comprehensive Income* | 165 |
| | *13.4.1   Presentation on the Face of the Statement— In Net Income* | 166 |
| | *13.4.2   Presentation as a Separate Disclosure in the Notes* | 167 |

13.5    *Earnings Per Share*                                          169
    13.5.1    *The Computation of the Simple EPS*                      169
    13.5.2    *The Computation of the Diluted EPS*                     171

14   **The Sub-Statement of Retained Earnings**                       175
    14.1    *General*                                                  175
    14.2    *Steps in Preparing the Statement
            of Retained Earnings*                                      175
    14.3    *Retained Earnings Formula*                                176
    14.4    *Changes in Retained Earnings*                             177
        14.4.1    *Accounting Changes
                  and Retained Earnings*                               177
        14.4.2    *Accounting Errors and Retained Earnings*            179

15   **The Computation of the Taxable Income**                        181
    15.1    *General*                                                  181
    15.2    *Differed Taxes and Assets*                                181
        15.2.1    *Temporary Differences for Revenue
                  and Expenses*                                        182
        15.2.2    *Permanent Differences*                              184
    15.3    *Net Operating Losses*                                     185
    15.4    *Undistributed Profits of Foreign Subsidiaries*            186
    15.5    *APB 23 and Indefinitely Reinvested Earnings*              188
    15.6    *ASC 740: Accounting for Uncertainty in Income
            Taxes (Formerly FIN 48)*                                   189
    15.7    *Financial Statement Reporting*                            191
        15.7.1    *Statement Reporting*                                191
        15.7.2    *Presentation*                                       191
        15.7.3    *Disclosure*                                         191

**Part III    The Statements of Cash Flows and Financial Ratios**

16   **Analysis of the Statements of Cash Flows**                     195
    16.1    *General*                                                  195
    16.2    *Classification of Cash Flows*                             196
        16.2.1    *Cash Flows from Operating Activities*               196
        16.2.2    *Cash Flows from Investing Activities*               197
        16.2.3    *Cash Flows from Financing Activities*               198

16.3    Content and Form of the Statement of Cash Flows        200
        16.3.1    Reporting Cash Flows from Operating
                  Activities                                    200
        16.3.2    Quick Analysis of the Operating Cash Flows    203
16.4    Examples                                                203
        16.4.1    Example of Operating Cash Flows               203
        16.4.2    Example with Investing Cash Flows             204
        16.4.3    Example with Financing Cash Flow
                  Activities                                    205
16.5    Noncash Investing and Financing Activities              205

17  Financial Ratios Analysis                                   207
17.1    General                                                 207
17.2    Liquidity Measurement Ratios                            207
17.3    Solvency Ratios                                         214
17.4    Profitability Indicator Ratios                          217
17.5    Efficiency Ratios                                       223
17.6    Debt Ratios                                             227
17.7    Operating Performance Ratios                            229
17.8    Cash Flow Indicator Ratios                              232
17.9    Investment Valuation Ratios                             234
17.10   Strategic Financial Ratios                              238
17.11   Bankruptcy Ratios                                       244
        17.11.1   Working Capital/Total Assets                  244
        17.11.2   Retained Earnings/Total Assets                245
        17.11.3   Earnings Before Interest and Taxes/Total
                  Assets                                        245
        17.11.4   Market Value of Equity/Book Value
                  of Total Debt                                 246
        17.11.5   Sales/Total Assets                            246
17.12   Limitations                                             247

Part IV   Pro-Forma Financial Statements

18  Forecasting Financial Statements' Analysis                  251
18.1    General                                                 251
18.2    The Forecasted Statement of Income                      251
        18.2.1    Sales Forecasting                             252

|  |  |  |
|---|---|---|
|  | 18.2.2 *Production and COGS Forecasting* | 252 |
|  | 18.2.3 *Expenses' Forecasting* | 252 |
| 18.3 | *The Forecasted Statement of Position* | 252 |
|  | 18.3.1 *Making Assumptions* | 253 |
| 18.4 | *The Forecasted Statements of Cash Flows* | 255 |
|  | 18.4.1 *Forecasting Operating Cash Flows* | 255 |
|  | 18.4.2 *Forecasting Financing Cash Flow* | 256 |
|  | 18.4.3 *Forecasting Investing Cash Flow* | 258 |

**Part V   Consolidated Financial Statements**

**19   Foreign Currency Accounting** — 261
| | | |
|---|---|---|
| 19.1 | *General* | 261 |
| 19.2 | *Determination of the Functional Currency of the Foreign Entity* | 261 |
|  | 19.2.1 *Factors to Be Considered* | 262 |
|  | 19.2.2 *Changing the Functional Currency* | 264 |
| 19.3 | *Translation Methods* | 264 |
|  | 19.3.1 *Current/Noncurrent Method* | 264 |
|  | 19.3.2 *Monetary/Nonmonetary Method* | 265 |
|  | 19.3.3 *Temporal Method* | 265 |
|  | 19.3.4 *Current Rate Method* | 266 |
| 19.4 | *Re-measurement into the Functional Currency* | 266 |
|  | 19.4.1 *The Foreign Entity Does Not Book or Record in Functional Currency* | 267 |
|  | 19.4.2 *Highly Inflationary Economies—US GAAP* | 267 |
| 19.5 | *Hedging Balance Sheet and Forecasted Exposure* | 268 |

**20   Consolidated Financial Statements** — 269
| | | |
|---|---|---|
| 20.1 | *Overview* | 269 |
| 20.2 | *Purpose of Consolidation* | 270 |
| 20.3 | *Consolidation Methods* | 271 |
| 20.4 | *Consolidation Theories* | 272 |
|  | 20.4.1 *Parent Company Theory* | 272 |
|  | 20.4.2 *Contemporary/Entity Theory* | 272 |
|  | 20.4.3 *Traditional/Hybrid Theory* | 272 |
| 20.5 | *The Consolidation Process* | 273 |
| 20.6 | *Pushdown Accounting* | 274 |

**21    Segment and Intermediary Financial Statements**    **277**
21.1    *General*    277
21.2    *Segment Statements*    277
    21.2.1    *Reportable Segments*    278
    21.2.2    *Identification of Additional Segment*    280
    21.2.3    *Disclosure Requirements*    282
    21.2.4    *Measurement*    283
    21.2.5    *Entity-Wide Information*    286
    21.2.6    *Goodwill Considerations*    289
21.3    *Intermediary Statements*    289
    21.3.1    *Accounting Principles and Practices*    289
    21.3.2    *Revenue*    289
    21.3.3    *Costs and Expenses*    290
    21.3.4    *Costs Associated with Revenue*    290
    21.3.5    *All Other Costs and Expenses*    291
    21.3.6    *Seasonal Revenue, Costs, or Expenses*    292
    21.3.7    *Extraordinary Items, Unusual and Infrequent Items, and Disposals of Components*    293
    21.3.8    *Accounting Changes in Interim Periods*    293
    21.3.9    *Adjustments Related to Prior Interim Periods of the Current Fiscal Year*    294
    21.3.10    *Guidelines for Preparing Interim Statements*    294
    21.3.11    *SEC Materials: Regulation S-X Rule 10-01, Interim Financial Statements*    297

**22    IFRS and GAAP**    **299**
22.1    *General*    299
22.2    *Principles-Based vs Rules-Based*    300
22.3    *Selected International Accounting Standards*    301
    22.3.1    *IAS 1—Presentation of Financial Statement*    301
    22.3.2    *IAS 2—Inventories*    303
    22.3.3    *IAS 5—Non-Current Assets Held for Sale and Discontinued Operations*    303
    22.3.4    *IAS 7-Statements of Cash Flows*    304
    22.3.5    *IAS16—Leases*    307
    22.3.6    *IAS 24 Related Disclosures*    309
    22.3.7    *IAS 27—Consolidated Financial Statements*    311

22.3.8    *IAS 32, Financial Instrument—*
          *Presentation*                                    316
22.3.9    *IAS 33—Earnings Per Shares*                      318
22.3.10   *IAS 34—Interim Financial Reporting*              320


**Part VI    Case Study**

**23    Apple and Microsoft Case Study**                    331
23.1    *Industry Analysis*                                 331
23.2    *Apple*                                             332
        23.2.1    *Overview*                                332
        23.2.2    *Business Strategy*                       333
        23.2.3    *Financial Statements*                    334
23.3    *Microsoft*                                         337
        23.3.1    *Overview*                                337
        23.3.2    *Business Strategy*                       340
        23.3.3    *Microsoft Financial Statements*          340
23.4    *Financial Analysis*                                342
        23.4.1    *Common-Size Income Statement Analysis*   342
        23.4.2    *Common-Size Balance Sheet Analysis*      345
        23.4.3    *Comparative Common-Size Analysis*        347
        23.4.4    *Financial Ratio Analysis*                347
        23.4.5    *Comparative Financial Ratio Analysis*    351

**Glossary**                                                353

**Bibliography**                                            361

**Index**                                                   365

# ABBREVIATIONS

| | |
|---|---|
| ABS | Asset-Backed Security |
| AIA | American Institute of Accountants |
| AICPA | American Institute of Certified Public Accountants |
| ARM | Accrual Reversal Method |
| ASC | Accounting Standard Committee |
| ASU | Accounting Standard Update |
| COGS | Cost of Goods Sold |
| EBITDA | Earnings Before Interest Tax Depreciation and Amortization |
| EFRAG | European Financial Reporting Advisory Group |
| EITF | Emerging Issues Task Force |
| EPS | Earnings per Share |
| ESOs | Employee Stock Options |
| FASB | Financial Accounting Standard Board |
| FIFO | First-in, First-out |
| FRC | Financial Reporting Council |
| GAAP | Generally Accepted Accounting Principles |
| GASB | Governmental Accounting Standards Board |
| IAS | International Accounting Standard |
| ICAI | Institute of Chartered Accountant of India |
| IFRS | International Financial Reporting Standards |
| ISOs | Incentive Stock Options |
| LIFO | Last-in, First-out |
| MBS | Mortgage-Backed Security |
| MD&A | Management Discussion & Analysis |
| NZASB | New Zealand Accounting Standards Board |
| OCI | Other Comprehensive Income |

| PBO | Projected Benefit Obligation |
| PCAOB | Public Company Accounting Oversight Board |
| PPE | Plants, Property, Equipment |
| ROA | Return on Assets |
| ROI | Return on Investment |
| SEC | Securities and Exchange Commission |
| SFAS | Statement of Financial Accounting Standard |

# LIST OF TABLES

| Table 8.1 | Starbucks (2014): Changes in the carrying amount of goodwill | 98 |
|---|---|---|
| Table 13.1 | Walmart (2014): Currency translation | 161 |
| Table 13.2 | Walmart (2014): Basic and Diluted Income per Common Share | 174 |
| Table 15.1 | Starbucks (2014): Tax effect of temporary differences and carryforward | 192 |
| Table 16.1 | PepsiCo (2014): Consolidated statements of cash flows | 199 |
| Table 23.1 | Apple—Consolidated statement of income | 335 |
| Table 23.2 | Apple—Consolidated balance sheet | 335 |
| Table 23.3 | Apple—Consolidated statement of shareholders' equity | 336 |
| Table 23.4 | Apple—Consolidated statement of cash flows | 337 |
| Table 23.5 | Microsoft—Consolidated statement of income | 341 |
| Table 23.6 | Microsoft—Consolidated balance sheet | 342 |
| Table 23.7 | Microsoft—Consolidated statement of shareholders' equity | 343 |
| Table 23.8 | Microsoft—Consolidated statement of cash flows | 344 |
| Table 23.9 | Apple—Common-sized income statement | 345 |
| Table 23.10 | Microsoft—Common-sized income statement | 345 |
| Table 23.11 | Apple—Common-sized balance sheet | 346 |
| Table 23.12 | Microsoft—Common-sized balance sheet | 347 |

# DISCLAIMER

While the author has made every effort to ensure that the information in this book is correct at the time of publication, he does not assume and hereby disclaims any liability to any party for any loss, damage, or disruption caused by errors or omissions, whether such errors or omissions result from negligence, accident, or any other cause.

This publication is designed to provide accurate and authoritative information in regard to the subject matter covered. It is sold on the understanding that the publisher is not engaged in rendering professional services. If professional advice or other expert assistance is needed, the services of a competent professional should be sought.

# PART I

# Overview of Financial Statements and the Statement of Financial Position

In the USA, financial statements are prepared and presented in accordance with the GAAP. However, correspondence between accounting numbers and the events/transactions those numbers purport to represent is far from giving the real picture.[1] Despite these inherent flaws, the statements as delivered to its readers still deserve considerable amount of scrutiny and analysis.

ASC 210-10 provides a general overview of the aspects of the balance sheet, which is also commonly referred to as a statement of financial position. The balance sheets of most entities show separate classifications of

- Current assets and current liabilities;
- Long-term assets and long-term;
- Shareholders' equity.

ASC 210-20 describes the concept of offsetting assets and liabilities in the balance sheet and notes the limited circumstances when it is allowed. ASC 210-20 includes the overview of the Subtopic.

This Subtopic provides criteria for offsetting amounts related to certain contracts and provides guidance on presentation. It is a general principle of accounting that the offsetting of assets and liabilities in the

---

[1] Lawrence Revsine (1991): "The Selective Financial Misrepresentation Hypothesis," *Accounting Horizons*, pp. 16–27.

balance sheet is improper except if a right of setoff exists. The general principle that the offsetting of assets and liabilities is improper except where a right of setoff exists is usually thought of in the context of unconditional receivables from and payables to another party. That general principle also applies to conditional amounts recognized for contracts under which the amounts to be received or paid or items to be exchanged in the future depend on future interest rates, future exchange rates, future commodity prices, or other factors.

# CHAPTER 1

# Overview of Financial Statements

## 1.1 GENERAL

Financial reporting is essentially a way of following standard practices to give to the readers of the financial statements an accurate depiction of a firm's finances, including its revenues, expenses, profits, capital, cash flows. Financial reporting is also a building block of a market-based monitoring of companies, which allows shareholders and the public at large to assess management performance.[1] In the wake of the international financial crisis of the 1990s, the international community embarked on a range of initiatives to strengthen the international financial architecture.[2] Financial reporting plays a crucial role in supporting the efficient functioning of the capital markets. Robust financial reporting increases investors' confidence, which in turn leads to better capital allocation decisions and economic growth.

---

[1] UNCTD (2004): International Accounting Reporting Issues, Chapter 3, p. 54, par. 2.
[2] UNCTD (2004): International Accounting Reporting Issues, Chapter 3, p. 59.

© The Author(s) 2018
F. I. Lessambo, *Financial Statements*,
https://doi.org/10.1007/978-3-319-99984-5_1

## 1.2   THE INTERNATIONAL
### ACCOUNTING STANDARD BOARD: IFRS

The concept of convergence first arose in the late 1950s in response to post-World War II economic integration and related increases in cross-border capital flows. Initially, the focus was put on harmonization. That is, reducing differences among the accounting principles used in major capital markets around the world. By the 1990s, the notion of harmonization was replaced by the concept of convergence. The International Accounting Standards Committee, formed in 1973, was the first international standards-setting body. It was reorganized in 2001 and became an independent international standard setter, the International Accounting Standards Board (IASB). As of 2013, the European Union and more than 100 other countries either require or permit the use of international financial reporting standards (IFRSs) issued by the IASB or a local variant of them. By 2016, approximately 120 countries and jurisdictions, including Hong Kong, Egypt, Canada, Australia, and the countries in the European Union, require or permit the use of IFRS or a local variant of IFRS.

The FASB and the IASB have been working together since 2002 to improve and converge USA generally accepted accounting principles (GAAP) and IFRS. As of 2013, Japan and China were also working to converge their standards with IFRSs. The Securities and Exchange Commission (SEC) consistently has supported convergence of global accounting standards. However, the Commission has not yet decided whether to incorporate IFRSs into the US financial reporting system. The Commission staff issued its final report on the issue in July 2012 without making a recommendation.

## 1.3   EUROPEAN FINANCIAL
### REPORTING ADVISORY GROUP (EFRAG)

EFRAG is an advisory body that participates in the European endorsement process of IFRS Standards. The European Union (EU) is not a single jurisdiction but, rather, an economic and political partnership between 28 European countries that together cover much of the continent of Europe. With respect to accounting, the European Union has enacted some laws, known as ("Directives") that all EU and EEA members must comply with. Some of those Directives address accounting issues. The most notable is Directive 2013/34/EU of the European Parliament and of the Council of June 26, 2013 on the annual financial statements, consolidated financial statements, and related reports. EU and EEA member states may enact additional accounting laws and regulations that add to the requirements of the Directives, but they cannot override the requirements of the Directives.

EFRAG serves the European public interest by developing and promoting European views in the field of financial reporting and ensuring these views are properly considered in the IASB standard-setting process and in related international debates. EFRAG ultimately provides advice to the European Commission on whether newly issued or revised IFRS meet the criteria in the IAS Regulation for endorsement for use in the EU, including whether endorsement would be conducive to the European public good. EFRAG seeks input from all stakeholders, and obtains evidence about specific European circumstances, throughout the standard-setting process and in providing our endorsement advice. The EFRAG is recognized as the European Voice in financial reporting.

## 1.4   THE USA: THE FASB

The FASB is an independent, private-sector organization that operates under the oversight of the Financial Accounting Foundation (FAF) and the US Securities and Exchange Commission ("SEC" or "Commission"). For nearly 40 years, the FASB has established standards of financial accounting and reporting for non-governmental entities, including both businesses (public and private) and not-for-profit organizations. Those standards—US GAAP—are recognized as authoritative by the SEC for public companies and by the American Institute of Certified Public Accountants (AICPA) for other non-governmental entities.

US GAAP is essential to the efficient functioning of the US economy because investors, creditors, donors, and other users of financial reports rely heavily on credible, transparent, comparable, and unbiased financial information. In today's dynamic financial markets, the need for integrity, transparency, and objectivity in financial reporting is increasingly critical to ensure the strength of US capital markets and provide investors with accurate and timely information.

In 2002, the US Congress enacted the Sarbanes–Oxley Act, which included provisions protecting the integrity of the FASB's accounting standards-setting process. The legislation provided the FASB with an independent, stable source of funding. The legislation established an ongoing source of funding for the FASB from annual accounting support fees collected from issuers of securities, as those issuers are defined in the Sarbanes–Oxley Act.

It is important to note that although the FASB has the responsibility to set accounting standards, it does not have the authority to enforce them. Officers and directors of a company are responsible for preparing financial reports in accordance with accounting standards. Auditors provide an opinion about whether those officers and directors appropriately applied accounting standards. The Public Company Accounting Oversight Board ("PCAOB") is charged with ensuring that auditors of public companies have performed an audit in accordance with the auditing standards of the PCAOB, which includes an auditor's analysis of whether a public company has complied with appropriate accounting standards. The SEC has the ultimate authority to determine whether public companies have complied with accounting standards.

- The Mission of the FASB

The FASB's mission is to establish and improve standards of financial accounting and reporting that foster financial reporting by non-governmental entities that provides useful decision-making information to investors and other users of financial reports. That mission is accomplished through a comprehensive and independent process that encourages broad participation, objectively considers all stakeholders' views, and is subject to oversight by the FAF's Board of Trustees. To accomplish its mission, the FASB acts to:

1. Improve the usefulness of financial reporting by focusing on the primary characteristics of relevance and reliability and on the qualities of comparability and consistency.
2. Keep standards current to reflect changes in methods of doing business and changes in the economic environment.
3. Consider promptly any significant areas of deficiency in financial reporting that might be addressed through the standards-setting process.
4. Improve the common understanding of the nature and purpose of information contained in financial reports.

As it works to develop accounting standards for financial reporting, the FASB is committed to following an open, orderly process that considers the interests of the many who rely on financial information.

- The Standards-Setting Process

An independent standards-setting process is paramount to producing high-quality accounting standards because it relies on the collective judgment of experts who are informed by the input of all interested parties through a deliberate process. The FASB sets accounting standards through processes that are thorough and open, accord due process to all interested parties, and allow for extensive input from all stakeholders. Such extensive due process is required by the Rules of Procedure, set by the Board within the parameters of the FAF's bylaws. The FASB process is similar to the Administrative Procedure Act process used by federal agencies for rulemakings but provides far more opportunities for interaction with all interested parties.

In short, the FASB actively seeks input from all of its stakeholders on proposals and processes. Wide consultation provides the opportunity for all stakeholders to be heard and considered, the identification of unintended consequences, and, ultimately, broad acceptance of the standards that are adopted. The Board's wide consultation also helps it to assess whether the benefits to users of improved information from proposed changes outweigh the costs of the changes to preparers and others.

The FASB meets regularly with the staff of the SEC and the PCAOB. Additionally, because banking regulators have a keen interest in US GAAP financial statements as a starting point in assessing the safety and soundness of financial institutions, the Board meets with them on a quarterly basis and otherwise, as appropriate. The FASB conducts outreach on a frequent and regular basis with the FASB's various advisory groups. The primary role of advisory group members is to share their views and experience with the Board on matters related to practice and implementation of new standards, projects on the Board's agenda, possible new agenda items, and strategic and other matters.

In addition to the FASB's various advisory groups, the Emerging Issues Task Force ("EITF") assists the FASB in improving financial reporting through the timely identification, discussion, and resolution of financial accounting issues relating to US GAAP. The EITF was designed to promulgate implementation guidance for accounting standards to reduce diversity in accounting practice on a timely basis. The EITF assists the FASB in addressing implementation, application, or other emerging issues that can be analyzed within existing US GAAP. Task Force members are drawn from a cross section of the FASB's stakeholders, including auditors, preparers, and users of financial statements. The chief accountant or the deputy chief accountant of the SEC attends Task Force meetings regularly as an observer with the privilege of the floor. The membership of the EITF is designed to include persons who are in a position to project emerging issues before they become widespread and before divergent practices become entrenched.

- Oversight of FASB

The FASB's accountability derives from oversight at two levels. First, the Board is overseen by the independent Board of Trustees of the FAF. Organized in 1972, the FAF is an independent, private-sector, not-for-profit organization. The FAF exercises its authority by having responsibility for oversight, administration, and finances of the FASB and its sister organization the Governmental Accounting Standards Board ("GASB"). The FAF's responsibilities consist of:

1. Selecting the members of the FASB, the GASB, and their respective Advisory Councils.
2. Overseeing the FASB's and the GASB's Advisory Councils (including their administration and finances).
3. Overseeing the effectiveness of the FASB's and the GASB's standards-setting processes and hold the Boards accountable for those processes.
4. Protecting the independence and integrity of the standards-setting process.
5. Educating stakeholders about those standards.

Second, the FASB is subject to oversight by the SEC with respect to standards setting for public companies. The SEC has the statutory authority to establish financial accounting and reporting standards for public entities. At the time of FASB's formation in 1973, the SEC formally recognized the FASB's pronouncements that establish and amend accounting principles and standards as "authoritative" in the absence of any contrary determination by the Commission. In 2003, the SEC issued a Policy Statement that affirms the FASB's status as a designated, private-sector standards setter.

## 1.5 THE UK: FINANCIAL REPORTING COUNCIL (FRC)

In the UK Accounting standards derive from a number of sources. The chief standard-setter is the Accounting Standards Board (ASB), which issues standards called Financial Reporting Standards (FRS). The ASB is part of the FRC, an independent regulator funded by a levy on listed companies, and it replaced the Accounting Standards Committee (ASC), which was disbanded in 1990 following a number of criticisms of its work. To the extent that the ASC's pronouncements, known as Statements of Standard Accounting Practice (SSAPs), have not been replaced by FRS, they remain in force. In 2015, the UK's FRC published a set of new reporting standards collectively known as the New UK GAAP. These new standards applied to all accounting periods starting on or after January 1, 2016. The Board comprises the Chairman, the Deputy Chairman, the Chief Executive, the Chair of the Codes and Standards Committee, the Chair of the Conduct Committee, and other non-executive directors (including the Chairs of the Corporate Reporting and Actuarial Councils). The Chairman and Deputy Chairman are appointed by the Secretary of State for Business, Energy & Industrial Strategy (BEIS).

The UK's FRC published five standards which together form the basis of the new UK regime. The Financial Reporting Standard for Smaller Entities will continue to be available for those that qualify to use it and will remain fundamentally unaltered for the time being. In March 2013 the FRC (now responsible for issuing accounting standards in the UK) issued FRS 102, The Financial Reporting Standard Applicable in the UK and Republic of Ireland. This followed the issue of FRS 100 Application of Financial Reporting Requirements and FRS 101—The Reduced Disclosure Framework in November 2012. Together these standards make up what is commonly being referred to by accountants as New UK GAAP, which takes mandatory effect for accounting periods commencing on or after January 1, 2015. The introduction of the New UK GAAP aimed to make financial reporting both easier and cheaper, while creating a more unified, coherent and succinct set of standards. Compared to the old standards, the New UK GAAP:

- Expands its definition of a "financial institution";
- Enables more organizations to apply for the UK GAAP, including a wider range of SMEs and micro-businesses;
- Creates new rules for some certain assets and sources of income, including biological assets and government grants; and
- Assumes all intangible assets have finite lives and must be amortized.

- UK GAAP for micro-entities

Under the New UK GAAP, a simpler accounting standard has been developed for "micro-entities." To be classified as a micro-entity, a company must meet at least two of the following requirements:

- An annual turnover of less than £632,000.
- A balance sheet total of less than £316,000.
- No more than 10 employees.

In 2016, the micro-entities regime was extended to include qualifying partnerships but some organizations, such as charities, still cannot qualify as micro-entities. The micro-entities standard is optional, and qualifying companies can follow the rules for larger organizations if they choose to do so.

According to this standard, micro-entities:

- Can produce a more simple balance sheet and profit and loss account;
- Are exempt from having to produce a directors' report;
- Are required to include less information and notes on their accounts—this is known as "minimum accounting items"; and
- Do not need to file their profit and loss account Companies House, only their balance sheet.

The Board is supported by three governance committees: (i) Audit Committee; (ii) Nominations Committee; and (iii) Remuneration Committee and by two business committees: (i) Codes & Standards Committee, and (ii) Conduct Committee.

The Codes & Standards Committee is supported by three Councils which advise on Corporate Reporting, Audit & Assurance and Actuarial matters. The CRR Committee, AQR Committee, and the Case Management Committee support the Conduct Committee and have specific responsibilities as set out in the FRC's monitoring, review, and disciplinary procedures. The Financial Reporting Review Panel and the Disciplinary Tribunal Panel are maintained pursuant to the Conduct Committee Operating procedures and the FRC's Disciplinary Schemes.

• UK GAAP Standard Process

The ASB has a formal exposure process for proposed standards. Early concepts are issued as Discussion Papers (DPs). These are released to the public and comments invited. Where a new standard is to be proposed, a Financial Reporting Exposure Draft (FRED) is released for comments. The standard in final form is only issued when comments have been incorporated or addressed. This aims to address the criticisms leveled at the ASC, whose comment process was less rigorous. Issues that require an immediate solution are considered by the Urgent Issues Task Force (UITF). The UITF comprises a number of senior figures from industry and accounting firms. It meets as necessary to consider pressing issues and issues abstracts which become binding immediately.

## 1.6   JAPAN: THE ACCOUNTING STANDARD BOARD OF JAPAN

Japanese GAAP are developed by the Accounting Standard Board of Japan (ASBJ) established in 2001. The ASBJ develops Accounting Standards in accordance with the "Rules on the Due Process for the Development of Japanese GAAP and Japan's Modified International Standards" ("Due Process Rules") set out by the Financial Accounting Standards Foundation (FASF). Japanese GAAP are one of the four sets of accounting standards listed companies in Japan can currently choose to use to file their consolidated financial statements. The other three sets of accounting standards are the IFRS, US GAAP, and Japan's Modified International Standards (JMIS). IFRS Standards have been permitted since 2010. Since then, a large number of Japanese companies have decided to use IFRS Standards for their financial statements; 164 listed companies have either already adopted or announced plans to adopt IFRS Standards, representing approximately 30% of total market capitalization of all listed companies in Japan. The ASBJ holds Board meetings at least once a month. The discussions of the Board meetings are generally open to the public unless, under limited circumstances, the Chairman of the ASBJ decides to make the meeting private. The video recordings of Board meetings are made available for a certain period of time on the FASF website. Furthermore, papers used for discussions at Board meetings are generally made available on the FASF web site unless they relate to drafts of Exposure Drafts (EDs) and accounting standards.

- Due Process

The Due Process Oversight Committee, set up by the FASF, ensures that the due process that the ASBJ must follow when developing Accounting Standards is followed indeed. The ASBJ is required to report to the Due Process Oversight Committee its compliance with the Due Process Rules whenever the ASBJ issues a new Accounting Standard or amends an existing Accounting Standard that is considered material, or whenever the ASBJ plans or conducts a post-implementation review. Furthermore, the ASBJ is required to report annually to the Due Process Oversight Committee a summary of its compliance with the Due Process Rules for the specific year. When developing accounting standards, the ASBJ is required to solicit the views of constituents in a sufficient and appropriate manner. When the ASBJ develops a new Accounting Standard or amends an existing Accounting Standard, the ASBJ generally issues an Exposure Draft and solicits comments from the general public. However, in rare cases such as when the proposal is immaterial, the Chairman of the ASBJ may decide to ask the ASBJ to vote for not issuing an Exposure Draft. Furthermore, when considered necessary, the ASBJ may issue a Discussion Paper prior to the issuance of an Exposure Draft and solicit the views of constituents. EDs and DPs generally have a comment period of two months or longer. However, considering the significance or urgency of the proposals, the ASBJ may vote to have a shorter comment period. Responses received on EDs and DPs, together with the name of the respondents, will be made available on the FASF web site. Responses received are considered by the ASBJ in a timely manner and the results of the ASBJ's considerations will be made available on the FASF web site. Before an Accounting Standard is issued, the ASBJ considers whether there is a need to re-expose its proposals.

## 1.7   AUSTRALIA: THE AUSTRALIAN ACCOUNTING STANDARD BOARD

The Australian Accounting Standard Board (AASB) is an agency of the Australian government under the Australian Securities and Investment Commission Act of 2001. The AASB provides and updates standards for public and private sector financial reporting for organizations in Australia. The Board comprises 11 members including the Chair. The Chair is appointed by the Minister for Superannuation and Corporate Law and members, from a variety of backgrounds, are appointed by the FRC. The Chair of the AASB reports to the Minister regarding the organization's operations.

- The functions of the AASB are to:

  - develop a conceptual framework for the purpose of evaluating proposed accounting standards and international standards;
  - make accounting standards under section 334 of the Corporations Act 2001 for the purposes of the corporations' legislation;
  - formulate accounting standards for other purposes;
  - participate in and contribute to the development of a single set of accounting standards for worldwide use; and
  - facilitate the Australian economy by reducing the cost of capital, enabling Australian entities to compete effectively overseas, leaving accounting standards that are clearly stated and easily to understand, and to maintain investor confidence in the Australian economy (including its capital markets).

Australia has adopted IFRSs since January 1, 2005, in line with a strategic direction from the FRC. Therefore, issues on the IASB work program and the IFRIC work program are also included on the AASB work program, although the degree of involvement by the AASB varies issue-by-issue and may be substantive or non-substantive.

- The Due Process

  - AASB standard-setting process starts with the identifying the technical issue. The technical issue can be identified by international organizations (including the IASB, IFRS) IPSASB, the AASB itself and the Australian organization/individual.

- AASB will develop a project proposal on the technical issue identified. The decision whether to place the issue to its agenda is based on the assessment of the project. Some considerations involved include the benefit and cost consideration (which is cost of not undertaking it), availability of resources and likely timing.
- Discussion on the agenda papers is then developed and presented by AASB on the research and consider issue stage. The agenda papers consider relevant material from other standard-setters and address the scope of issue, alternative approaches, and timing of outputs.
- On the consultation with stakeholder's stage, the AASB involves various stakeholders to make comment and discussion via one of the following document: EDs is a draft of a proposed (or amendment) standard. Invitations to Comment (ITCs) aim to seek feedback on broad proposals. Draft Interpretations is a draft of a proposed interpretation of a standard.
- DPs outline wide range of possible accounting policies on the issue. Roundtable discussions are the formal discussions for the proposals issued for comment with a range of stakeholders. Focus Groups consist of two groups, the User Focus Group and the Not-For-Profit Focus Group. The User Focus Group represents the financial statement users and NFP Focus Group comprises representative of NFP sector. Project Advisory Panels provides advises and comments the agenda papers and this group members are the expertise in that topic. Interpretation Advisory Panels comprise preparers, users, auditors and regulators to preparing alternative views on an issue and recommendations for consideration by the AASB.
- The document issued for comment will be formally submitted to the IASB an IPSASB to achieve the objective of high-quality international accounting standards. The issuance of a pronouncement may include a standard, an interpretation, or a conceptual framework document. The pronouncement to be applied to for-profit entities will be made consistent with IFRSs). One of the main roles of AASB is placed at the final stage of the standard-setting process, which is implementation and compliance of accounting standards and interpretations in Australia.
- If the standards are deemed to be inappropriate to be implemented in Australia, AASB will lead the revision or submission to propose changes to IASB or IPSASB.

## 1.8   New Zealand: The New Zealand Accounting Standards Board (NZASB)

In New Zealand, accounting standards are issued by the NZASB, a Committee of the External Reporting Board (XRB). The XRB is an independent "Crown Entity" established under New Zealand law, particularly the Financial Reporting Act 2013 (and its precursor, the Financial Reporting Act 1993). Compliance with Accounting Standards developed by the NZASB) and approved by the XRB is mandated under the Financial Reporting Act 2013. The NZASB has up to 10 members with a focus on diversity of experience and perspective. Members of the NZASB are appointed by the XRB and are all part time. New Zealand has adopted New Zealand equivalents to IFRS Standards (NZ-IFRS) for all public companies. NZ-IFRS are substantively identical to IFRS Standards as issued by the IASB Board with three additional New Zealand-specific standards. Foreign companies are required to use NZ-IFRS unless specific exemption is granted allowing them to use another financial reporting framework including IFRS Standards as issued by the IASB.

## 1.9   India: The Council of the Institute of Chartered Accountants of India (ICAI)

In India, Accounting Standards are formulated by the Council of the Institute of Chartered Accountants of India (ICAI) through its ASB, created in 1977. Thereafter, those Accounting Standards are considered by the National Advisory Committee on Accounting Standards (NACAS) of the Ministry of Corporate Affairs (MCA), which recommends the Standards to the Central Government for notifying under the Companies Act. The Government, on accepting the recommendation of the Committee, notifies the Standards under the Companies Act by publishing them in the Gazette of India. Notified standards are authoritative under the law. In January 2015, the Indian MCA released a revised roadmap that reflects that, in essence, companies with a net worth of Rs. 500 crore or more will have to mandatorily follow Indian Accounting Standards (Ind AS), which are largely converged with IFRSs, from April 1, 2016. Corporates having a net worth of less than Rs. 500 crore but are listed, or in the process of getting listed, and companies with a net worth of Rs. 250 crore or more will have to follow the new norms from

April 1, 2017. For banking, insurance, and non-banking finance companies, which were exempt from the general roadmap, a separate one has was drawn up in January 2016 that will see a phased approach with Ind AS adoption beginning from April 1, 2018. This was later deferred to April 1, 2019.

## 1.10  CHINA: ACCOUNTING STANDARD FOR BUSINESS ENTERPRISES

The accountancy standards for companies were put into effect by the Ministry of Finances (MOFs). China established its first complete standards specific to accountancy in 1997 and the Ministry of Finance (MOF) promulgated an additional 13 standards more specific to accountancy since then. Chinese Accounting Standards for Business Enterprises (ASBEs) are mandatory for listed Chinese enterprises. Other Chinese enterprises are encouraged to apply the ASBEs, which are substantially in line with IFRS, except for certain modifications that reflect China's circumstances and environment. China is committed to converge with IFRS. Foreign Invested Enterprises (FIE) may prepare financial statements in accordance with other accounting standards or in other languages for global consolidation purposes. However, the Chinese authorities will only recognize and accept accounts in Chinese that are prepared based on Chinese accounting standards. Chinese companies whose securities trade on the Stock Exchange of Hong Kong may choose among IFRS, Hong Kong Financial Reporting Standards (HKFRS), and ASBEs for purposes of financial reporting to Hong Kong investors. However, those financial reports are in addition to the ASBE financial reports that the Chinese companies issue within mainland China.

## 1.11  THE FINANCIAL STATEMENT MATERIALS

The main purpose of financial accounting is to prepare financial reports that provide information about a firm's financial position to external parties such as investors and creditors. Such information is intended to be useful in making economic decisions by providing information that reflects the underlying economics of a firm's transactions. Public companies must follow the rules and provide financial statements require by their regulators.

Financial statements refer to a set of four core statements: the balance sheet, the statement of income (or the statement of comprehensive income), the statement of changes in equity, the statement of cash flows as well as the notes thereto. In a broader sense, financial statements include the four aforementioned plus a series of other materials, including the proxy statement, the management discussion, and analysis (MD&A).

### 1.11.1 The Proxy Statement

A proxy is a voting ballot sent by a corporation to its stockholders.

As it is almost impossible for all shareholders of a corporation to physically attend annual meetings, most corporations anticipate the "unattendance" by sending out proxy statement to those shareholders who could not make it. A company is required to file its annual proxy statement with the SEC no later than the date proxy materials are first sent or given to shareholders. The SEC requires that shareholders of a company whose securities are registered under Section 12 of the Securities Exchange Act of 1934 receive a proxy statement prior to a shareholder meeting, whether an annual or special meeting. The information contained in the statement must be filed with the SEC before soliciting a shareholder vote on the election of directors and the approval of other corporate action. Solicitations, whether by management or shareholders, must disclose all important facts about the issues on which shareholders are asked to vote.

### 1.11.2 The Management Discussion & Analysis (MD&A)

MD&A is a narrative explanation of the financial statements and other statistical data that the registrant believes will enhance a readers' understanding of its financial condition, changes in financial condition and results of operation.

The objectives of MD&A are:

a. To provide a narrative explanation of a company's financial statements that enables investors to see the company through the eyes of management;
b. To enhance the overall financial disclosure and provide the context within which financial information should be analyzed; and
c. To provide information about the quality of, and potential variability of, a company's earnings and cash flow so that investors can ascertain the likelihood that past performance is indicative of future performance.

## 1.12    INTERIM STATEMENTS AND SUBSEQUENT & ADJUSTING EVENTS

### 1.12.1    *Interim Financial Statements*

Quarterly and semiannual financial statements are called interim financial statements and are normally prepared in a condensed form. It means that the disclosures required in them are far less than those required in annual financial statements. Quarterly financial statements are normally unaudited but semiannual reports need to be at least reviewed by an auditor who is a qualified professional accountant authorized to attest the authenticity of financial statements.

### 1.12.2    *Subsequent Events*

Subsequent events (also called events after balance sheet date) can be defined as the events that occur after the balance sheet date but before the authorization of financial statements for issue. Under IFRS they are termed as "events after the reporting period" and are also commonly called "events after the balance sheet date" and the accounting treatment is prescribed by IAS 10 Events after the Reporting Period.

- Date of Financial Statements

The date of the financial statements is the balance sheet's date (i.e., it is the point of time to which a balance sheet relates. For example, if a balance sheet is prepared to show the assets, liabilities, and equity of a company as at December 31, 2014 then December 31, 2014 is the date of the financial statements.

### 1.12.3    *Adjusting Events*

IAS 10 Events after the Reporting Period (Balance Sheet Date) Adjusting Events Non-Adjusting Events Going Concern Exception Introduction Events may occur between the end of the reporting period and the date when financial statements are authorized for issue which may present information that should be considered in the preparation of financial statements. IAS 10 Events after the Reporting Period provides guidance as to which events should lead to adjustments in the financial statements and which events shall be disclosed in the notes to financial statements. Date of Authorization for Issue Events after reporting period are those that occur between the end of the reporting period and when the financial statements are authorized for issue. The date of authorization for issue is usually taken to be the date when the board of directors authorizes the issue of financial statements. Where management is required to issue its financial statements to a supervisory board or shareholders for approval, the authorization is considered to be complete upon the management's authorization for issue of financial statements rather than when the supervisory board or shareholders give their approval. Events after the Reporting Period Events after the end of reporting period may be classified into two types: Adjusting Events—those events that provide further evidence about conditions that existed at the end of reporting period. Non-Adjusting Events—those events that reflect conditions that arose after the end of reporting period. Adjusting Events if any events occur after the end of the reporting period that provide further evidence of conditions that existed at the end of reporting period (i.e., Adjusting Events), then the financial statements must be adjusted accordingly.

- Example

Detection of fraud or errors after the reporting period may indicate that the financial statements are misstated. Financial statements may be adjusted to reflect accounting for those errors or frauds that relate to the present or prior reporting periods in accordance with IAS 8 Accounting Policies, Changes in Accounting Estimates and Errors.

Non-Adjusting Events Entity shall not adjust the financial statements in respect of those events after the end of reporting period that reflect conditions that arose after the end of reporting period (i.e., Non-Adjusting Events).

## Examples of Non-Adjusting Events

- Declaration of dividends after the reporting date does not indicate existence of liability to pay dividends at the reporting date and shall not therefore trigger the recognition of liability in financial statements in accordance with IAS 37 Provisions, Contingent Liabilities, and Contingent Assets.

- Destruction of assets of the entity by floods occurring after the reporting period does not indicate that the assets of the entity were impaired at the end of reporting period. Hence, the financial statements should not be adjusted to account for the impairment loss that arose after the end of reporting period.
- Initiation of litigation against the company arising out of events that occurred after the reporting period does not indicate the existence of liability at the reporting date and shall not therefore trigger the recognition of liability in the financial statements in accordance with IAS 37 Provisions, Contingent Liabilities, and Contingent Assets.
- The nature and estimate of the financial impact of material Non-Adjusting Events shall be disclosed in the financial statements. Non-Adjusting Events are considered material if they could influence the economic and financial decisions of the users of financial statements.

## Examples of Material Non-Adjusting Events

- Management's plan to discontinue or significantly curtail its activities in major geographic segments.
- Initiation of a major litigation against the company arising out of events that occurred after the reporting period.
- Major losses suffered as a result of a natural disaster occurring after the end of reporting period.

Going Concern Exception Entity shall not prepare financial statements on the going concern basis if events after the reporting period indicate that the entity shall not be able to continue as a going concern irrespective of whether such events are indicative of conditions that arose after the end of reporting period or not. If financial statements are not prepared on the going concern basis, it shall disclose this fact in the financial statements along with any major uncertainties that may cast considerable doubt regarding the entity's ability to operate as a going concern.

## 1.13   Users of Financial Statements

The same financial statements prepared and released by a corporation would be of particular interest to several groups:

- Investors and Financial Analysts: Investors need the information to estimate the intrinsic value of the entity and to decide whether to buy, hold, or sell the entity's shares. Equity research analysts use financial statements to conduct their research on earnings expectations and price targets.
- Employee groups: Employees and their representative groups are interested in information about the solvency and profitability of their employers to decide about their careers, assess their bargaining power, and set a target wage for themselves.
- Lenders: Lenders are interested in information that enables them to determine whether their loans and the interest earned on them will be paid when due.
- Suppliers and other trade creditors: Suppliers and other creditors are interested in information that enables them to determine whether amounts owing to them will be paid when due and whether the demand from the company is going to increase, decrease, or stay constant.
- Customers: Customers want to know whether their supplier is going to continue as an entity, especially when they have a long-term involvement with that supplier. For example, Apple is interested in long-term viability of Intel because Apple uses Intel processors in its computers and if Intel ceases operations at once, Apple will suffer difficulties in meeting its own demand and will lose revenue.
- Governments and their agencies: Governments and their agencies are interested in financial accounting information for a range of purposes. For example, the tax-collecting authorities, such as IRS in USA, are interested in calculating taxable income of the tax-paying entities and finding their tax payable. Antitrust authorities, such as Federal Trade Commission, are interested in finding out whether an entity is engaged in monopolization. The governments themselves are interested in efficient allocation of resources and they need financial accounting information of different sectors and industries to decide on federal and state budget allocation, etc. The bureaus of

statistics are interested in calculating national income, employment, and other measures.

- Public: The public is interested in an entity's contribution toward the communities in which it operates, its corporate social responsibility updates, its environmental track record, etc.

CHAPTER 2

# Cash and Cash Equivalents

## 2.1   GENERAL

Balance sheet (also known as the statement of financial position) provides the value of firm's assets, liabilities, and equity on a particular date. There is no general requirement within the US GAAP as to the layout of the balance sheet. However, Codification Topic 210 provides guidance concerning the balance sheet. The balance sheet is made of assets, liabilities, and shareholders' equity.

The value of assets will equal the value of liabilities plus owner's equity (or $A = L + E$). Assets are subdivided into (i) current assets[1] (i.e., cash, marketable securities, accounts receivable, inventory, prepaid expenses, and other current assets), (ii) long-term/fixed assets (e.g., equipment, land), and (iii) intangibles (i.e., goodwill, patents, deferred charges). Likewise, the liabilities portion of the balance sheet is subdivided into (i) current liabilities[2] (i.e., bank advances, income tax payable, accounts payable, accrued expenses) and (ii) long-term liabilities (i.e., leases, pensions, long-term bonds). Finally, the third component of the balance sheet, the shareholder's equity, includes share capital (par or stated value of shares received at the time of original issue), paid-in-capital (when

---

[1] Current assets are assets that are expected to be realized within a year or normal operating cycle, whichever is longer.

[2] Current liabilities are liabilities that are expected to liquidate within a year or normal operating cycle, whichever is longer.

© The Author(s) 2018
F. I. Lessambo, *Financial Statements*,
https://doi.org/10.1007/978-3-319-99984-5_2

shares are sold for more than the par or stated value), retained earnings/deficit (undistributed earnings), and foreign currency translation adjustment (fluctuation in the value of assets of foreign subsidiaries due to changes in exchange rates). Equity is also expressed as "residual interest" ($E = A - L$). If E is negative, the firm is technically bankrupt.

Net worth or book value refers to what is available to common shareholders and is given by:

Total Assets − Total Liabilities − Preferred Stock = Net Worth

Net worth divided by number of common shares outstanding provides the book value per share. The market value is equal to the price per share times the number of shares outstanding (also referred to as the market capitalization of a company). We can estimate the intrinsic value of stock by using discounted cash flow models.

All assets (except land) lose their value over time and this is accounted for through depreciation (for fixed assets), depletion (for natural resources), and amortization (for intangible assets/deferred charges).

Limitations of Balance Sheet: The balance sheet records the values of assets and liabilities in terms of their original cost. This is especially misleading for fixed assets (that could have significantly changed in value). Also, it is difficult to value intangible assets. Current assets are less troublesome, partly because of their short-term nature (inventories and marketable securities are listed at lower of their cost or market values). Liabilities are also not biased (since they are generally contractual, and market values will be equal to their book values. For example, if the company has taken a loan, the dollar amount of loan obligation does not change with time). Also, an analyst should pay close attention to "off-balance sheet items."

## 2.2    CASH AND CASH EQUIVALENTS

Cash and cash equivalents is an asset that appears on the statement of financial position of a business and includes currency (coins and banknotes) held by a business (in hand and in bank accounts) and cash equivalents.

Cash is a medium of exchange, a store of value and a unit of account and a business needs to have sufficient cash in order to be able to pay its liabilities. Higher cash ratio (ratio of cash and cash equivalents to current liabilities) suggests that the business is liquid (i.e., it is expected not to face any difficulty in paying its very short-term liabilities).

A business generates cash from sale of products and services, sale of assets, borrowings from banks and other creditors and from capital contributions by its owners. It uses cash to pay for its operating and capital expenditure, its liabilities and in paying dividends to its owners. Information about sources and uses of cash are presented in the statement of cash flows.

Businesses keep a small amount of cash (called petty cash) for day-to-day cash expenses and keep a larger percentage of cash at its bank. Control over cash is vital for efficient and profitable operations of a business that is why businesses prepare their cash and bank reconciliations periodically.

Cash equivalents are not precisely coins and banknotes but are marketable securities of very short-term maturity (typically always less than 3 months) which are not expected to deteriorate significantly in value till maturity. They are treated as equivalent to cash under IAS 7 Statements of cash flows.

### 2.2.1   Bank Reconciliation

A company's cash balance at bank and its cash balance according to its accounting records usually do not match. This is due to the fact that, at any particular date, checks may be outstanding, deposits may be in transit to the bank, errors may have occurred, etc. Therefore companies have to carry out bank reconciliation process which prepares a statement accounting for the difference between the cash balance in company's cash account and the cash balance according to its bank statement.

Following are the transactions which usually appear in company's records but not in the bank statement:

- Deposits in Transit: Deposits which have been sent by the company to the bank but have not been received by the bank at proper time before the issuance of bank statement.
- Checks Outstanding: Checks which have been issued by the company but were not presented or cleared before the issuance of bank statement.

Following are the transactions which usually appear in bank statement but not in company's cash account:

- Service Charges: Service charges may have been deducted by the bank. Such charges are usually not known to the company before the issuance of bank statement.
- Interest Income: If any interest income has been earned by the company on its bank account, it is not usually entered in company's cash account before the issuance of bank statement.
- NSF Checks: NSF stands for "not sufficient funds." These are the checks deposited by the company in bank account but the bank is unable to receive payment on those checks due to insufficient funds in the payer's account.

## Example

Company A's bank statement dated Dec 31, 2011, shows a balance of $24,594.72. The company's cash records on the same date show a balance of $23,196.79. Following additional information is available:

1. Following checks issued by the company to its customers are still outstanding:

|                          |          |
|--------------------------|----------|
| No. 846 issued on Nov 29 | $320.00  |
| No. 875 issued on Dec 26 | 49.21    |
| No. 878 issued on Dec 29 | 275.00   |
| No. 881 issued on Dec 31 | 186.50   |

2. A deposit of $400.00 made on Dec 31 does not appear on bank statement.
3. An NSF check of $850 was returned by the bank with the bank statement.
4. The bank charged $50 as service fee.
5. Interest income earned on the company's average cash balance at bank was $1237.22.
6. The bank collected a note receivable on behalf of the company. Amount received by the bank on the note was $550. This includes $50 interest income. The bank charged a collection fee of $10.
7. A deposit of $430 was incorrectly entered as $340 in the company's cash records.

Task: Prepare a bank reconciliation statement using the above information.

## Solution

Company A
Bank reconciliation
December 31, 2011

| | | |
|---|---|---|
| Balance as per Bank, Dec 31 | | $24,594.72 |
| Add: Deposit in transit | | 400.00 |
| | | $24,994.72 |
| Less: Outstanding checks: | | |
| No. 846 issued on Nov 29 | $320.00 | |
| No. 875 issued on Dec 26 | 49.21 | |
| No. 878 issued on Dec 29 | 275.00 | |
| No. 881 issued on Dec 31 | 186.50 | |
| | | 830.71 |
| Adjusted bank balance | | $24,164.01 |
| Balance as per books, Dec 31 | | $23,196.79 |
| Add: | | |
| Interest income from bank | $1237.22 | |
| Note receivable collected by bank | 500.00 | |
| Interest income from note receivable | 50.00 | |
| Deposit understated | 90.00 | |
| | | 1877.22 |
| | | $25,074.01 |
| Less: | | |
| NSF check | $850.00 | |
| Bank service fee | 50.00 | |
| Bank collection fee | 10.00 | |
| | | 910.00 |
| Adjusted book balance | | $24,164.01 |

### 2.2.2   Bank Overdraft

When a business' bank account has a negative balance, it is said to be running a bank overdraft (more precisely an actual bank overdraft). It is a form of financing in which the bank honors presented checks even when there is no balance in the business account which results in negative balance in the bank account.

There is a special type of bank overdraft called "book bank overdraft" which represents situation in which the balance as per cash book is negative while the balance as per bank book is positive. It arises when the checks written exceed the bank balance available thereby resulting in negative bank balance in books but since those checks are not yet presented so the bank balance is not negative and there is no "actual bank overdraft."

### 2.2.2.1 Balance Sheet Treatment of Bank Overdraft

When the bank has a right to offset the overdraft balance with another bank account of the business, the overdraft is netted off against the other bank accounts maintained with the same bank and the net bank balance is shown as the balance of cash at bank.

When the bank has no such right to offset, the overdraft is reported as a liability and when it is material it should be reported separately from other liabilities.

### 2.2.2.2 Bank Overdraft and Statement of Cash Flows

For the purpose of statement of cash flows, under US GAAP any changes in bank overdrafts for a period are appropriately reported as cash flows from financing activities.

Under IFRS, however, bank overdraft is treated as part of cash and cash equivalents and movement in bank overdraft is not reported anywhere in the statement of cash flows.

### Example

Earth Inc. has four bank accounts: Accounts A and B which are maintained at Mars Bank. A has a balance of $20 million while B has an overdraft of $2 million. Accounts C and D are maintained at Venus Bank. C has a balance of $50 million and D has a balance of −$10 million. On Mars, banks are entitled to set off any negative bank balances with positive balances while Venetian banks have no such luxury. Earth applies US GAAP and Accounts B and D have no balance at the start of the year. Comment on balance sheet and statement of cash flows presentation of the overdraft.

### Solution

On its balance sheet, Earth Inc. shall report cash and cash equivalents of $68 million ($20 million in Account A minus $2 million in Account B plus $50 million in Account C). It will show a corresponding bank overdraft liability of $10 million.

On its statement of cash flows, it shall report a cash inflow from "changes in overdrafts" of $10 million under cash flows from financing activities.

### 2.2.3    Petty Cash

Petty cash fund is a relatively small amount of cash that businesses keep on hand for the purpose of small transactions such as providing change to customers, postage expenses, highway tolls. In such transactions, the use of checks is time consuming, costly, or illogical.

Usually, a custodian is appointed to administer the petty cash and it is his/her duty to account for the expenses incurred out of petty cash fund. Whenever the custodian makes any payment from the fund to an employee or a customer, etc., he or she must record the amount being disbursed, the name of the person to whom the payment is being made, and the reason for the disbursement.

Following are the typical transactions connected to petty cash fund.

1. Creation: Petty cash fund may be created by drawing a check on the company's checking account and handing it over to the custodian of the fund. The journal entry is to debit petty cash and credit cash at bank.
2. Disbursements: Individual disbursements from petty cash are not recorded via a journal entry. Instead, journal entry is passed at the time of each replenishment and at the end of the period for the total amount disbursed.
3. Replenishment: When the balance in petty cash becomes low, a journal entry is passed debiting various expense accounts and crediting petty cash for the sum of disbursements made. Then petty cash is replenished usually via a check.
4. Raising Fund Level: When the volume of transactions to be handled by the petty cash grows, the fund level is raised. The journal entry is to debit the petty cash and credit cash at bank.

### Example

Company A created a petty cash fund of $900 on Jan 1, 2012. The journal entry is:

(DR) Petty Cash 900
(CR) Cash at Bank 900
During January 2012, following disbursements were made from the fund:

| Office Supplies | $300 |
|---|---|
| Highway Toll | 50 |
| Postage | 30 |
| Freight-In | 350 |

## 2.3    MARKETABLE EQUITY SECURITIES AND FAIR VALUE MEASUREMENT

Following a lengthy debate over the pertinence of the historical cost principle, some have argued that historical cost no longer, "faithfully represent(s) the economic realities of today's complex instruments" and needed to be supplement by an update measurement for specific assets.

SFAS 115, effective for fiscal years beginning after December 15, 1993, addresses the accounting and reporting for investments in equity securities that have readily determinable fair values and for all investments in debt securities. Those investments are to be classified into three categories and accounted for as follows:

- Debt securities that the enterprise has the positive intent and ability to hold to maturity are classified as held-to-maturity securities and reported at amortized cost.
- Debt and equity securities that are bought and held principally for the purpose of selling them in the near term are classified as trading securities and reported at fair value, with unrealized gains and losses included in earnings.
- Debt and equity securities not classified as either held-to-maturity securities or trading securities are classified as available-for-sale securities and reported at fair value, with unrealized gains and losses excluded from earnings and reported in a separate component of shareholders' equity.

Fair value measurement was deemed relevant because it accurately reflects current market conditions, accurately portrays the effect of economic events on an entity over time.

The journal entry to record the about disbursements from petty cash is:
(DR) Office Supplies 300
(DR) Highway Toll 50
(DR) Postage 30
(DR) Freight-In 350
 (CR) Petty Cash 730
- The company replenished the fund via a check of $730. The journal entry is:
(DR) Petty Cash 730
 (CR) Cash at Bank 730

The FASB updated the SFAS 115 with two additional pronouncements: SFAS 157[3] and SFAS 159,[4] and extended the list of financial statements items that may be value at fair value to include:

- loans receivable and payable
- investments in equity securities
- rights and obligations under insurance contracts
- rights and obligations related to warranty agreements
- host financial instruments that are separated from embedded derivative instruments
- firm commitments involving financial instruments
- written loan commitments.

The raise and expansion of the fair value measurement do not go without fierce criticisms. Some have argued that the FASB's movement toward fair value accounting principles as biased in a desire to be in compliance with international standards, that, "the reliability offered by historical financial reporting is infinitely more valuable to the vast majority of financial report users than the collective accumulation of statistical probabilities offered by fair value."[5]

[3] SFAS 157: Fair value measurements.

[4] SFAS 159: The fair value option for financial liabilities.

[5] McCarthy, P. D. (2004): Unnecessary Complexity in Accounting Principles. *The CPA Journal* 74 (3): 18–19.

## 2.4   ACCOUNTING FOR FINANCIAL INSTRUMENTS

The financial reporting rules for financial instruments determine whether a particular type of instrument should be recorded at historical cost or at fair value.

Historical cost is a measure of value based on the nominal or original cost at the time of acquisition, while fair value is a measure of value based on current market prices at the financial statement date and is comparable to mark-to-market in the Internal Revenue Code.[6] GAAP has adopted a set of rules for valuing financial instruments that contains elements of both the fair value and historical cost approaches, often referred to as the "mixed attribute" model. The determination of whether debt or equity instruments are recorded at fair value or historical cost is made according to the type of instrument (debt or equity), the firm's proportional ownership share of any equity investment, and the firm's intent with respect to the holding period of the security. Marketable securities include, inter alia, treasury bills, treasury notes, and commercial papers. The primary purpose of investing in marketable securities is the opportunity to capture returns on a business excess of cash, while still maintaining easy access to cash flow.

GAAP provides different accounting treatment for three separate categories of debt instruments: (i) held-to-maturity securities, (ii) trading securities, and (iii) available-for-sale securities.[7] The management of the firm often considers several variables before investing in marketable securities. These variables include: <u>Safety</u> (or the likelihood of getting back the same number of dollars you originally invested), <u>Marketability</u> (or the ability to sell a significant volume of securities in a short period of time in the secondary market without significant price concession), <u>Interest Rate</u> (or Yield) Risk, and <u>Maturity</u> (or the remaining life of the security).

* Held-to-maturity securities

Held-to-maturity securities are debt instruments that a firm has the positive intent and the ability to hold to maturity. They are valued at historical amortized cost, reduced by any other-than-temporary losses.

---

[6]US Congress (2011): Present Law and Issues Related to the Taxation of Financial Instrument and Products—A Report to the Joint Committee on Taxation, p. 49.

[7]ASC 825—Financial Instruments.

The term "other-than-temporary" is designed to distinguish certain declines in value from those that are temporary.[8] Any impairment in value need not be considered permanent to be classified as other-than-temporary. ASC 320 provides many factors that must be considered in making a determination of whether a decline is temporary or not. Other-than-temporary losses must be charged to earnings in the period in which the loss occurs. Thus, temporary unrealized gains and losses are not reported in the firm's earnings. By valuing debt instruments held for long-term investment at historical cost, firms avoid earnings volatility related to temporary changes in the market value of debt instruments they intend to redeem for the full face amount at maturity.[9]

- Trading securities

Trading securities are debt instruments bought and held primarily for sale in the near term. They are valued at fair value, and all unrealized holding gains and losses (both temporary and other-than-temporary) are included in earnings. From accounting perspective, there are four accounting events to consider while dealing with trading securities: (a) the purchase of marketable securities; (b) the receipt of related cash dividends; (c) the sale of securities (at gain or loss); and (d) the change in the fair value (i.e., market price) of securities at the end of an accounting period.

### Example

On January 1, 2016, Yin Corp. acquires 100 shares issued by Grump LLC for $10,000. These shares were acquired merely for trading purposes.

To record the purchase of the trading securities, Yin Corporation makes the following journal entry:

(DR) Trading security 10,000
(CR) Cash 10,000

---

[8] US Congress (2011): Present Law and Issues Related to the Taxation of Financial Instrument and Products—A Report to the Joint Committee on Taxation, p. 49.

[9] US Congress (2011): Present Law and Issues Related to the Taxation of Financial Instrument and Products—A Report to the Joint Committee on Taxation, p. 50.

On March 25, 2016, Yin Corp. sold the 50 shares at $80 per share (fair market value). Yin Corp. makes the following journal entry to recognize the receipt of cash:

(DR) Cash (50 shares × $80) 4000
(DR) Realized loss on sale of trading securities 1000
  (CR) Trading securities 5000

Note: The realized loss on sale of trading securities would be included in Yin Corp. income statement accounts. More specifically, in the "Other revenues and expenses" section of the income statement.

- Available-for-sale securities

Debt instruments that do not meet the criteria to be classified as either held-to-maturity or trading (available-for-sale securities) are valued at fair value, but unrealized gains and losses are reported in OCI as opposed to earnings. A fair value election is allowed for available-for-sale securities. If the election is made, unrealized gains and losses are reported in earnings.

### Example

On January 1, 2016, Doonya Corp. acquires 100 short-term securities (i.e., treasury notes) for $10,000. The management considers the investments to be available-for-sale securities. Doonya Corp. makes the following journal entry:

(DR) Available-for-sale Securities 10,000
  (CR) Cash 10,000

On March 25, 2016, the market price of these treasury notes climbed to $125 a treasury note due to the performance of the US economy. Doonya Corp. makes the following journal entry:

(DR) Available-for-sale Securities 2500
  (CR) Unrealized gain on Available-for-sale Securities 2500

> Note: The changes in the fair value of available-for-sale securities are reported as a separate component of stockholders' equity.

## 2.5 ACCOUNTING FOR DERIVATIVES

The objective of a fair value measurement is to arrive at an appropriate exit price within the bid-offer spread, and ASC 820 notes that mid-market pricing may (but is not required to) be used a practical expedient.[10]

Under US Generally Accepted Accounting Principles (GAAP), at the close of every business day, companies that own derivatives, including credit derivatives, must establish their fair value. Under GAAP, fair value is defined as "the price that would be received to sell an asset or paid to transfer a liability in an orderly transaction between market participants at the measurement date." GAAP explains that deriving fair value assumes a hypothetical transaction but is nonetheless a market-driven exercise using the best available information at hand. GAAP specifies a hierarchy of three categories of information that should be used when calculating the fair value of a derivative, placing a priority on observed market prices:

- Level 1 consists of quoted prices in active markets for identical assets or liabilities.
- Level 2 consists of inputs other than quoted prices included within Level 1 that are observable for the asset or liability, either directly or indirectly. They include, for example, quoted prices for similar assets in either active or inactive markets.
- Level 3 consists of unobservable inputs, such as pricing models used when no actual market prices are available.

To establish the fair value of a derivative that is traded in a dealer's market, such as credit derivatives, GAAP focuses on the prices actually used by the dealers. The daily price range is often referred to as the "bid-ask spread," meaning the prices that dealers offer to buy or sell a derivative during the course of a trading day. GAAP states: "The price within the

---

[10]US Congress (2011): Present Law and Issues Related to the Taxation of Financial Instrument and Products—A Report to the Joint Committee on Taxation, pp. 90–94.

bid-ask spread that is most representative of fair value in the circumstances shall be used to measure fair value."

Determining what price within a given price range is most representative of fair value in the circumstances permits market participants to exercise a degree of subjective judgment. GAAP also supports using mid-market pricing... as a practical expedient for fair value measurements within a bid-ask spread.[11] By "mid-market pricing," it means the price in the middle of the day's price range. For that reason, many market participants routinely use the midpoint price of a derivative's bid-ask spread in their daily financial reporting. Some financial firms employ independent price reporting services to identify, for a fee, the bid-ask spread and midpoint prices of specified derivatives for use in their financial reporting. Still other firms use their own personnel to identify the daily bid-ask spread and midpoint prices for their derivatives. Although GAAP essentially provides a safe harbor for midpoint prices, it does not compel firms to use them. Because GAAP requires derivative values to be recorded each business day in accordance with market values, derivatives are often characterized as "mark-to-market." The values or prices assigned to the derivatives each day are often referred to as the daily "marks." Under GAAP, the value of every derivative must be recorded or "mark-to-market" each day in a company's books, even if the derivative was not actually purchased, sold, or otherwise actively traded. The daily gain or loss is typically reported internally by each business line within a firm and rolled up into a firm-wide daily profit and loss statement.

Because derivative values often fluctuate, parties to a derivative agreement often agree to post cash collateral on an ongoing basis to cover the cost of settling the derivatives contract. The amount of cash collateral that has to be posted typically changes periodically to reflect the fair value of the derivative. If a dispute arises over the value of the derivative and the amount of collateral to be posted, the parties typically negotiate a resolution of the "collateral dispute."

As part of establishing the fair value of derivatives, pricing adjustments are also sometimes made when the derivatives are traded in less liquid markets, or are part of a large holding whose size might affect the price. Parties with derivative portfolios may also establish a reserve, known as

---

[11] Accounting Standards Codification Topic 820-10-30, Fair Value Measurements and Disclosures (ASC 820).

a fair value adjustment, based on such considerations as the illiquidity of the market, the creditworthiness of its derivative counterparties, the extent to which it holds a concentrated block of assets, and the uncertainties associated with its pricing methodology.

## 2.6   ACCOUNTING FOR HEDGING

The objective of hedge treatment for financial reporting purposes is a proper matching of the timing of gain or loss recognition on a derivative instrument used for hedging purposes with the income or expense recognition related to the item being hedged.[12] For financial reporting purposes, the hedging instrument and the underlying asset are both marked to market. Identification of the hedge at the onset of a contract and substantial documentation are required to qualify an instrument for hedge treatment. GAAP defines three separate categories for risks that can be hedged: (i) fair value hedge, (ii) cash flow hedge, and (iii) net investment hedge.

- Fair value hedge

For a derivative designated to hedge the exposure to changes in the fair value of an asset, liability, or a firm commitment, a timing difference arises if the derivative instrument is valued at fair value while the underlying asset is required to be valued at historical cost (such as a held-to-maturity debt security) or the lower of cost or market value (such as inventory). GAAP addresses this inconsistency by creating an exception that allows the hedged item to be marked to market.[13] Thus, the gain or loss recognized on the derivative is offset by the gain or loss on the hedged item, resulting in a net effect in earnings only to the extent to which the hedge is not perfectly effective in offsetting changes in the fair value of the hedged item. GAAP deems a hedge effective to the extent that the changes in fair value or cash flow of the hedged item and the hedging derivative offset each other. Any remaining gain or loss that does not offset with the change in the value of the hedged item

---

[12] US Congress (2011): Present Law and Issues Related to the Taxation of Financial Instrument and Products—A Report to the Joint Committee on Taxation, p. 53.
[13] ASC 815-20-25.

considered to be ineffective. By electing the fair value option for an asset or a liability that is otherwise valued at historical cost, a firm may be able to replicate hedge accounting treatment for a fair value hedge by electing to mark the hedged item to market, as would be permitted for a hedge, while avoiding the identification and documentation requirements of hedge accounting.

• Cash flow hedge

For a derivative designated to hedge the exposure to variable cash flows of an upcoming, forecasted event, a different type of timing mismatch can occur for which the firm may wish to enter into a cash flow hedge.[14]

## Example

If a firm expects to purchase steel in the future, the firm is exposed to variability in the future price of steel. The firm may enter into a forward contract to purchase steel at a price of \$700/ton to hedge this exposure. A subsequent decrease in the price of steel to \$650/ton has no economic impact on the firm because the contract offsets the benefit of the price decrease. The forward contract constitutes a liability, as it requires the firm to purchase steel at a price (\$700/ton) above the current market price. However, the firm's balance sheet does not recognize an obligation related to the expected price of future purchases. Current recognition of the unrealized gains and losses on the forward contract creates a timing mismatch because the future cash flow that is being offset does not affect earnings until a later period. GAAP addresses this inconsistency by allowing the portion of the gain or loss that is determined to be effective as a hedge to be initially reported as OCI. The gains and losses are subsequently reclassified into earnings at the time the underlying cash flow affects earnings. Like the fair value hedge, the ineffective portion of the gain or loss is reported in earnings immediately.

---

[14]ASC 815-20-25-3—Derivatives and Hedging.

- Net investment hedge

For a derivative designated as hedging the foreign currency exposure of an investment in a foreign operation, a timing mismatch can occur because translation gains and losses are included in OCI rather than earnings. GAAP addresses this inconsistency by allowing the portion of the gain or loss that is determined to be effective to be reported in OCI rather than earnings. Like the fair value hedge and cash flow hedge, the ineffective portion of the gain or loss is reported in earnings immediately. Hedges of foreign currency risk that do not relate to an investment in a foreign operation, such as a foreign currency hedge on an available-for-sale security, are treated as a fair value hedge or a cash flow hedge, as appropriate.

# CHAPTER 3

# Short-Term Assets: Inventories

## 3.1 GENERAL

Inventory includes the raw materials, work in process, and finished goods that a company has on hand for its own production processes or for sale to customers. Inventory is considered an asset, so the accountant must consistently use a valid method for assigning costs to inventory in order to record it as an asset. The primary basis of accounting for inventories is cost, which is the price paid or consideration given to acquire an asset. Although principles for the determination of inventory costs may be easily stated, their application, particularly to such inventory items as work in process and finished goods, is difficult because of the variety of considerations in the allocation of costs and charges. In certain cases, a departure from the cost basis of pricing the inventory is required when the utility of the goods is no longer as great as their cost. That is, where there is evidence that the utility of goods, in their disposal in the ordinary course of business, will be less than cost, whether due to physical deterioration, obsolescence, changes in price levels, or other causes, the difference shall be recognized as a loss of the current period. This is generally accomplished by stating such goods at a lower level commonly designated as market.

The valuation of inventory is not a minor issue, because the accounting method used to create a valuation has a direct bearing on the amount of expense charged to the cost of goods sold in an accounting period and therefore on the amount of income earned. The basic formula for determining the cost of goods sold in an accounting period is:

© The Author(s) 2018
F. I. Lessambo, *Financial Statements*,
https://doi.org/10.1007/978-3-319-99984-5_3

Beginning inventory + Purchases − Ending inventory = Cost of goods sold

## 3.2   INVENTORY METHODS

There are two main types of inventory systems: the perpetual inventory system and the periodic inventory system.

### 3.2.1   The Perpetual Inventory System

The perpetual inventory method is one in which inventory data is updated continuously. When an order is placed or received, that data immediately is entered into the system to update the quantity and inventory availability right away. Thus, a perpetual inventory system has the advantages of both providing up-to-date inventory balance information and requiring a reduced level of physical inventory counts. The system works best when coupled with a computer database of inventory quantities and bin locations, which is updated in real time by the warehouse staff using wireless bar code scanners, or by sales clerks using point of sale terminals. It is least effective when changes are recorded on inventory cards, since there is a significant chance that entries will not be made, will be made incorrectly, or will not be made in a timely manner. Thus, technology makes keeping this type of inventory control system even easier to use.

The perpetual inventory system debits the purchases of inventory and related cost directly to the account "inventory" and credits the sales or thefts of inventories to the same inventory account.

Illustration: Assuming that Yin Corp. opts for the perpetual system of inventory and has the following transactions:

- purchase of $1500 of widgets
- freight cost associated with the delivery of inventory
- sale of widgets from inventory for $3000, for which the associated inventory cost is $1800
- downward inventory adjustment of $800, caused by inventory theft.

## Example

Assuming that Yin Corp. opts for the perpetual system of inventory and has the following transactions:

- purchase of $1500 of widgets
- freight cost associated with the delivery of inventory
- sale of widgets from inventory for $3000, for which the associated inventory cost is $1800
- downward inventory adjustment of $800, caused by inventory theft.

Under the perpetual inventory method, Yin Corporation would have to record—Journal Entries:

1. To record a purchase of $1500 of widgets that are stored in inventory:
   (DR) Inventory 1500
     (CR) Accounts payable 1500
2. To record $300 of inbound freight cost associated with the delivery of inventory:
   (DR) Inventory 300
     (CR) Accounts payable 300
3. To record a sale of widgets from inventory for $3000, for which the associated inventory cost is $1800:
   (DR) Accounts receivable 3000
     (CR) Revenue 3000
   (DR) Cost of goods sold 1800
     (CR) Inventory 1800
4. To record a downward inventory adjustment of $800, caused by inventory theft, and detected during an inventory count:
   (DR) Inventory shrinkage expense 800
     (CR) Inventory 800

### 3.2.2   The Periodic Inventory System

The periodic inventory system only updates the ending inventory balance in the general ledger when a physical inventory count is conducted. In the meantime, the inventory account in the accounting system continues to show the cost of the inventory that was recorded as of the last physical inventory count. Under the periodic inventory system, all purchases made between physical inventory counts are recorded in a purchases account. When a physical inventory count is done, then the balance in the purchases account is shifted into the inventory account, which in turn is adjusted to match the cost of the ending inventory.

---

### Example

Assuming that Yin Corporation has the following transactions for the reported period:

- beginning inventory of $100,000,
- purchases of $170,000 for, and
- its physical inventory count reveals an ending inventory cost of $80,000. The calculation of its cost of goods sold is:
- $100,000 Beginning inventory + $170,000 Purchases − $80,000 Ending inventory = $190,000 Cost of goods sold

Under a periodic inventory system, inventory purchases made by a company are initially stored in a purchases (asset) account with the following journal entry:

(DR) Purchases $170,000
(CR) Accounts payable $170,000

At the end of the accounting period, the entire balance in the purchases account is shifted in the inventory (asset) account. This means that the purchases account is really an accumulation account for a single accounting period, rather than an account that holds a balance over multiple periods. The entry at the end of the period is:

(DR) Inventory XXXX
(CR) Purchases XXXX

---

The calculation of the cost of goods sold under the periodic inventory system is:

Beginning inventory + Purchases = Cost of goods available for sale

Cost of goods available for sale − Ending inventory = Cost of goods sold

The final periodic inventory entry in an accounting period arises immediately after the physical count of the inventory, when the accounting staff establishes the actual cost of the inventory on hand at the end of the month. It then subtracts this actual ending inventory cost from the cost that has accumulated in the inventory account, and charges the difference to the cost of goods sold account with this entry:

(DR) Cost of goods sold XXXX
    (CR) Inventory XXXX

A variation on the last two entries is to not shift the balance in the purchases account into the inventory account until after the physical count has been completed. By waiting, you can then merge the final two entries together and apportion the balance in the purchases account between the inventory account and the cost of goods sold, using the following entry. The end result is the same, but with fewer entries.

The periodic inventory system is most useful for smaller businesses that maintain minimal amounts of inventory. For them, a physical inventory count is easy to complete, and they can estimate cost of goods sold figures for interim periods. However, there are several problems with the system:

- Minimal information. It does not yield any information about the cost of goods sold or ending inventory balances during interim periods when there has been no physical inventory count.
- Estimation errors. You must estimate the cost of goods sold during interim periods, which will likely result in a significant adjustment to the actual cost of goods whenever you eventually complete a physical inventory count.
- Large adjustments. There is no way to adjust for obsolete inventory or scrap losses during interim periods, so there tends to be a significant (and expensive) adjustment for these issues when a physical inventory count is eventually completed.
- Not scalable. It is not an adequate system for larger companies with large inventory investments, given its high level of inaccuracy at any given point in time (other than the day when the system is updated with the latest physical inventory count).

## 3.3    OWNERSHIP ISSUES

In some situations, the identification of items that should be included in inventory is more difficult. Consider, for example, goods in transit, goods on consignment, and sales returns. That is, when examining a company's inventory on hand. Goods consigned in and out to others would need a reclassification depending on either the consignment agreement. Another issued that may arise of common inventory is where more than a single business entity has the right to sale to customers. When the items are classified as to identify what goods belong to which entities, the ownership issue is plain. Whether the issue becomes complex when the entities involved did not bother themselves to separate their ownerships.

## 3.4    VALUATION OF INVENTORY

Cost for inventory purposes may be determined under any one of several assumptions as to the flow of cost factors, such as first-in, first-out (FIFO), average, and last-in, first-out (LIFO). The major objective in selecting a method should be to choose the one which, under the circumstances, most clearly reflects periodic income.

There are three basis approaches to valuing inventory that are allowed by GAAP:

(a) FIFO: Under FIFO, the cost of goods sold is based on the cost of material bought earliest in the period, while the cost of inventory is based on the cost of material bought later in the year. This results in inventory being valued close to current replacement cost. During periods of inflation, the use of FIFO will result in the lowest estimate of cost of goods sold among the three approaches and the highest net income.

(b) LIFO: Under LIFO, the cost of goods sold is based on the cost of material bought toward the end of the period, resulting in costs that closely approximate current costs. The inventory, however, is valued on the basis of the cost of materials bought earlier in the year. During periods of inflation, the use of LIFO will result in the highest estimate of cost of goods sold among the three approaches and the lowest net income.

(c) Weighted Average: Under the weighted average approach, both inventory and the cost of goods sold are based on the average cost of all units bought during the period. When inventory turns over rapidly this approach will more closely resemble FIFO than LIFO.

Firms often adopt the LIFO approach for the tax benefits during periods of high inflation, and studies indicate that firms with the following characteristics are more likely to adopt LIFO: rising prices for raw materials and labor, more variable inventory growth, an absence of other tax loss carryforwards, and large size. When firms switch from FIFO to LIFO in valuing inventory, there is likely to be a drop in net income and a concurrent increase in cash flows (because of the tax savings). The reverse will apply when firms switch from LIFO to FIFO.

Given the income and cash flow effects of inventory valuation methods, it is often difficult to compare firms that use different methods. There is, however, one way of adjusting for these differences. Firms that choose to use the LIFO approach to value inventories have to specify in a footnote the difference in inventory valuation between FIFO and LIFO, and this difference is termed the LIFO reserve. This can be used to adjust the beginning and ending inventories, and consequently the cost of goods sold, and to restate income based on FIFO valuation.

## 3.5   THE LIFO RESERVE

The difference between the cost of an inventory calculated under the FIFO and LIFO methods is known as the LIFO reserve. This reserve is essentially the amount by which an entity's taxable income has been deferred by using the LIFO method.

During times of increasing costs, the balance in the LIFO reserve account will have a credit balance, meaning that less cost reported in inventory. Remember, under LIFO the latest (higher) costs are expensed to the cost of goods sold, while the older (lower) costs remain in inventory. The credit balance in the LIFO reserve reports the difference in the inventory costs under LIFO versus FIFO since the time that LIFO was adopted. The change in the balance during the current year represents the current year's inflation in costs.

LIFO reserve = FIFO inventory − LIFO inventory.

**Example**

Yuco Industries Inc., a producer of over 15,000 types of multi-purpose and flexible packaging films, reported fiscal second-quarter earnings on June 9, 2016, with a LIFO reserve change of $9.1 million for the quarter. Analysts excluded this LIFO reserve change to derive an increase in gross profit of $13.4 million for the quarter. This gross profit number was compared to prior year periods in the company analysis.

## 3.6    LIFO Liquidation

In the case of LIFO liquidation, a company sells more than it acquired in a given period and assumes that it is selling some of the older merchandise. This can result in inflation in profits, because older inventory is usually purchased at a lower cost price than newer inventory as a result of inflation, but it is sold at the current asking price. Consequently, LIFO liquidation makes it look like a company made more money in a given accounting period.

For tax purposes, this can be a problem. Making more money on sales results in a higher tax liability. Moreover, it can also be used to make a company's financial situation look more solid on paper than it is in real life. Accounting statements may show that a company realized a large profit with a LIFO liquidation, reassuring investors and other concerned parties, but the company can still be in financial trouble.

Learning to read accounting and inventory statements is important for people who want to collect meaningful information from public filings. Understanding the accounting and inventory methods used by a company will provide important clues about what is going on between the lines. In the case of a LIFO liquidation, for example, it could mean that the company is struggling and needs cash, or that it just had a month of unanticipated sales volume, and is actually doing very well.

## 3.7    Comprehensive Example

Jiang LLC provides the following transactions concerning its inventory on October 2015:
- October 1: beginning inventory 60 units @ $14 per unit
- October 5: purchase of 200 units @ $15 per unit
- October 12: purchase of 100 units @ $16 per unit
- October 20: sale of 250 units @ $20 per unit
- October 25: purchase of 50 units @ $18 per unit
- October 30: sale of 100 units @ $25 per unit

*Task*: (i) determine Jiang LLC COGS and ending inventory under FIFO assuming that the management would like to know the numbers under both (a) the perpetual system and (b) the periodic method.
(ii) determine Jiang LLC COGS and ending inventory under LIFO assuming that the management would like to know the numbers under both (a) the perpetual system and (b) the periodic method.

**Solutions**:

(i) (a) FIFO perpetual system

| Date | Purchases | | | Sales | | | Balances | | |
|------|----------|-------|-------|----------|-------|-------|----------|-------|-------|
| | Quantity | Price | Total | Quantity | Price | Total | Quantity | Price | Total |
| 10/1 | | | | | | | 60 | 14 | 840 |
| 10/5 | 200 | 15 | 3000 | | | | 60 | 14 | 840 |
| | | | | | | | 200 | 15 | 3000 |
| 10/12 | 100 | 16 | 1600 | | | | 60 | 14 | 840 |
| | | | | | | | 200 | 15 | 3000 |
| | | | | | | | 100 | 16 | 1600 |
| 10/20 | | | | 60 | 14 | 840 | 10 | 15 | 150 |
| | | | | 190 | 15 | 2850 | 100 | 16 | 1600 |
| 10/25 | 50 | 18 | 900 | | | | 10 | 15 | 150 |
| | | | | | | | 100 | 16 | 1600 |
| | | | | | | | 50 | 18 | 900 |
| 10/30 | | | | 10 | 15 | 150 | 10 | 16 | 160 |
| | | | | 90 | 16 | 1440 | 50 | 18 | 900 |
| | | | | | | | 60 | | 1066 |

(i) (b) FIFO periodic system
- Units available for sale $= 60 + 200 + 100 + 50 = 410$
- Units sold $= 250 + 100 = 350$
- Units end $= 60$
- COGS $= 350$
- Ending inventory $= (10 \times 16) + (50 \times 18) = \$1160$

| Transactions | Units quantity | Unit price | Total(s) |
|---|---|---|---|
| Beginning inventory | 60 | 14 | 840 |
| 10/5 purchase | 200 | 15 | 3000 |
| 10/12 purchase | 90 | 16 | 1440 |
| 10/25 purchase | 0 | 18 | 0 |
| | 350 | | 5280 |

(ii) (a) Perpetual system—LIFO

| Dates | Purchases | | | Sales | | | Balances | | |
|---|---|---|---|---|---|---|---|---|---|
| | Quantity | Price | Total | Quantity | Price | Total | Quantity | Price | Total |
| 10/1 | | | | | | | 60 | 14 | 840 |
| 10/5 | 200 | 15 | 3000 | | | | 60 | 14 | 840 |
| | | | | | | | 200 | 15 | 3000 |
| 10/12 | 100 | 16 | 1600 | | | | 60 | 14 | 840 |
| | | | | | | | 200 | 15 | 3000 |
| | | | | | | | 100 | 16 | 1600 |
| 10/20 | | | | 100 | 16 | 1600 | 60 | 14 | 840 |
| | | | | 150 | 15 | 2250 | 50 | 15 | 750 |
| 10/25 | 50 | 18 | 900 | | | | 60 | 14 | 840 |
| | | | | | | | 50 | 15 | 750 |
| | | | | | | | 50 | 18 | 900 |
| 10/30 | | | | 50 | 15 | 750 | 60 | 14 | 840 |
| | | | | 50 | 18 | 900 | | | |

(ii) (b) Periodic system—LIFO
- Units available for sale $= 60 + 200 + 100 + 50 = 410$
- Units sold $= 250 + 100 = 350$
- Units end $= 60$
- COGS $= 350$
- Ending inventory $= 60 \times 14 = \$840$

| Transactions | Units quantity | Unit price | Total(s) |
|---|---|---|---|
| 10/20 Sale | 100 | 16 | 1600 |
| | 150 | 15 | 2250 |
| 10/30 Sale | 50 | 15 | 750 |
| | 50 | 18 | 900 |
| | 350 | | 5500 |

## 3.8   RESTRICTIONS ON THE USE OF LIFO

Though the Obama administration has lobbied since 2011 for the repeal of the LIFO standard, discussions are still ongoing in 2016. Regardless, the accounting method is still subject to increased restrictions in both the USA and internationally. Basically, once a business uses LIFO, it cannot use any other method that year. If LIFO is used on a taxpayer's tax return, then no other method can be used to value inventory to calculate income, profit, or loss in any report or statement covering the same tax year that is provided to shareholders and other owners or to creditors.

In the USA, the IRS strictly enforces this rule. Meanwhile, LIFO is banned by International Financial Reporting Standards (IFRS), a set of common rules for accountants who work across international borders. While many nations have adopted IFRS, the USA still operates under the guidelines of Generally Accepted Accounting Principles (GAAP). If this country were to ban LIFO, the USA would clear an obstacle to adopting IFRS, thus streamlining accounting for global corporations. Because of the current discrepancy, however, US-based companies that use LIFO must convert their statements to FIFO in the footnotes of their financial statements.

It should be noted that standards in both the USA and internationally are moving away from LIFO and FIFO. Many US-based companies have switched to FIFO; some companies still use LIFO within the USA as a form of inventory management, but translate it to FIFO for tax reporting. Only a select few large companies within the USA are still able to use LIFO for the purpose of tax reporting. Many companies believe the repeal of LIFO would result in a tax increase for both large and small businesses, though many other companies use FIFO with little financial repercussion.

# CHAPTER 4

# Account Receivables

## 4.1 GENERAL

Receivables include all amounts due from third parties. Receivable is a general term which refers to all monetary obligations owed to the business by its customers or debtors. Receivables can be broadly classified as trade receivables and non-trade receivables.

Trade receivables are those receivables which originate from sales of goods and services by a business to its customers in ordinary course of business. There are two main accounts used for trade receivables which are accounts receivable and notes receivable. When the customers orally promise to pay, the receivables are recorded as accounts receivable. However, if the customers' promise is written one, the receivables are recorded as notes receivable. Notes receivable usually require the debtor to pay interest. Both accounts receivable and notes receivable may be current and non-current.

Non-trade receivables are the amounts due from third parties for transactions outside its normal course of business of selling goods and services. Example of non-trade receivables are loans to employees, tax refunds owed to the business by tax authorities.

As long as a business expects to recover the money from the debtors, it records its receivables as assets in its balance sheet because it expects to derive future benefits (i.e., cash) from them. It does not matter whether they are due in the current period or not.

© The Author(s) 2018
F. I. Lessambo, *Financial Statements*,
https://doi.org/10.1007/978-3-319-99984-5_4

A company is required to provide the following new disclosures about its financing receivables:

- Credit quality indicators of financing receivables at the end of the reporting period by class
- The aging of past due financing receivables at the end of the reporting period by class
- The nature and extent of troubled debt restructurings that occurred during the period by class and their effect on the allowance for credit losses
- The nature and extent of financing receivables modified as a result of troubled debt restructurings within the previous 12 months that defaulted during the reporting period by class, and their effect on the allowance for credit losses.

## 4.2    CASH DISCOUNT ON SALES

Cash discount is the discount offered by seller for paying cash early. Cash discount is only offered on credit sales where the customers do not pay at the time of sale but promise to pay latter. There are two methods of accounting for sales that offer cash discounts: (i) the gross method and (ii) the net method.

### 4.2.1    The Gross Method

According to gross method, the company would initially record the sale at gross or full price. Subsequently, if the customer pays within 10 days, he would be entitled to avail the cash discount. However, if the customer does not pay within 10 days, they would not be entitled to avail the cash discount.

### 4.2.2    The Net Method

According to the net method the company would initially record the sale at net price.

## 4.3    BAD DEBTS CONCEPT

Accounts receivable are not always collected in full due to various reasons. Sometimes customers simply evade payment and the cost of pursuing them is more than the recoverable amount, sometime they become bankrupt, sometimes the debt becomes time-barred etc. A debt which is determined to be uncollectible, i.e., there is no chance that the debt would be collected, is called a bad debt. Bad debts are written off from accounts as soon as they are determined. This is because a business does not expect future economic benefits from a bad debt and it no longer remains an asset.

Although bad debts are a grim reality of doing business on credit, this does not mean that one should stop selling on credit since a good credit policy outweighs this drawback by a great margin. Selling goods on credit increases sales volume because customers like to have the ability to purchase on credit.

Accounting Standards Update No. 2010-20, expand the disclosures that companies provide about the credit quality of their financing receivables and the related allowance for credit losses. Financing receivables include loans and trade accounts receivable. Exempt from these disclosure amendments are: (i) short-term trade accounts receivable; (ii) receivables measured at fair value or lower of cost or fair value; and (iii) debt securities.

It is expected that these improvements will help investors assess credit risk in a company's receivables portfolios and the adequacy of its allowance for credit losses. The disclosure amendments apply to all companies with financing receivables, whether public or nonpublic.

Companies shall now disclose more information about the credit quality of their financing receivables, such as (i) aging of past due receivables; (ii) credit quality indicators; and (iii) modifications of financing receivables.

### 4.3.1    Rebates

310-10-05-7 Rebates represent refunds of portions of the pre-computed finance charges on installment loans or trade receivables, if applicable, that occur when payments are made ahead of schedule. Rebate calculations generally are governed by state laws and may differ from unamortized finance charges on installment loans or trade receivables because many states require rebate calculations to be based on the Rule of 78s or other methods instead of the interest method.

### 4.3.2    Doubtful Accounts

Doubtful accounts are the accounts receivable which are likely to be uncollected or, in other words, these are potential bad debts.

### 4.3.3    Accounting for Bad Debts

There are two methods of accounting for bad debts:

1. Direct Write-Off Method

Under the direct method, whenever an invoice is discovered to be uncollectible, it must be removed from the accounts receivable. That is it must be expensed or written off.

### Example

Journal Entry to Record Bad Debt
- Yin Corporation sold wigs for $1000 to Dan. After several unsuccessful invoices, Yin Corp. discovered that the $1000 would never be collected.
  (DR) Bad debt expense $1000
  (CR) Account receivables $1000

The direct method conflicts with the matching principle. Thus, no accepted under the GAAP.

2. Allowance Method

The allowance method estimates doubtful debts and transfers them to a reserve account before they are actually determined as uncollectible. Allowance method is according to GAAP. The Allowance for doubtful accounts is a contra-asset account which is subtracted from accounts receivable on the balance sheet. In practice, a firm can its allowance for doubtful account estimate based on the following facts:

- Size of the receivables
- Age of the receivables
- Past loss experience

---

### Example

Record of the Allowance
- Yuco Manufacturing sold pipes to Bald LLC for $1000
- The account receivable is far overdue (18 months late)
- Based on Yuco Manufacturing past experience, such a receivable would never be collected
  (DR) Bad Debt Expense $1000
     (CR) Allowance for Doubtful Accounts $1000

---

## 4.4    Accounts Receivable Aging Method

Accounts receivable aging is a technique to estimate bad debts expense by classifying accounts receivable of a business according to of length of time for which they have been outstanding and then estimating the probability of non-collection for each category. The classification of accounts receivable in the accounts receivable aging schedule also helps the business to identify the customers who take longer to pay so that they can restrict sales to those customers to reduce risk of bad debts.

Typically receivables are categorized into periods which are multiples of payment terms. For example, if company sells at payment terms of n/20, the typical classification in aging schedule will be 0–30 days, 30–60 days, 60–90 days. Most businesses prepare an accounts receivable aging schedule at the end of each month. Typical accounts receivable aging schedule consists of 6 columns:

- Column 1 lists the name of each customer with an accounts receivable balance.
- Column 2 lists the total amount due from the customers listed in Column 1.

- Column 3 is the "current column." Listed in this column are the amounts due from customers for sales made during the current month.
- Column 4 shows the unpaid amount due from customers for sales made in the previous month. These are the customers with accounts 1–30 days past due.
- Column 5 lists the amounts due from customers for sales made two months prior. These are customers with accounts 31–60 days past due.
- Column 6 lists the amount due from customers with accounts over 60 days past due.

| Clients' names | Amount receivables ($) | Amount owed ($) | Amount still outstanding (days) ($) | | |
|---|---|---|---|---|---|
| | | | 1–30 | 31–60 | 61–90 |
| Alexandra | 2000 | 500 | 1500 | | |
| Naomi | 2000 | 400 | | 1600 | |
| Jonathan | 4000 | 800 | | | 3200 |
| Aaron | 1000 | 200 | | 800 | |
| Yanick | 4500 | 900 | | 3600 | |
| Tanya | 5000 | 1500 | 3500 | | |

## 4.5    ASSIGNMENT OF ACCOUNTS RECEIVABLE

Assignment of accounts receivable is an agreement between a lending company and a borrowing company in which the latter assigns its accounts receivable to the former in return for a loan. By assignment of accounts receivable, the lender gets a right to collect the receivables of the borrowing company if it fails to repay the loan in time. The lender also receives finance charges and service charges.

It is important to note that the receivables are not sold/transferred under an assignment agreement. If the receivables have been transferred, the agreement would be of sale/factoring of accounts receivable. Usually, the borrowing company would itself collect the assigned receivables and remit the loan amount as per agreement. It is only when the borrower fails to pay as per agreement, that the lender gets a right to collect the assigned receivables on its own.

The assignment of accounts receivable may be general or specific. A general assignment of accounts receivable entitles the lender to proceed to collect any accounts receivable of the borrowing company whereas in case of specific assignment of accounts receivable, the lender is entitled only to collect the accounts receivable specifically assigned to the lender.

The following example shows how to record transactions related to assignment of accounts receivable via journal entries:

### Example

On March 1, 2016, Company A borrowed $50,000 from a bank and signed a 12% one month note payable. The bank charged 1% initial fee. Company A assigned $73,000 of its accounts receivable to the bank as a security. During March 2066, the company collected $70,000 of the assigned accounts receivable and paid the principle and interest on note payable to the bank on April 1. $3000 of the sales were returned by the customers.

Task: Record the necessary journal entries by Company A.

### Solution

- Journal Entries on March 1:
  (DR) Cash 49,500
  (DR) Finance Charge 500
    (CR) Notes Payable 50,000
  (DR) Accounts Receivable Assigned 73,000
    (CR) Accounts Receivable 73,000

- Journal Entries on April 1:
  (DR) Cash 70,000
  (DR) Sales Returns 3000
    (CR) Accounts Receivable Assigned 73,000
  (DR) Notes Payable 50,000
  (DR) Interest Expense 500
    (CR) Cash 50,500

## 4.6    FACTORING OF ACCOUNTS RECEIVABLE

Factoring is the sale of accounts receivable of a company to a financing company at discount. The financing company which buys the receivables is called a factor. Factoring helps a business convert its receivables immediately into cash instead of waiting for due dates of payment by customers.

Factoring arrangements are a means of discounting accounts receivable on a non-recourse, notification basis. Accounts receivable are sold outright, usually to a transferee (the factor) that assumes the full risk of collection, without recourse to the transferor in the event of a loss. Debtors are directed to send payments to the transferee.

The parties to the factoring agreement assess the recoverability of the accounts receivable, decide whether or not the factoring agreement will be with recourse and then they agree on a suitable discount factor to calculate the amount of fee to be charged by the factor. After deducting such fee from the value of accounts receivable, the factor pays in cash to originating company. The factor may also withheld an additional amount as a refundable security against bad debts which may arise.

### 4.6.1    Recourse vs Non-recourse Factoring

Under non-recourse factoring, the factor may set off the sum retained as a security, if any, against any bad debts that may arise but the factor is not entitled to be reimbursed by the originating company if the total of bad debts exceed the amount of security. In other words, the additional loss on bad debts under non-recourse factoring is borne by the factor. Under a factoring agreement with recourse, the company factoring its receivables agrees to pay bad debts in full to the factor. So if the security falls short of the total bad debts, the factor is entitled to be reimbursed for bad debts in full.

Non-recourse factoring is riskier than factoring with recourse for the factor, resulting in higher discount rates over factoring with recourse in general.

### 4.6.2    Factoring vs Loan

To determine if factoring is a better alternative than a business loan you just need to ask yourself these questions:

1. Does my company provide goods or services that are completed when I invoice my customers?
2. Are my customers not paying within the credit terms I am offering?
3. Are you turning away sales because you do not have the cash?
4. With cash, is your business growth potential greater than 20%?

If your answers were yes to these questions, then factoring your accounts receivable invoices is better for you than a traditional loan that you can obtain from banks. Accounts receivable factoring provides a business with financing flexibility based on your sales. A properly structured factoring program eliminates slow payment cycles by providing your business with cash to grow your business.

As a business owner, you should be aware and open to all financing products available to you by either a bank or commercial financing company and choose the one that best fits your company's needs.

### Example

Factoring Without Recourse
- Dylan Walker Corporation factored its accounts receivable to Bennet Finance LLP, a factoring business based in New Heaven.
- The accounts receivable had a book value of $1,200,000.
- The transfer was made without recourse.
- Bennett Finance LLP assesses the quality of accounts receivable and charges a fee of 8%. It also retains an amount equal to 12% of the accounts receivable for probable adjustments against discounts, returns, and allowances etc.

Task: Record the transactions in a journal entry for Dylan Walker Corp.


(DR) Cash 960,000
(DR) Due from factor [1,200,000 × 12%] 144,000
(DR) Loss on sale of receivables [1,200,000 × 8%] 96,000
   (CR) Accounts receivable 1,200,000

## Example

Factoring with Recourse
- Dylan Walker Corporation factored its accounts receivable to Bennet LLP, a factoring business based in New Heaven.
- The accounts receivable had a book value of $1,200,000.
- The transfer was made without recourse.
- Bennett LLP remit 85% of the factored amount to Dylan Walker Corp. and retains 15%.
- Under the parties' arrangement, when Bennett LLP collects the receivables, it will remit to Dylan Walker Corp. the retained amount less 5% fee.
- Dylan Corporation anticipated a $60,000 recourse obligation.
Task: Record the transactions in a journal entry for Dylan Corp.

(DR) Cash ($1,200,000 × 85%) 1,020,000
(DR) Loss on sale of receivables ($1,200,000 × 5%) 60,000
(DR) Receivable from factor ($1,200,000 × 15%) 180,000
  (CR) Recourse liability 60,000
  (CR) Account receivables 1,2000,000

### 4.6.3    Factoring vs Assignment of Receivables

Factoring is different from a financing agreement involving assignment of receivables because the later uses receivables as a collateral security for a loan, but the actual ownership of receivables and the right to collect them is not.

It is important to note that the type of factoring influences the amount of fee charged and the amount of security held by the factor and the scenario in this example is only for the purpose of comparing the two types. The amount of security retained may be zero under factoring with recourse because the agreement guarantees the factor that any debts that may turn out to be irrecoverable will be reimbursed.

## 4.7   SECURITIZATION OF RECEIVABLES

Securitization is the creation and issuance of debt securities, or bonds, whose payments of principal and interest derive from cash flows generated by separate pools of assets. It has grown from a non-existent industry in 1970 to $6.6 trillion as of the second quarter of 2003. To initiate a securitization, a company must first create what is called a special purpose vehicle (SPV) in the parlance of securitization. The SPV is legally separate from the company, or the holder of the assets. Typically a company sells its assets to the SPV.

Securitization can either be a sale or a secured borrowing. ASC 860 stipulates that a transfer of an entire financial asset, a group of entire financial assets, or a participating interest in an entire financial asset needs to be evaluated for relinquishment of control over those transferred assets. To determine whether control over the transferred financial assets has been surrendered, facts such as the transferor's or any of its consolidated affiliates' continuing involvement with the transferred assets, as well as other arrangements between the parties to the transaction that were entered into either contemporaneously with, or in contemplation of, the transfer must be considered in the analysis.

### 4.7.1   Sale Accounting Criteria

For a financial asset transfer to be accounted for as a sale, the transferor must surrender control over the assets transferred. Control is considered to be surrendered in a securitization only if all three of the following conditions are met: (1) the assets have been legally isolated, (2) the transferee has the ability to pledge or exchange the assets, and (3) the transferor otherwise no longer maintains effective control over the assets.

1. Legal isolation.

The transferred assets have to be isolated—put beyond the reach of the transferor, or any consolidated affiliate of the transferor, and their creditors (either by a single transaction or a series of transactions taken as a whole)—even in the event of bankruptcy or receivership of the transferor or any consolidated affiliate.

> ### Example
>
> The seller/company transfers assets to an SPE that, although wholly owned, is designed in such a way that the possibility that the transferor or its creditors could reclaim the assets is remote. This first transfer is designed to be judged a true sale at law, in part because it does not provide excessive credit or yield protection to the SPE. Legal isolation must be determined from the perspective of the transferor and all of its consolidated affiliates.

2. Ability of transferee to pledge or exchange the transferred assets.

When the transferee is a securitization vehicle that is constrained from pledging or exchanging the transferred assets, each third-party holder of its beneficial interests must have the right to pledge or exchange those beneficial interests. No condition can constrain the holder from taking advantage of its right to pledge or exchange if it provides more than a trivial benefit to the transferor.

3. Surrender effective control.

The transferor, its consolidated affiliates, or its agents cannot effectively maintain control over the transferred assets or third-party beneficial interests related to those transferred assets through:

- An agreement that requires the transferor to repurchase the transferred assets before their maturity (in other words, the agreement both entitles and obligates the transferor to repurchase as would, for example, a forward contract or a repo).
- The ability to unilaterally cause the SPE to return specific assets, other than through a cleanup call, that conveys more than a trivial benefit to the transferor.
- An agreement that permits the transferee to require the transferor to repurchase the transferred assets that is priced so favorably that it is probable that the transferee will, in fact, require the transferor to repurchase them.

Under ASC 860, sale accounting must be applied only to a financial asset in its entirety, a pool of financial assets in its entirety, or participating interests highlights that, inherent in this concept, is that a financial asset (or pool of assets) may not be divided into components prior to transfer unless all of the components meet the definition of a participating interest.

Under ASC 860, one can sell only an entire financial asset, an entire pool of assets, or a participating interest; no part sale/part financing.

When a securitization is structured as a sale for accounting purposes, income is accrued over the life of the transaction. The rate at which income is recognized, or accrual rate, is found by finding the yield given a set of cash flows and a beginning basis, or book value.

To calculate the gain or loss, sellers must:

- First accumulate the elements of carrying value of the pool of assets securitized, including any premiums and discounts, capitalized fees or costs, lower-of-cost-or-fair-value valuation reserves and allowances for losses.
- Second, sellers must identify any assets received and any liabilities incurred as part of the securitization.
- Third, sellers must estimate carefully the fair values of every element received or incurred based on current market conditions. This estimate must use realistic assumptions and appropriate valuation models for only existing assets that have actually been transferred (without anticipating future transfers).
- Finally, for those transfers that qualify as a sale, sellers must: (i) recognize gain or loss on the assets sold by comparing the net sale proceeds (after transaction costs and liabilities incurred) to the carrying value attributable to the assets sold and (ii) record as proceeds, and, on the balance sheet at fair value, any beneficial interest received in the transferred assets, which may include (1) a separate servicing asset or liability and/or (2) debt or equity instruments in the special purpose entity, and (3) subtract from proceeds and record on the balance sheet the fair value of any new liabilities issued, including guarantees; recourse obligations or derivatives, such as put options written; forward commitments; and interest rate or foreign currency swaps.

### 4.7.2    Secured Borrowing

If the securitization does not qualify as a sale, the proceeds are accounted for as a liability—a secured borrowing. The assets will remain on the balance sheet with no change in measurement, meaning that no gain or loss is recognized. With no gain or loss recognized, the assets should be classified separately from other assets that are unencumbered.

The securities relating to the transferred assets that are legally owned by the transferor or any consolidated affiliate (i.e., the securities that are not issued for proceeds to third parties) do not appear on the transferor's consolidated balance sheet. They are economically represented as being the difference between the securitization-related assets and the securitization-related liabilities on the balance sheet. When a securitization is treated as a financing for accounting purposes, the loans and associated debt remain on the balance sheet (on-balance sheet financing).

## 4.8    RECEIVABLES—TROUBLED
## DEBT RESTRUCTURINGS BY CREDITORS

When a debtor cannot face the original term of a debt arrangement, the creditor may consider making some concessions to accommodate him. A modification of the terms of a loan would qualify as a troubled debt restructurings when a borrower is troubled and a financial institution grants a concession to the borrower that it would not otherwise consider. ASC Subtopic 310-40 addresses receivables that are TDR. ASU 2011-02 identifies several indicators a creditor must consider in determining whether a debtor is experiencing financial difficulties. A troubled debt restructuring may include, but is not necessarily limited to, one or a combination of the following:

- Transfer of assets to the creditor to fully or partially satisfy the borrower's debt)
- Issuing an equity interest in the borrower to the creditor (i.e., converting the borrower's debt to equity
- Modification of terms of a debt.

If the receivable in the TDR is settled at the time of the restructuring, that is, the debt or pays whether in cash, non-cash, or equity, the creditor simply records a loss for the difference between the carrying amount of the receivable and the fair value of the assets or equity received.

## Example

- Arline Corporation owes $50 million to Wells Fargo Bank, N.A. under a 10% note with two years remaining to maturity.
- Due to Arline Corp. financial difficulties last year, Wells Fargo was not able to collect the previous year interest of $5 million ($50 million × 10%).
- Wells Fargo agreed to settle the receivable (and accrued interest receivable) in exchange for Arline Corporation building located in Manhattan for $40 million.

Task: Record the TDR settlement in Wells Fargo's journal entry.

### Solution

(DR) Building (fair value) 40 million
(DR) Loss on TDR 15 million
    (CR) Accrued interest receivable (10% of %50m) 5 million
    (CR) Note Receivable 50 million

# CHAPTER 5

# Prepaid Expenses, Unearned Income, and Other Current Assets

## 5.1 GENERAL

In the due course of everyday operating activities, firms end up paying for goods or services before they actually receive delivery of them. This includes items like employee labor, which the company records into a prepaid salaries account until it cuts paychecks. ASC 340-10 provides guidance concerning the nature of prepaid expenses. GAAP dictate that expenses that are paid before they are due belong on the balance sheet.

## 5.2 PREPAID EXPENSES

Prepaid expense is an expenditure that is paid for in one accounting period, but for which the underlying asset will not be entirely consumed until a future period. An example of a prepaid expense is insurance, which is frequently paid in advance for multiple future periods; an entity initially records this expenditure as a prepaid expense and then charges it to expense over the usage period. A prepaid expense is listed within the current assets section of the balance sheet until the prepaid item is consumed. Once consumption has occurred, the prepaid expense is removed from the balance sheet and is instead reported in that period as an expense on the income statement. If the total ending balance in the prepaid expenses account is quite small, it may be aggregated with other assets and reported within an "other expenses" line item in the balance sheet.

© The Author(s) 2018
F. I. Lessambo, *Financial Statements*,
https://doi.org/10.1007/978-3-319-99984-5_5

Prepaid expense is expense paid in advance but which has not yet been incurred. Expense must be recorded in the accounting period in which it is incurred. Therefore, prepaid expense must not be shown as expense in the accounting period in which it is paid, but instead it must be presented as such in the subsequent accounting periods in which the services in respect of the prepaid expense have been performed. Entity should therefore recognize an asset in respect of expense it has paid in advance until such time as the services that are due in relation to the prepaid expense have been performed by the suppliers/contractors. That is, at the end of each month, your client's accounting personnel need to prepare a journal entry to book the expired portion of the prepaid expense.

Examples of a prepaid expense would include insurance, library subscriptions or periodicals, multi-year equipment service contracts, or any types of advance paid to a third party or employees. At year-end, an analysis should be performed and entries should be made to record prepaid expenses as assets on the statement of net assets.

A prepaid expense might be recorded initially as (1) an expense or (2) as an asset.

1. If a prepaid expense is recorded initially as an expense, then at the end of an accounting period, only the true expense amount for the period should remain in the expense account. The future expense (the portion that has not yet expired; the unexpired part) must be credited to the expense account and debited to the prepaid asset account.

2. If a prepaid expense is recorded initially in a prepaid asset account, the true expense of the period (the expired portion) needs to be removed and debited to the related expense account. The remaining amount in the prepaid asset account should be the unexpired portion.

### Example

Assuming that an insurance premium of $6000 is paid on December 1. This cost covers the six-month period of December 1 through May 31. As a result, the monthly expense will be $1000. Let's also assume that the company did not have any insurance prior to December 1.

1. On December 1, the account Insurance Expense was initially debited for $6000 and Cash was credited for $6000. On December 31, an adjusting entry will be needed to debit Prepaid Insurance for $5000 and to credit Insurance Expense for $5000. After this adjusting entry is recorded, the balance in Insurance Expense will be December's true expense of $1000 (original debit of $6000 minus the adjusting entry credit of $5000) and the balance in Prepaid Insurance will be the debit of $5000. This represents five months of cost that has not yet expired (5 months × $1000 per month).

2. On December 1, the account Prepaid Insurance was initially debited for $6000 and Cash was credited for $6000. On December 31, an adjusting entry will be needed to debit Insurance Expense for $1000 (the amount that expired during December) and to credit Prepaid Insurance for $1000. After this adjusting entry is recorded, the balance in the asset Prepaid Insurance will be $5000 (the initial debit of $6000 minus the credit of $1000, and the unexpired amount consisting of 5 months × $1000 per month). The account Insurance Expense will report the debit of $1000.

Usually, there would be insurance coverage prior to December 1. In that case, the year-to-date balance in the expense account should be equal to the expired insurance cost during the year-to-date period. If there is a conflict between getting the prepaid asset balance to be correct and the expense balance to be correct, make certain that the prepaid asset balance is correct.

A prepaid expense is listed within the current assets section of the balance sheet until the prepaid item is consumed. Once consumed, the prepaid expense is removed from the balance sheet and is instead reported in that period as an expense on the income statement. If the total ending balance in the prepaid expenses account is quite small, it may be aggregated with other assets and reported within an "other expenses" line item in the balance sheet.

## 5.3    Unearned Income

Under Generally Accepted Accounting Principles (GAAP), unearned income, also known as deferred revenue, is a liability that is created when monies are received by a company for goods/or services not yet delivered or provided. Deferred revenue stems from the accounting concept of revenue recognition, under which revenues are recognized only when the earnings process is complete. Thus, anytime a business receives funds before the delivery or providing of service, the earning's process is not complete. A "pure" thus revenue cannot be recognized; instead, a deferred revenue liability is recorded. The unearned revenue is considered a liability—or at least a contra-asset—because it represents an obligation to perform a service in the future arising from a past transaction.

---

**Example**

Daxa Inc. is a US domestic corporation in business of repairing roofs.

On September 30, 2015, Ms. Chintan contacted Daxa Inc. to fix her apartment roof. Daxa Inc. manager informed her that the overall work would cost $5000 and that a $3000 deposit is required before it will begin work on the customer's special order.

Ms. Chintan gave the company $3000 on December 20, 2015, and the company will begin work by January 10, 2016.

On December 20, 2015, Daxa Inc. records the transaction as follows:

(DR) Cash $3000

(CR) Unearned Revenue $3000.

Note that Daxa Inc. reports no revenue in December 2015 since the company has not yet performed any work.

When the special order is completed in January 10, 2016, the company will debit the liability account for $3000 and will credit a revenue account as follows:

(DR) Unearned Revenue $3000

(CR) Cash $3000

## 5.4   OTHER CURRENT ASSETS

Other current assets are a default classification of "current asset." They represent current assets, which are recorded so rarely, or are so immaterial, that they are not accorded a separate "major" account within the general current assets classification. Examples of other current assets may include cash surrender value of life insurance policies, advances paid to suppliers, advances paid to employees. Accounts included in the other current assets classification are often aggregated for presentation in a single line item in the balance sheet. Whenever the ending balance of this account (or items) becomes significant, businesses would have to shift some of the balance into a separate line item that is more specifically identified, so that the reader of a balance sheet can have a better understanding of the nature of the recorded items.

### Example

Daxa Inc. is a US domestic corporation. On November 30, 2015, Daxa Inc. management has decided to dispose of an old PPE with net book value of $5000.

– The transaction is expected to be closed shortly.

Thus, Daxa Inc. moves the PPE from the long-term side into the short-term side of the balance sheet.

# CHAPTER 6

# Short-Term Liabilities and Working Capital

## 6.1 General

Current liabilities refer to liabilities that are expected to liquidate within a year or normal operating cycle, whichever is longer. The main current liabilities accounts are account and not payable. Some businesses also report a liability known as other current liability. Working capital refers to the difference between the net current assets and the net current liabilities for a given accounting cycle.

## 6.2 Accounts Payable

Accounts payable, listed under current liabilities on the balance sheet represent payments a company has promised or is committed to pay. A/P is a promise of short-term debt obligations and is generally used when dealing with suppliers and creditors.

If accounts payable are not paid within the payment terms agreed to with the supplier, the payables are considered to be in default, which may trigger a penalty or interest payment, or the revocation or curtailment of additional credit from the supplier.

When individual accounts payable are recorded, this may be done in a payables sub-ledger, thereby keeping a large number of individual transactions from cluttering up the general ledger. Alternatively, if there are few payables, they may be recorded directly in the general ledger.

© The Author(s) 2018
F. I. Lessambo, *Financial Statements*,
https://doi.org/10.1007/978-3-319-99984-5_6

Accounts payable are considered a source of cash, since they represent funds being borrowed from suppliers. From a management perspective, it is of some importance to have accurate accounts payable records, so that suppliers are paid on time and liabilities are recorded in full and timely acquitted. Otherwise, suppliers will be less inclined to grant credit, and the financial results of a business may be incorrect.

Other types of payables that are not considered accounts payable are wages payable and notes payable.

## Example

Caroll Company purchases office supplies for $500.00. Caroll Company uses its store credit to pay for them. The transaction will be recorded as follows:
  (DR) Office Supplies $500.00
  (CR) Accounts Payable $500.00

## 6.3   NOTES PAYABLE

Notes payable are payments or liabilities due for payment within one year, or the operating cycle, whichever is longer. Notes payable represent obligations or short-term liabilities in the form of written notes (e.g., promissory notes). Notes payable are often used instead of accounts payable because they give the lender written documentation of the obligation in case legal remedies are needed to collect the debt. Notes payable usually require the borrower to pay interest and frequently are issued to meet short-term financing needs.

A proper classification of a note payable is of interest from the accounting department to see if notes are coming due in the near future and whether the corporation has money to pay for. When a company borrows money under a note payable, it debits a cash account for the amount of cash received and credits a notes payable account to record the liability. For example, a bank loans ABC Company $1,000,000; ABC records the entry as follows:

(DR) Bank $1,000,000
  (CR) Account Payable $1,000,000

## 6.4    Current Maturities of Long-Term Debt

The current portion of a long-term debt should be included in current liabilities. Current maturities of long-term debt are frequently identified in the current liabilities portion of the balance sheet as long-term debt due within one year. It is not necessary to prepare an adjusting entry to recognize the current maturity of long-term debt.

---

### Example

Assume that Zhing Corporation borrows $10,000,000 from Wells Fargo Bank. The loan is not due for five years, Zhing Corporation records the portion of the loan that is not due within the next 12 months as a long-term liability. However, the portion that is due within the next 12 months (say it's $125,000), is the current portion of long-term debt and is recorded as a current liability.
(DR) Loan payment $125,000
(CR) Current liability $125,000

---

## 6.5    Other Current Liabilities

Other current liabilities include short-term liabilities that are too insignificant to be identified separately. The most commonly reported are sales tax, income tax, payroll, and customer advances (deferred revenue).

## 6.6    Working Capital

Working capital, sometimes called net working capital, is represented by the excess of current assets over current liabilities and identifies the relatively liquid portion of total enterprise capital which constitutes a margin or buffers for meeting obligations within the ordinary operating cycle of the business.[1] Working capital is a common measure of a company's liquidity, efficiency, and overall health.

The working capital of a borrower has always been of prime interest to grantors of credit; and bond indentures, credit agreements, and

---

[1] ARB 43: Restatement and Revision of Accounting Research Bulletins—Chapter 3.

preferred stock agreements commonly contain provisions restricting corporate actions which would effect a reduction or impairment of working capital. Working capital indicates the optimal investment needs of a business in a short run. Excessive investment in current assets would reduce productivity and inadequately investment could lead to insolvency. A business working capital can be positive, negative, or nil. Positive working capital indicates that a company is well-able to pay off its short-term liabilities as they become due. Conversely, negative working capital indicates that a company is unable to pay its short-term liabilities as they become due. Financial analysts are sensitive to the trend of working capital. A useful tool for determining working capital needs is the operating cycle. A firm working capital policy is reflected in its current ratio, quick ratio, turnover of cash, and securities, etc.

Working capital = current assets − current liabilities

### 6.6.1    Determinants of Working Capital

Several factors influence the level of the working capital of a business: (i) the basic nature of the business, (ii) the business cycle fluctuations, (iii) the size of the business, (iv) the production policy, (v) the seasonal operations, (vi) the growth and expansion of the business, (vii) the market competitiveness, (viii) the supply conditions, (ix) the credit policy, and (x) the manufacturing or production cycle.

### 6.6.2    Financing of Working Capital

The appropriate way to finance working capital is to match the maturity of the assets with the maturity of the financing. This approach is known as the moderate approach. However, in times of credit restrictions or contractions when interest rates are higher, some firms manage to consider a more aggressive approach of using short-term financing to finance permanent assets.

### 6.6.3   Computation of Working Capital: Example

| Current Assets | 2014 | 2013 |
|---|---|---|
| Cash & cash equivalents | 6000 | 5000 |
| Marketable securities | 1800 | 1500 |
| Accounts receivable | 50,000 | 40,000 |
| Inventories | 80,000 | 70,000 |
| Prepaid expenses & other current assets | 5200 | 6500 |
| Total | 144,000 | 123,000 |

| Current Liabilities | 2014 | 2013 |
|---|---|---|
| Accounts payable | 60,000 | 55,000 |
| Notes payable | 40,000 | 45,000 |
| Accrued expenses | 20,000 | 25,000 |
| Income tax payable | 15,000 | 25,000 |
| Other liabilities | 5000 | 10,000 |
| Current portion of LT debt | 2000 | 4000 |
| Total | 142,000 | 164,000 |

*Solution*
Current assets − current liabilities = working capital

| Working Capital in 2014 | Working Capital in 2013 |
|---|---|
| 144,000 − 142,000 = 2000 | 123,000 − 164,000 = −41,000 |
| (positive working capital) | (negative working capital) |

# CHAPTER 7

# Long-Term Assets:
# Plant, Property, and Equipment

## 7.1 GENERAL

Capital expenditures are significant for many companies. For example, at Jet Blue Airways, plant assets are 69% of its total assets. For Wal-Mart Stores, Inc., it's 53%. Conversely, Microsoft's percentage is just 3%.

Thus, not only do companies have to be careful in planning the proper amount of capital expenditures, but users must understand the impact of these expenditures on measures of financial performance. As illustrated by the examples above, the level of capital expenditures, depreciation expense, cash flow from operations, and net income all play a role in assessing a company's ability to generate future cash flows.

## 7.2 PROPERTY, PLANT, AND EQUIPMENT

Companies like Boeing, Target, and Starbucks use assets of a durable nature. Such assets are called property, plant, and equipment. Other terms commonly used are plant assets and fixed assets. Property, plant, and equipment include land, building structures (offices, factories, warehouses), and equipment (machinery, furniture, tools).

The major characteristics of property, plant, and equipment are as follows.

© The Author(s) 2018
F. I. Lessambo, *Financial Statements*,
https://doi.org/10.1007/978-3-319-99984-5_7

1. They are acquired for use in operations and not for resale. Only assets used in normal business operations are classified as property, plant, and equipment. For example, an idle building is more appropriately classified separately as an investment. Land developers or subdividers classify land as inventory.
2. They are long-term in nature and usually depreciated. Property, plant, and equipment yield services over a number of years. Companies allocate the cost of the investment in these assets to future periods through periodic depreciation charges. The exception is land, which is depreciated only if a material decrease in value occurs, such as a loss in fertility of agricultural land because of poor crop rotation, drought, or soil erosion.
3. They possess physical substance. Property, plant, and equipment are tangible assets characterized by physical existence or substance. This differentiates them from intangible assets, such as patents or goodwill. Unlike raw material, however, property, plant, and equipment do not physically become part of a product held for resale.

### 7.2.1   Acquisition of Property, Plant, and Equipment

Most companies use historical cost as the basis for valuing property, plant, and equipment. Historical cost measures the cash or cash equivalent price of obtaining the asset and bringing it to the location and condition necessary for its intended use.

Subsequent to acquisition, companies should not write-up property, plant, and equipment to reflect fair value when it is above cost. The main reasons for this position are as follows.

1. Historical cost involves actual, not hypothetical, transactions and so is the most reliable.
2. Companies should not anticipate gains and losses but should recognize gains and losses only when the asset is sold.

Even those who favor fair value measurement for inventory and financial instruments often take the position that property, plant, and equipment should not be revalued. The major concern is the difficulty of developing a reliable fair value for these types of assets.

A long-lived asset classified as held for sale should be measured at the lower of its carrying amount or fair value less costs to sell. In that case, a reasonable valuation for the asset can be obtained, based on the sales price. A long-lived asset is not depreciated if it is classified as held for sale. This is because such assets are not being used to generate revenues.

### 7.2.2    Cost of Land

All expenditures made to acquire land and ready it for use are considered part of the land cost. Thus, when Wal-Mart Stores, Inc. or Home Depot purchases land on which to build a new store, its land costs typically include (1) the purchase price; (2) closing costs, such as title to the land, attorney's fees, and recording fees; (3) costs incurred in getting the land in condition for its intended use, such as grading, filling, draining, and clearing; (4) assumption of any liens, mortgages, or encumbrances on the property; and (5) any additional land improvements that have an indefinite life.

### Example

In some cases, when Home Depot purchases land, it may assume certain obligations on the land such as back taxes or liens. In such situations, the cost of the land is the cash paid for it, plus the encumbrances. In other words, if the purchase price of the land is $50,000 cash but Home Depot assumes accrued property taxes of $5000 and liens of $10,000, its land cost is $65,000.

Home Depot also might incur special assessments for local improvements, such as pavements, street lights, sewers, and drainage systems. It should charge these costs to the Land account because they are relatively permanent in nature. That is, after installation, they are maintained by the local government. In addition, Home Depot should charge any permanent improvements it makes, such as landscaping, to the Land account. It records separately any improvements with limited lives, such as private driveways, walks, fences, and parking lots, as land improvements. These costs are depreciated over their estimated lives.

Generally, land is part of property, plant, and equipment. However, if the major purpose of acquiring and holding land is speculative, a company more appropriately classifies the land as an investment. If a real estate concern holds the land for resale, it should classify the land as inventory.

### 7.2.3    Cost of Buildings

The cost of buildings should include all expenditures related directly to their acquisition or construction. These costs include (1) materials, labor, and overhead costs incurred during construction and (2) professional fees and building permits. Generally, companies contract others to construct their buildings. Companies consider all costs incurred, from excavation to completion, as part of the building costs.

### 7.2.4    Cost of Equipment

The term "Of equipment" in accounting includes delivery equipment, office equipment, machinery, furniture and fixtures, furnishings, factory equipment, and similar fixed assets. The cost of such assets includes the purchase price, freight and handling charges incurred, insurance on the equipment while in transit, cost of special foundations if required, assembling and installation costs, and costs of conducting trial runs. Costs thus include all expenditures incurred in acquiring the equipment and preparing it for use.

## 7.3    VALUATION
## OF PROPERTY, PLANT, AND EQUIPMENT

Like other assets, companies should record property, plant, and equipment at the fair value of what they give up or at the fair value of the asset received, whichever is more clearly evident. However, the process of asset acquisition sometimes obscures fair value. For example, if a company buys land and buildings together for one price, how does it determine separate values for the land and buildings?

## 7.4    Amortization, Depreciation, and Depletion

The GAAP provides several methods of amortization, depreciation, and depletion. Thus, the choice relies upon the management to pick up the one that best suits the company's financial goals.

### 7.4.1    Straight-Line Method of Depreciation

In straight-line depreciation method, depreciation is charged uniformly over the life of an asset. We first subtract residual value of the asset from its cost to obtain the depreciable amount. The depreciable amount is then divided by the useful life of the asset in number of accounting periods to obtain depreciation expense per accounting period. Due to the simplicity of the straight-line method of depreciation, it is the most commonly used depreciation method.

The formula to calculate the straight-line depreciation of an asset for a full accounting period is:

Depreciation = Cost − Salvage Value/Life in Number of Periods

### Example 1

On Jan 1, 2014, Company A purchased a vehicle costing $20,000. It is expected to have a value of $5000 at the end of 4 years.
Tasks: (i) prepare the amortization table; (ii) calculate depreciation expense on the vehicle for the year ended Dec 31, 2014; and (iii) Record the amortization within a journal entry.

### Solution

We will first find the depreciable amount which is $15,000 ($20,000 cost minus $5000 residual value). Then we divide the depreciable amount by the 4 which is the useful life of the vehicle. This will give a figure of $3750 for the yearly depreciation.

Depreciation

$$(\$20{,}000 - \$5000) \div 4 = \$3750$$

### Example 2

Assumed that the corporation acquires the PPE on January 1, 2014. That is not always the case. A corporation can acquire a PPE anytime during a fiscal year. If so the yearly amortization must be adjusted as in Example 2.

### Solution

Occasionally, we may need to charge depreciation for a period less than full financial year. For example, if the vehicle was purchased on July 1, the depreciation should be charged only for a portion of the financial year. In such situation, we multiply the full year straight-line depreciation formula by the fraction the asset has been used in the current accounting period. This is illustrated below.

Depreciation Expense
$$(6 \text{ months} / 12 \text{ months}) \times [(\$20,000 - \$5000) \div 4] = \$1875$$
Tasks: Same as in Example 1.

### 7.4.2    Declining Balance Method of Depreciation

Declining balance method of depreciation is a technique of accelerated depreciation in which the amount of depreciation that is charged to an asset declines over time. In other words, more depreciation is charged during the beginning of the lifetime and less is charged during the end.

Why more depreciation is charged in beginning years? The reason is that assets are usually more productive when they are new and their productivity declines gradually. Thus, in the early years of their lifetime, assets generate more revenue as compared to the revenue generated in later years of their life. According to the matching principle of accounting, we should depreciate more of the asset's cost in early years to match the depreciation expense with the revenue earned from the use of the asset.

Declining balance depreciation is calculated using the following formula:

Depreciation = Depreciation Rate × Book Value of Asset

Depreciation rate is given by the following formula:

$$\text{Depreciation Rate} = \text{Accelerator} \times \text{Straight Line Rate}$$

Note: In the above formula, accelerator is a multiplication factor which accelerates depreciation. Book value is the difference between cost of an asset and its accumulated depreciation. During the first accounting period, accumulated depreciation is zero so book value is equal to cost. Since the book value decreases after each depreciation charge, depreciation expense declines in successive charges.

Depreciation is charged according to the above method as long as book value is less than the salvage value of the asset. No more depreciation is provided when book value equals salvage value.

### 7.4.3  Double Declining Balance Depreciation Method

Double declining balance depreciation method is a type of declining balance depreciation method in which depreciation rate is double the straight-line depreciation rate. For straight-line depreciation rate of 8%, double declining balance rate will be $2 \times 8\% = 16\%$.

### Example 1

An asset costing $20,000 has estimated useful life of 5 years and salvage value of $4500.
Tasks: (i) Prepare the amortization table; (ii) Calculate the depreciation for the first year of its life using double declining balance method; and (iii) Record the depreciation within a journal entry.

### Solution

Straight-line Depreciation Rate $= 1 \div 5 = 0.2 = 20\%$
Declining Balance Rate $= 2 \times 20\% = 40\%$
Depreciation $= 40\% \times \$20,000 = \$8000$

## Example 2

Referring to Example 1, calculate the depreciation of the asset for the second year of its life.

### Solution

Declining Balance Rate $= 40\%$
Book Value $=$ Cost $-$ Accumulated Depreciation $= \$20,000 - \$8000 = \$12,000$
Depreciation $= 40\% \times \$12,000 = \$4800$

## Example 3

Calculate the depreciation of the asset mentioned in the above examples for the third year.

### Solution

Declining Balance Rate $= 40\%$
Book Value $= \$20,000 - \$8000 - \$4800 = \$7200$
Depreciation $= 40\% \times \$7200 = \$2880$

The depreciation calculated above will decrease the book value of the asset below its estimated residual value ($\$7200 - \$2880 = \$4320 < \$4500$). Therefore depreciation would only be allowed up to the point where book value $=$ salvage value. Thus,
Depreciation Allowed $= \$7200 - \$4500 = \$2700$.

### 7.4.4    Units of Production Method of Depreciation

In units of production method of depreciation, depreciation is charged according to the actual usage of the asset. In units of production method, higher depreciation is charged when there is higher activity and less is charged when there is low level of operation. Zero depreciation is charged when the asset is idle for the whole period. This method is similar to straight-line method except that life of the asset is estimated in terms of number of operations or number of machine hours etc.

Such a method is useful where a company has many fixed assets with varying usage.

The following formula is used to calculate depreciation under this method:

$$\text{Depreciation} = \text{Number of Units Produced} \times (\text{Cost} - \text{Salvage Value})/\text{Life in Number of Units}$$

### Example 1

A plant costing $110 million was purchased on April 1, 2010. The salvage value was estimated to be $10 million. The expected production was 150 million units. The plant was used to produce 15 million units till the year ended December 31, 2010. Calculate the depreciation on the plant for the year ended December 31, 2011.

### Solution

Depreciation = (15/150) × ($110 million − $10 million) = $10 million.

### Example 2

A coal mine was purchased by X Corporation for $16 million. It was estimated that the mine has capacity to produce 200,000 tons of coal. The company extracted 46,000 tones during its first year of operation. Calculate the depreciation.

### Solution

Depreciation = (46,000/200,000) × $16 million = $3.68 million.

### *7.4.5   Sum of the Years' Digits Method of Depreciation*

Sum of the years' digits method of depreciation is one of the accelerated depreciation techniques which are based on the assumption that assets are generally more productive when they are new and their productivity decreases as they become old. The formula to calculate depreciation under SYD method is:

$$SYD \, Depreciation = Depreciable \, Base \times Remaining \, Useful$$
$$Life/Sum \, of \, the \, Years' \, Digits$$

In the above formula, depreciable base is the difference between cost and salvage value of the asset and sum of the years' digits is the sum of the series:

1, 2, 3, ..., n; where n is the useful life of the asset in years.

Sum of the years' digits can be calculated more conveniently using the following formula:

Sum of the years' digits method can also be applied on monthly basis, in which case the above formula to calculate the sum of the years' digits becomes much useful.

## Example

Use sum of the years' digits method of depreciation to prepare a depreciation schedule of the following asset:
Cost $45,000
Salvage Value $5000
Useful Life in Years 4
Asset is Depreciated Yearly

## Solution

Sum of the Years' Digits $= 1 + 2 + 3 + 4 = 4(4 + 1) \div 2 = 10$
Depreciable Base $= \$45,000 - \$5000 = \$40,000$

Year Depreciable
Base Depreciation
Factor Depreciation Expense Accumulated
Depreciation
1    $40,000 4/10 4/10 × 40,000 = 16,000 $16,000
2    $40,000 3/10 3/10 × 40,000 = 12,000 $28,000

3   $40,000 2/10 2/10 × 40,000 = 8000 $36,000
4   $40,000 1/10 1/10 × 40,000 = 4000 $40,000

## 7.5   Disposition of Property, Plant, and Equipment

A company, like Intel, may retire plant assets voluntarily or dispose of them by sale, exchange, involuntary conversion, or abandonment. Regardless of the type of disposal, depreciation must be taken up to the date of disposition. Then, Intel should remove all accounts related to the retired asset. Generally, the book value of the specific plant asset does not equal its disposal value. As a result, a gain or loss develops.

The reason: Depreciation is an estimate of cost allocation and not a process of valuation. The gain or loss is really a correction of net income for the years during which Intel used the fixed asset.

### 7.5.1   Sale of Plant Assets

Companies record depreciation for the period of time between the date of the last depreciation entry and the date of sale. To illustrate, assume that Barret Company recorded depreciation on a machine costing $18,000 for 9 years at the rate of $1200 per year. If it sells the machine in the middle of the tenth year for $7000, Barret records depreciation to the date of sale as:

The entry for the sale of the asset then is:

The book value of the machinery at the time of the sale is $6600 ($18,000–$11,400). Because the machinery sold for $7000, the amount of the gain on the sale is $400.

### 7.5.2   Involuntary Conversion

Sometimes an asset's service is terminated through some type of involuntary conversions such as fire, flood, theft, or condemnation. Companies report the difference between the amount recovered (e.g., from a condemnation award or insurance recovery), if any, and the asset's book value as a gain or loss. They treat these gains or losses like any other type of disposition. In some cases, these gains or losses may be reported as extraordinary items in the income statement if the conditions of the disposition are unusual and infrequent in nature.

To illustrate, Camel Transport Corp. had to sell a plant located on company property that stood directly in the path of an interstate highway. For a number of years, the state had sought to purchase the land on which the plant stood, but the company resisted. The state ultimately exercised its right of eminent domain, which the courts upheld. In settlement, Camel received $500,000, which substantially exceeded the $200,000 book value of the plant and land (cost of $400,000 less accumulated depreciation of $200,000). Camel made the following entry.

If the conditions surrounding the condemnation are judged to be unusual and infrequent, Camel's infrequent, Camel's gain of $300,000 is reported as an extraordinary item.

Some object to the recognition of a gain or loss in certain involuntary conversions. For example, the federal government often condemns forests for national parks. The paper companies that owned these forests must report a gain or loss on the condemnation. However, companies such as Georgia-Pacific contend that no gain or loss should be reported because they must replace the condemned forest land immediately and so are in the same economic position as they were before. The issue is whether condemnation and subsequent purchase should be viewed as one or two transactions. GAAP requires "that a gain or loss be recognized when a nonmonetary asset is involuntarily converted to monetary assets even though an enterprise reinvests or is obligated to reinvest the monetary assets in replacement nonmonetary assets."

### 7.5.3    Miscellaneous Problems

If a company scraps or abandons an asset without any cash recovery, it recognizes a loss equal to the asset's book value. If scrap value exists, the gain or loss that occurs is the difference between the asset's scrap value and its book value. If an asset still can be used even though it is fully depreciated, it may be kept on the books at historical cost less depreciation.

Companies must disclose in notes to the financial statements the amount of fully depreciated assets in service. For example, Petroleum Equipment Tools Inc. in its annual report disclosed, "The amount of fully depreciated assets included in property, plant, and equipment at December 31 amounted to approximately $98,900,000."

# CHAPTER 8

# Long-Term Assets: Intangibles

## 8.1 General

FASB 142 provides guidance for the initial recognition of intangible assets either acquired or internally developed. It also provides companies with guidance on how to account for any intangible asset in periods following the asset's initial recognition. A company should measure an intangible asset at its fair value at the time of acquisition. The costs of internally developing, maintaining, or restoring intangible assets generally should be expensed as incurred (with some exceptions). Intangible assets other than goodwill may or may not be amortized depending on their useful lives to the entity: Assets with finite lives are amortized; assets with indefinite lives are not. Goodwill is not amortized. Prior to Statement No. 142 the amortization period of an asset was limited to 40 years. Under FASB 142, there is no arbitrary ceiling on the useful life of an amortized asset. The amortization method should reflect the pattern in which the company uses up the benefits the asset provides, with the straight-line method the default choice.

The amortization process is a systematic write-off of the cost of an intangible asset to an expense, which effectively allocates a portion of the intangible asset's cost to each accounting period in the economic or legal life of the asset (an amortization expense).

Intangible assets have a useful life that is either identifiable or indefinite. Intangible assets with identifiable useful lives are amortized on a straight-line basis over their economic or legal life, whichever is shorter.

© The Author(s) 2018                                                                     95
F. I. Lessambo, *Financial Statements*,
https://doi.org/10.1007/978-3-319-99984-5_8

The finite useful life of an intangible asset is considered to be the length of time it is expected to contribute to the cash flows of the reporting entity. Pertinent factors that should be considered in estimating the useful lives of intangible assets include legal, regulatory, or contractual provisions that may limit the useful.

Like tangibles long-term a corporation can only include in the basis for amortization the immediate purchase costs of an intangible asset, which do not include the costs associated with internal development or self-creation of the asset. If an intangible asset is internally generated in its entirety, none of the costs related to the asset are capitalized.

### Example

Yin Corporation purchases a patent for $100,000, which enables the owner to manufacture, sell, lease, or otherwise benefit from an invention for 10 years. Yin Corp. would have to recognize an intangible asset valued at $100,000 and amortize that cost over 10 years. Each year, Yin Corp. will recognize an expense of $10,000 in addition to decreasing the value of the patent reported on the balance sheet by $10,000.

Intangible assets other than that a company is not amortizing shall be reevaluated in each reporting period to determine whether amortization should begin (if the assets' useful lives go from indefinite to definite). Companies shall test intangible assets, including goodwill, for impairment at least annually and recognize an impairment loss in any period where the asset's recorded value is higher than its fair value.

## 8.2    THE GOODWILL

Goodwill is an intangible asset associated with a business combination. Goodwill is recorded when a company acquires (purchases) another company and the purchase price is greater than the combination or net of (i) the fair value of the identifiable tangible and intangible assets acquired and (ii) the liabilities that were assumed.

## 8.2.1    Goodwill Impairment[1]

Goodwill of a reporting unit shall be tested for impairment on an annual basis and between annual tests in certain circumstances. The annual goodwill impairment test may be performed any time during the fiscal year provided the test is performed at the same time every year. Exceptionally, Goodwill of a reporting unit shall be tested for impairment between annual tests if an event occurs or circumstances change that would more likely than not reduce the fair value of a reporting unit below its carrying amount.

In evaluating whether it is more likely than not that the fair value of a reporting unit is less than its carrying amount, an entity shall assess relevant events and circumstances. Examples of such events and circumstances include the following:

- Macroeconomic conditions such as a deterioration in general economic conditions, limitations on accessing capital, fluctuations in foreign exchange rates, or other developments in equity and credit markets;
- Industry and market considerations such as a deterioration in the environment in which an entity operates, an increased competitive environment, a decline in market-dependent multiples or metrics (consider in both absolute terms and relative to peers), a change in the market for an entity's products or services, or a regulatory or political development;
- Cost factors such as increases in raw materials, labor, or other costs that have a negative effect on earnings and cash flows;
- Overall financial performance such as negative or declining cash flows or a decline in actual or planned revenue or earnings compared with actual and projected results of relevant prior periods;
- Other relevant entity-specific events such as changes in management, key personnel, strategy, or customers; contemplation of bankruptcy; or litigation;
- Events affecting a reporting unit such as a change in the composition or carrying amount of its net assets, a more-likely-than-not expectation of selling or disposing all, or a portion, of a reporting unit, the testing for recoverability of a significant asset group within

[1] ASC 350.

a reporting unit, or recognition of a goodwill impairment loss in the financial statements of a subsidiary that is a component of a reporting unit; and

• If applicable, a sustained decrease in share price (consider in both absolute terms and relative to peers).

If, after assessing the totality of the aforementioned events or circumstances, an entity determines that it is more likely than not that the fair value of a reporting unit is less than its carrying amount, then the entity shall perform the first step of the two-step goodwill impairment test. If the carrying amount of a reporting unit is greater than zero and its fair value exceeds its carrying amount, goodwill of the reporting unit is considered not impaired; thus, the second step of the impairment test is unnecessary. On the reverse, if the carrying amount of a reporting unit exceeds its fair value, the second step of the goodwill impairment test shall be performed to measure the amount of impairment loss, if any. In the later case, the impairment test shall be performed to measure the amount of impairment loss (Table 8.1).

**Table 8.1**  Starbucks (2014): Changes in the carrying amount of goodwill

*Goodwill*

Changes in the carrying amount of goodwill by reportable operating segment *(in millions)*:

| | Americas | EMEA | China / Asia Pacific | Channel Development | All Other Segments | Total |
|---|---|---|---|---|---|---|
| Balance at September 30, 2012 | | | | | | |
| Goodwill prior to impairment | $ 235.9 | $ 60.0 | $ 75.3 | $ 23.8 | $ 12.7 | $ 407.7 |
| Accumulated impairment charges | (8.6) | — | — | — | — | (8.6) |
| Goodwill | $ 227.3 | $ 60.0 | $ 75.3 | $ 23.8 | $ 12.7 | $ 399.1 |
| Acquisitions/(divestitures) | (3.7) | — | — | — | 467.5 | 463.8 |
| Other[1] | (2.0) | 2.2 | (0.2) | — | — | — |
| Balance at September 29, 2013 | | | | | | |
| Goodwill prior to impairment | $ 230.2 | $ 62.2 | $ 75.1 | $ 23.8 | $ 480.2 | $ 871.5 |
| Accumulated impairment charges | (8.6) | — | — | — | — | (8.6) |
| Goodwill | $ 221.6 | $ 62.2 | $ 75.1 | $ 23.8 | $ 480.2 | $ 862.9 |
| Impairment | — | — | — | — | (0.8) | (0.8) |
| Other[1] | (2.6) | (3.1) | (0.2) | — | — | (5.9) |
| Balance at September 28, 2014 | | | | | | |
| Goodwill prior to impairment | $ 227.6 | $ 59.1 | $ 74.9 | $ 23.8 | $ 480.2 | $ 865.6 |
| Accumulated impairment charges | (8.6) | — | — | — | (0.8) | (9.4) |
| Goodwill | $ 219.0 | $ 59.1 | $ 74.9 | $ 23.8 | $ 479.4 | $ 856.2 |

[1] Other is primarily comprised of changes in the goodwill balance as a result of foreign exchange fluctuations

*Source* SEC—Starbucks 2014

From the goodwill table above, the carrying amount of the goodwill varies largely from one segment to another, the Americas' segment bearing the largest portion of the overall charges and changes.

**In summary:**

- Step 1

The first step of the goodwill impairment test identifies potential impairment and compares the fair value of a reporting unit with its carrying amount, including goodwill.

- Step 2

The second step of the goodwill impairment test measures the amount of impairment loss and compares the implied fair value of reporting unit goodwill with the carrying amount of that goodwill.

In determining the implied fair value of a reporting unit, an entity shall assign the fair value of a reporting unit to all of the assets and liabilities of that unit (including any unrecognized intangible assets) as if the reporting unit had been acquired in a business combination or an acquisition by a not-for-profit entity.

After a goodwill impairment loss is recognized, the adjusted carrying amount of goodwill shall be its new accounting basis. Subsequent reversal of a previously recognized goodwill impairment loss is prohibited once the measurement of that loss is recognized.

### Example of Goodwill Impairment

- On January 1, 2005, Mozes LLC purchased a building for $2 million.
- The building estimated useful life at that date was 20 years, and Mozes LLC uses the straight-line depreciation method.
- On December 31, 2009, the government embarked on a plan to construct a flyover adjacent to the building and the related installation reduced the access to the building thereby decreasing the value of the building.

- Mozes LLC estimated that it can sell the Building for $1 million but it has to incur cost of $50,000. Alternatively, if Mozes LLC continued to use the building, the present value of the net cash flows from the building will help in generating is estimated to $1.2 million.

Task: Determine the goodwill impairment, if any?

### Solution

- First, we need to determine the carrying amount of the building:
  - The building has a cost of $2 million, useful life of 20 years, and was used for 5 years (2005–2009). Thus, the carrying value $2 million−500,000 = 1,500,000
- Second, we need to determine the recoverable amount: The recoverable amount is the higher of the fair value minus the cost to sell, and the value in use.
  - Fair value minus cost to sell = $1 million−50,000 = $950,000
  - The value in use is the present value of future cash flows which amounts to $1.2 million.
- Third, determination of the impairment: The carrying amount is $1.5 million, while the recoverable amount is $1.2 million. Thus, the impairment is $300,000
- The impairment would be recorded as follows:

(DR) Impairment loss 300,000
(CR) Accumulated impairment losses 300,000

IFRS for Goodwill.[2]

International Accounting Standard 36, Impairment of Assets, requires an entity to test goodwill for impairment using a single-step quantitative test performed at the level of a cash-generating unit or group of

---

[2] IAS 36.

cash-generating units. The test must be performed at least annually and between annual tests whenever there is an indication of impairment. IAS 36 requires an entity to compare the carrying amount of a cash-generating unit with its recoverable amount. An entity would record the excess of the carrying amount over the recoverable amount as an impairment loss, and the amount of that impairment loss is not limited to the carrying amount of goodwill recorded in the cash-generating unit.

IFRS for small- and medium-sized entities requires goodwill to be amortized over its estimated useful life, or a 10-year period if a reliable estimate of the useful life cannot be made. An entity reporting under IFRS for small- and medium-sized entities is required to assess, on the basis of qualitative factors, whether there is any indication that goodwill may be impaired at each reporting date.

## 8.3   Computer Software

The guidance in the software topic applies to computer software to be sold, leased, or otherwise marketed as a separate product or as part of a product or process. However, the guidance does not apply to (a) software created for internal use or for others under a contractual agreement and (b) research and development assets acquired in a business combination or an acquisition by a not-for-profit entity.

### 8.3.1   Research and Development Costs of Computer Software

All costs incurred to establish the technological feasibility of a computer software product to be sold, leased, or otherwise marketed are research and development costs. Those costs shall be charged to expense when incurred. The technological feasibility of a computer software product is established when the entity has completed all planning, designing, coding, and testing activities that are necessary to establish that the product can be produced to meet its design specifications including functions, features, and technical performance requirements.

### 8.3.2   Production Costs of Computer Software

Software production costs for computer software that is to be used as an integral part of a product or process shall not be capitalized until both of the following conditions have been met:

- Technological feasibility has been established for the software.
- All research and development activities for the other components of the product or process have been completed.

Capitalization of computer software costs shall cease when the product is available for general release to customers. Costs of maintenance and customer support shall be charged to expense when related revenue is recognized or when those costs are incurred, whichever occurs first.

### 8.3.3    Purchased Computer Software

The cost of purchased computer software to be sold, leased, or otherwise marketed that has no alternative future use shall be accounted for the same as the costs incurred to develop such software internally. The cost of software purchased to be integrated with another product or process shall be capitalized only if technological feasibility is established for the software component and if all research and development activities for the other components of the product or process are completed at the time of purchase. If purchased software has an alternative future use, the cost shall be capitalized when the software is acquired and accounted for in accordance with its use. The alternative future use test also applies to purchased software that will be integrated with a product or process in which the research and development activities for the other components are not complete.

### 8.3.4    Amortization of Capitalized Software Costs

Capitalized software costs shall be amortized on a product-by-product basis. Amortization shall start when the product is available for general release to customers. The annual amortization shall be the greater of the amounts computed using the following:

- The ratio that current gross revenues for a product bear to the total of current and anticipated future gross revenues for that product.
- The straight-line method over the remaining estimated economic life of the product including the period being reported on.

Because a net realizable value test, which considers future revenues and costs, must be applied to capitalized costs, amortization shall be based on estimated future revenues. In recognition of the uncertainties involved in estimating revenue, amortization shall not be less than straight-line amortization over the product's remaining estimated economic life. At each balance sheet date, the unamortized capitalized costs of a computer software product shall be compared to the net realizable value of that product. The amount by which the unamortized capitalized costs of a computer software product exceed the net realizable value of that asset shall be written off. The net realizable value is the estimated future gross revenues from that product reduced by the estimated future costs of completing and disposing of that product, including the costs of performing maintenance and customer support required to satisfy the entity's responsibility set forth at the time of sale. The reduced amount of capitalized computer software costs that have been written down to net realizable value at the close of an annual fiscal period shall be considered to be the cost for subsequent accounting purposes, and the amount of the write-down shall not be subsequently restored.

### 8.3.5 Presentation and Disclosure of Software Costs

In an entity's balance sheet, capitalized software costs having a life of more than one year or one operating cycle shall be presented as another asset because the costs are an amortizable intangible asset. Both of the following shall be disclosed in the financial statements:

- Unamortized computer software costs included in each balance sheet presented.
- The total amount charged to expense in each income statement presented for both of the following: (i) amortization of capitalized computer software costs and (ii) amounts written down to net realizable value.
- The amortization and write-down amounts may be combined with only the total of the two expenses being disclosed.

### 8.3.6 Software Purchased Before Technological Feasibility Established

An entity may purchase software before technological feasibility has been established. For example, an entity purchases software for $100,000 that can be resold for $75,000. The amount of $25,000 would be charged to research and development, and $75,000 would be capitalized. If the software product reached technological feasibility, the $75,000 would be included in the cost of the software product. If the technological feasibility of the software was never established, the $75,000 would be classified as inventory.

### 8.3.7 Disclosure of Risks and Uncertainties Related to Capitalized Software Costs

Software Inc. develops and markets computer programs. In 20X3, it acquired a software entity. A significant portion of the purchase price was allocated to (capitalized) Product A (present net book value of $5 million), the most significant and profitable software program currently being marketed by the acquired entity. Only nominal amounts of other software costs have been capitalized. Software Inc. expects Product A and its derivatives to be among its most significant products over the next several years. However, a competitor has recently released a new product designed to compete directly with Product A. Software Inc. amortizes the capitalized software costs of Product A by the greater of the following:

- The ratio that current gross revenues for a product bear to the total of current and anticipated future gross revenues for that product.
- The straight-line method over the remaining estimated economic life of the product including the period being reported on.

# CHAPTER 9

# Long-Term Liabilities: Leases

## 9.1 GENERAL

In 2016, FASB has revisited previous accounting rules (GAAP) concerning leases and issued—leases—Topic 842.[1] The new standard applies to leases (and subleases) of all assets except:

- Leases of intangible assets, inventory, biological assets, assets under construction;
- Leases to explore for the use of minerals, oil, natural gas, and similar resources.

## 9.2 LEASE

### 9.2.1 Legal Definition of a Lease

Topic 842 defines a lease as a contract, or part of a contract, that conveys the right to control the use of identified property, plant, or equipment (an identified asset) for a period of time in exchange for consideration. Control over the use of the identified asset means that the customer has both (1) the right to obtain substantially all of the economic benefits from the use of the asset and (2) the right to direct the use of the asset.

---

[1] FASB—Accounting Standards Update—No. 2016-02.

© The Author(s) 2018
F. I. Lessambo, *Financial Statements*,
https://doi.org/10.1007/978-3-319-99984-5_9

More, Topic 842 requires an entity to separate the lease components from the non-lease components (i.e., maintenance services or other activities that transfer a good or service to the customer) in a contract. The right to control the use of the underlying property, plant, or equipment is conveyed if any of the following conditions is met:

a. The purchaser has the ability or right to operate the property, plant, or equipment or direct others to operate the property, plant, or equipment in a manner it determines while obtaining or controlling more than a minor amount of the output or other utility of the property, plant, or equipment. The purchaser's ability to operate the property, plant, or equipment may be evidenced by (but is not limited to) the purchaser's ability to hire, fire, or replace the property's operator or the purchaser's ability to specify significant operating policies and procedures in the arrangement with the owner–seller having no ability to change such policies and procedures. A requirement to follow prudent operating practices (or other similar requirements) generally does not convey the right to control the underlying property, plant, or equipment. Similarly, a contractual requirement designed to enable the purchaser to monitor or ensure the seller's compliance with performance, safety, pollution control, or other general standards generally does not establish control over the underlying property, plant, or equipment.
b. The purchaser has the ability or right to control physical access to the underlying property, plant, or equipment while obtaining or controlling more than a minor amount of the output or other utility of the property, plant, or equipment.
c. Facts and circumstances indicate that it is remote that one or more parties other than the purchaser will take more than a minor amount of the output or other utility that will be produced or generated by the property, plant, or equipment during the term of the arrangement, and the price that the purchaser (lessee) will pay for the output is neither contractually fixed per unit of output nor equal to the current market price per unit of output as of the time of delivery of the output.

The definition of a lease does not include agreements that are contracts for services that do not transfer the right to use property, plant, or equipment from one contracting party to the other. Further, although specific property, plant, or equipment may be explicitly identified in an arrangement, it is not the subject of a lease if fulfillment of the arrangement is not dependent on the use of the specified property, plant, or equipment. However, addition, a contractual provision (contingent or otherwise) permitting or requiring the owner–seller to substitute other property, plant, or equipment for any reason on or after a specified date does not preclude lease treatment before the date of substitution.

A lease is either an operating lease in which the risks and rewards inherent in the asset are not transferred to the lessee or it is a finance lease (also called capital lease in US GAAP) in which the risks and rewards inherent in the asset are transferred to the lessee. Substance-over-form principle is applied to determine whether risks and rewards have transferred or not, which means that transfer of legal ownership is not very relevant in deciding whether a lease is an operating lease or a finance lease.

### 9.2.2   Advantages and Disadvantages of Leasing

Lessees engage in leases because it allows them financial flexibility. Instead of paying off all of the cost of expensive equipment at one time, the burden is spread out over a period of time which frees resources for other cash flows requirements. Further, lease guards the lessee against obsolescence. Whenever new technology is available, it can switch over to the newer technology by terminating the lease. A fully owned technology on the other hand is not easy to replace. The main drawback to a lease is its financial cost. Lease is a kind of credit facility, and the lessee has to pay interest expense over the period. In many cases, leases might not be that easy to exit owing to their exit penalties, etc.

## 9.3   Types of Leases

The new guidance retains the distinction between finance leases and operating leases. The treatment is substantially similar to the previous guidance distinctions between capital and operating leases.

### 9.3.1   Finance Lease

Under financing leases, the lease recognizes (i) the right-to-use asset and (ii) lease liability are both recognized and discounted to present value. Each payment has two components (interest and principal).

A lease qualifies as a finance/sales-type lease if it satisfies one or more of the five criteria below:

1. The agreement specifies that ownership of the asset transfers to the lessee.
2. The agreement contains a purchase option that the lessee is reasonably certain to exercise (bargain purchase option).
3. The lease term is for the "major part" of the remaining economic life of the underlying asset.
4. The present value of the lease payments equals or exceeds "substantially all" of the fair value of the underlying asset.
5. The underlying asset is of such a specialized nature that it is expected to have no alternative use to the lessor at the end of the lease term.

**Example**

- On January 1, 2018, McCoy LLC leased an airplane from MatFinancing Inc.
- MatFinancing has purchased the airplane from Boeing Inc. for 800,000.
- The lease agreement specifies eight annual payments of $125,000 beginning as from January 1, 2018 (the beginning of the lease) and at each December 31 thereafter through 2025.
- The eight-year lease term ending on December 31, 2025 is equal to the estimated useful life of the airplane.
- MatFinancing Inc. owed interest rate at 10% to Boeing Inc.
Task: Record the lease in the journal entry of both McCoy LL and MatFinancing Inc.

**Solution**

- McCoy Journal:
    At the beginning of the lease
    (DR) Right-of-use asset 800,000
        (CR) Lease Payable 800,000
    - First lease payment
    (DR) Lease payable 125,000
        (CR) Cash 125,000
- MatFinancing journal:
    - At the beginning of the lease

(DR) Lease receivable 800,000
  (CR) Equipment 800,000
− First lease collection
(DR) Cash 125,000
  (CR) Lease Receivable 125,000

### 9.3.2  Operating Lease

Operating lease is a lease which does not satisfy the criteria for recognition as a capital lease (also known as finance lease). Therefore, operating leases satisfy neither of the following conditions:

- The leased asset is transferred to the lessee at the end of the lease;
- The present value of minimum lease payments is equal to substantively all (>90%) of the fair value of the leased asset;
- The lease contains a bargain purchase option; or
- The lease term is the major part (>70%) of the useful life of the leased asset.

The lease recognizes: (i) a right-of-use asset and (ii) a lease liability at the present value of the lease payments not yet paid, discounted using the discount rate for the lease at lease commencement. More, the lease recognizes interest on the lease liability separately from amortization of the right-of-use asset in the income statement. Overall cost of the lease is allocated over the lease term on a straight-line basis.

#### Example

- On January 1, 2018, McCoy LLC leased an airplane from MatFinancing Inc.
- MatFinancing has purchased the airplane from Boeing Inc. for 650,000.
- McCoy LLC borrowing rate for comparable transactions is 10%.
- The lease agreement specifies six annual payments of $125,000 beginning as from January 1, 2018 (the beginning of the lease) and at each December 31 thereafter through 2025.
- The useful life of the airplane is estimated to be 5 years.

Task: Record the lease in the journal entry of both McCoy LL and MatFinancing Inc.

### Solution

– The present value of an annuity due of $1: $n=6$, $i=10\%$ is 4.1699. Thus, $125,000 \times 4.1699 = 421,237.50$
  - At the beginning of the lease, the lease records:
    (DR) Right-of-use asset 421,237.50
        (CR) Lease payable 421,237.50
  - At First Lease Payment, the lease records:
    (DR) Lease payable 125,000
        (CR) Cash 125,000

## 9.4    SALE–LEASEBACK[2]

ASU 2016-02 represents a substantial change from previous US GAAP related to sale and leaseback transactions. The seller–lessee in a sale and leaseback transaction is required to evaluate the transfer of the underlying asset (sale) under the requirements of ASC 606 to determine whether the transfer qualifies as a sale. The existence of a leaseback by itself would not indicate that control has not been transferred unless the leaseback is classified as a finance lease. In addition, if the arrangement includes an option for the seller–lessee to repurchase the asset, the transaction would not qualify as a sale unless both of the following criteria are met: (i) The option is priced at the fair value of the asset on the date of exercise and (ii) there are alternative assets that are substantially the same as the transferred asset and readily available in the marketplace.

If the transaction does not qualify as a sale, the seller–lessee and buyer–lessor would account for the transaction as a financing arrangement. Conversely, if the transaction qualifies as a sale, the leaseback is accounted for in the same manner as all other leases (i.e., the seller–lessee and buyer–lessor would account for the leaseback under the new accounting guidance for lessees and lessors, respectively).

[2] Topic 842-40-55-22.

### 9.4.1   Sale–Leaseback Advantages

The core advantage of the sale and leaseback arrangement is that entity selling and then leasing the asset is essentially releasing the cash tied up in that asset prior to selling it, while it continues to benefit from the usage of the asset. More, depending on the terms of the arrangement, the sale and leaseback arrangement may be cheaper than financing the purchase of the asset with a bank loan.

### 9.4.2   Accounting Analysis

The analysis of the sale–leaseback transaction leads to consider that two transactions happen in a sale–leaseback transaction:

(i) Seller–lessee receives cash from the sale of the asset.
(ii) Seller–lessee pays periodic rent payments to the buyer–lessor to retain the use of the asset.

Under Topic 842, sale–leaseback can be accounted for under sale-lease-back approach, or financing arrangement. A sale–leaseback arrangement is viewed as a single transaction in which the sale and leaseback are interdependent and negotiated together as a package. The sale–lease-back approach records two transactions: (i) the sale of the asset including applicable gain or loss and (ii) a lease for the leaseback portion in accordance with standard lease guidance. Conversely, under the financing arrangement approach, the arrangement is not considered as a sale, but as a loan by the lessor to the lessee for the "sale" price. Thus, the asset remains on the lessee's books, and the leaseback is accounted for as debt. The lease payments are deemed to be repayment of the loan. It should be noted that the sale–leaseback approach is allowed only in situations where the leaseback qualifies as an operating lease.

### Example

Sale–Leaseback Under the Sale–Leaseback Approach
– Facing a huge shift in their industry, McCoy LLC raised $1 billion by selling and leasing back its headquarter for 10 years.
– The building had an original cost of $2 billion and a carrying value of $800,000. The sale date is December 31, 2018.

- The lease annual payment is $125,000, beginning December 31, 2018.
- The building estimated remaining useful life is 20 years.
- The annual lease payments (present value of $950,000) provide the lessor with 8% rate of return on the financing arrangement.
  Task: Record the transactions in McCoy LLC journal?
  Answer: The seller–lessee should:
- Recognize the transaction price for the sale at the point in time the buyer–lessor obtains control of the asset;
- Adjust the transaction price for any off-market terms and recognize the entire gain/loss on the sale of the asset;
- Derecognize the carrying amount of the underlying asset; and
- Account for the lease in accordance with ASC 842.
  - December 31, 2108
    (DR) Cash 1,000,000
    (DR) Accumulated depreciation 1,200,000
      (CR) Building 2,000,000
      (CR) Gain on sale–leaseback 200,000
    (DR) Right-of-use (PV of lease payments) 950,000
      (CR) Lease Payable 950,000
    (DR) Lease Payable 125,000
      (CR) Cash 125,000

## Example

Failed Sale and Leaseback Transaction
- Seller sells an asset to an unrelated entity (buyer) for cash of $2 million.
- Immediately before the transaction, the asset has a carrying amount of $1.8 million and has a remaining useful life of 21 years.
- At the same time, seller enters into a contract with buyer for the right to use the asset for 8 years with annual payments

of $200,000 payable at the end of each year and no renewal options.
- Seller's incremental borrowing rate at the date of the transaction is 4%.
- The contract includes an option to repurchase the asset at the end of year 5 for $800,000.

Task: Record the transaction in the seller journal?

Solution

- The exercise price of the repurchase option is fixed and, therefore, is not the fair value of the asset on the exercise date of the option.
- Consequently, the repurchase option precludes accounting for the transfer of the asset as a sale.
- Absent the repurchase option, there are no other factors that would preclude accounting for the transfer of the asset as a sale.

• At the commencement date,

- Seller accounts for the proceeds of $2 million as a financial liability and continues to account for the asset.

(DR) Cash 2,000,000
  (CR) Note payable 2,000,000

(DR) Note Payable 200,000
  (CR) Cash 200,000

## 9.5   SHORT-TERM LEASE

For leases with a term of 12 months or less, a lessee is permitted to make an accounting policy election by class of underlying asset not to recognize lease assets and lease liabilities. If a lessee makes this election, it should recognize lease expense for such leases generally on a straight-line basis over the lease term.

### Example

- On January 1, 2018, McCoy LLC leased a copier machine from Boom-Boom Leasing Inc.
- The lease agreement specifies four quarterly payment of 15,000 beginning January 1, 2018, the beginning of the lease, and at the first day of each of the next three quarters.
- The useful life of the equipment is estimated to be four years.

    Task: Record the lease (short-term) in the lease journal entry

### Solution

- At the beginning of the lease (January 1, 2018), there should be no recording because this is a short-term lease
- At the beginning of each quarter, McCoy LLC would record:
    (DR) Lease expense 15,000
    (CR) Cash 15,000

## 9.6    LEASE DISCLOSURE

### 9.6.1    In the Balance Sheet

- Operating and financing right-to-use assets should be presented separately from one another and from other assets. The treatment is the same for lease liabilities, and no netting of the assets and liabilities is allowed.
- In finance leases, interest expense and amortization of the right-to-use can be presented together, but only if that treatment is consistent with how interest expense and depreciation/amortization are presented for other types of assets.
- In operating leases, lease expense is included in income from continuing operations.

### 9.6.2    In the Statement of Cash Flows

- For cash flows, principal payments of the lease liability for financing leases are financing activities.

- Interest expense is an operating activity consistent with statement of cash flows (Topic 230).
- Payments for operating leases are classified as operating activities, and the same holds true for variable lease payments or short-term lease payments.

Finally, the qualitative and quantitative information is required concerning the lease arrangement. These include, among other things: general details about leases, significant judgments made, as well as the amounts recognized in the financials related to those judgments.

# CHAPTER 10

# Long-Term Liabilities: Pension and Postretirement Liabilities

## 10.1   GENERAL

Employee benefits represent the compensation paid to employees in return for the services they provide to the company. A few categories of employee benefits include: short-term employee benefits, post-employment benefit plan, termination benefits, etc.

Short-term employee benefits are "current" employee benefits, i.e., these are expected to be settled within 12 months of the end of the period in which the related services were received from employees. These include wages, salaries and social security contributions, paid annual leave, paid sick leave, profit-sharing arrangements, bonuses (if current). These also include certain non-monetary benefits such as housing, transportation, subsidized services, and medical care.

Post-employment benefits (also called postretirement medical benefits) are employee benefits which are payable after retirement. However, they do not include termination benefits. They include pensions, retirement benefits and postretirement medical facility.

Post-employment benefit plans (also called postretirement employee benefit plans) are arrangements between a company and its employees under which it provides retirement benefits to its employees. There are normally two types of post-employment benefit plans: the defined contribution plan and the defined benefit plan.

© The Author(s) 2018
F. I. Lessambo, *Financial Statements*,
https://doi.org/10.1007/978-3-319-99984-5_10

Termination benefits are employee benefits paid to an employee when his employment is prematurity terminated or he opts for a voluntary redundancy scheme by himself.

## 10.2    Types of Pension Plans

### 10.2.1    Defined Contribution Plan

Defined contribution plan is an employee benefit plan in which the employer undertakes to contribute a specific amount each period to the fund. Since the employer is responsible only for his contributions and nothing else, he does not bear the risks related to the plan rather those risks are borne by employees. The contributions made by the employer are based on the current number of employees and their current salary levels.

- Attributes
  - Promise fixed annual contributions to a pension fund (i.e., employer contributes 5% of the employees' pay).
  - Promise fixed periodic contributions to a pension fund, without further commitment regarding benefit amounts at retirement. Sometimes the amount the employer contributes is tied to the amount of the employee contribution.
- Accounting for a defined contribution plan.

Accounting for defined contribution plan is straightforward. The employer records pension expense equal to the contributions which it is required to make to the plan in accordance with the fund characteristics. The pension plan has no further accounting complications for the employer because the contributions are managed by a trust representing the employees and the employer shares no gain or loss on those funds.

If a plan promises an annual contribution equal to 5% of an employee's salary that amounts to $200,000 in a particular year, the employer simply recognizes pension expense for the amount of the contribution. Thus, the employer would record the following in a journal entry:

(DR) Pension expenses 10,000
   (CR) Cash 10,000

- Components of pension expenses

Pension expenses are made of different components:

---

### Components of Pension Expenses

+ Service cost ascribed to employee service during the period
+ Interest accrued on the pension liability
− Return on the plan assets

- Including the amortized portion of:
+ Prior service cost attributed to employee service before an amendment to the pension plan
+ or − Losses or gains from revisions in the pension liability or from investing plan assets

---

= Pension expense

---

### Example

- John Aristote, Inc. Company has a defined contribution plan. According to employment contracts, it has entered into with its 200 employees it is required to contribute an amount one average monthly salary per employee to the plan.
- Average salary for the financial year ended December 31, 2017 is $60,000.
- The yearly contribution which DCP should record as pension expense amounts to $12,000,000 ($60,000 multiplied by 200).
- The contributions are collected by a trust which represents employees and manages the contributions received for John Aristote, Inc. on their behalf.
- Note also, that any future increase in salary level, decrease in mortality rate, increase in expected inflation and expected return, and prevailing market return, etc. has no impact on the company's expense and liability related to the plan.

### 10.2.2    Defined Benefit Plan

Defined benefit plans provide a fixed, pre-established benefit for employees at retirement. Employees often value the fixed benefit provided by this type of plan. On the employer side, businesses can generally contribute (and therefore deduct) more each year than in defined contribution plans. However, defined benefit plans are often more complex and, thus, more costly to establish and maintain than other types of plans. Promise fixed retirement benefits defined by a designated formula. Pension formula bases retirement pay on the employees' (a) years of service, (b) annual compensation, and sometimes (c) age.

---

### Example

An employee retires after 25 years of service with a final salary of $200,000. The annual benefits are calculated as 1.5% times 25 years times final year's salary:
   $1.5\% \times 25 \times 200,000 = \$75,000$ a year.

---

## 10.3    NET PENSION ASSET/LIABILITY

On the balance sheet the employee presents a net pension asset or a net pension liability. A net pension asset arises when the plan assets are higher than the present value of debit benefit obligation (PVDBO) (also known as projected benefit obligation) while a net pension liability arises when the PVDBO (or PBO) is higher than the plan assets.

---

### Example

Actuaries have calculated that project benefit obligation of EBP's pension plan is $30 million and $36 million in 2010 and 2011, respectively. At the end of 2010, EBP had plan assets of $32 million. During 2011, EBP contributed as amount of $2 million to the fund and paid out benefits of $5 million.

   EBP will report a net pension asset of $2 million for the financial year 2010 ($32 million plan assets −$30 million obligation). At the end of financial year 2011, its obligation is $36 million and its plan assets are $29 million ($32 million+2 million (contribution)−5million (benefits paid out)). It will report a net pension liability of $7 million at the end of financial year 2011 (difference between plan assets of $29 million and obligation of $36 million).

## 10.4   PROJECTED BENEFIT OBLIGATIONS

- Are estimates retirement benefits by applying the pension formula using projected future compensation levels less reliable, but more relevant and representationally faithful.
- It is the measurement of the pension liability used to report amounts in the balance sheet and income statement.

Steps to calculate the projected benefit obligation:

1. Use the pension formula (including a projection of future salary levels) to determine the retirement benefits earned to date.
2. Find the present value of the retirement benefits as of the retirement date (i.e., end of 2046).
3. Find the present value of retirement benefits as of the current date (i.e., end of 2016).

### Example

Jessica Farrow was hired by Global Communications in 2007. The company has a defined benefit pension plan that specifies annual retirement benefits equal to:

1.5% × Service years × Final year's salary

Farrow is expected to retire in 2046 after 40 years of service. Her retirement period is expected to be 20 years. At the end of 2016, 10 years after being hired, her salary is $100,000. The interest rate is 6%. The company's actuary projects Farrow's salary to be $400,000 at retirement.

## 10.5   PLAN ASSETS

Resources with which a company will provide the retirement benefits. Netted together with the PBO to report either a net pension asset (debit balance) or a net pension liability (credit balance) in the balance sheet.

ASC 715 requires the disclosure of the allocation of pension plan assets by type of investment. The allocation of assets in pension plans is an important determinant of the plan's overall investment performance. Moreover, assets allocation strongly influences volatility in the plan's funded status and the plan sponsor's cash and accounting cost.

Reconciliation between opening plan assets and closing plan assets would look like follows:

| | |
|---|---|
| Opening plan assets | XXX |
| Add: contributions received from employer | XXX |
| Add: actual return on plan assets | XXX |
| Less: Benefits paid | (XXX) |
| Add/Less: actuarial gains and losses | XXX |
| Closing plan assets | XXX |

### Example

CE Ltd. has a funded defined benefit plan. Its plan assets had a fair value of $25 million as at January 1, 2011. They include $15 million equity investments and $10 investment in bonds. Equity investments are expected to pay a dividend of $1 million during the year. Bonds are expected to pay an interest of 6%. The fund received contributions of $5 million during the year and paid out $3 million to employees. The fair value of the investments as at December 31, 2011 is $30 million. Reconcile the opening balance of plan assets with closing balance.

## 10.6    REPORTING PENSIONS PLANS
## ON FINANCIAL STATEMENTS

### 10.6.1    In the Statement of Income

To calculate a pension expense, the employer must report the service and interest cost, expected return on plan assets, amortization of prior service cost, and effects of gains and losses.

- Service Cost

The service cost represents the present value of projected retirement benefits earned by covered employees in the current year. Put differently, service cost refers to the required amount the employer must set aside each year to cover employees' pension benefits upon retirement.

- Interest Cost

Interest cost refers to the interest accumulated on the unpaid balance of the projected benefit obligation as an employee's service time increases. Projected benefit obligation refers to the current value of all benefits employees earn during employment. Employers record interest cost at a discounted rate.

- Return on Plan Assets

The return on plan assets represents the current year's earnings on invested plan assets. An employer figures the rate of return by multiplying the assets' fair value at the start of the year by the estimated long-term assets' rate of return. The employer must subtract gains and add losses when computing pension expense.

- Amortization of Prior Service Cost

The amortization of prior service represents the cost of providing retroactive benefits over the remaining service years of the covered employees.

- Gains and Losses

The gains or losses components illustrate the changes in the employer's projected benefit obligation and the market impact on plan assets. For example, prior service cost generally increases the employer's pension expense, but can decrease the expense if the employer does not provide retroactive pension benefits. Service and interest costs always increase pension expenses.

Thus, companies report the service cost component of pension expense in the income statement as part of the total compensation costs, separate from the other components of pension expense. It should be noted that the nature of service cost is different from that of the other elements of pension cost.

### Example

Chintan, Inc. reported the following pension expenses in 2017 ($ in million):

| | |
|---|---|
| –Service cost: | 50 |
| –Interest cost: | 20 |
| –Expected return on assets: | (35) |
| –Amortization of prior service cost: | 6 |
| Amortization of net loss: | 4 |
| –*Pension expense* | $ 45 |

Chintan, Inc. would have to record the following in its income statement:

(DR) Pension expense (total amount): 45
(DR) Expected return on assets 35
  (CR) PBO ($50 of service cost + $20 of interest cost) 70
  (CR) Amortization of prior service cost 6
  (CR) Amortization of net loss 4

### 10.6.2    In the Balance Sheet

All of the assets of the pension plan are retained by the employer until paid out to the employees at retirement. Thus, the pension obligation is determined by the terms of the pension plan and is not satisfied until retirement payments are made.

## 10.7    FUNDED STATUS

Funded status is the net liability or net asset related to a company's defined benefit plans. At any point of time, it equals the fair value of total plan assets minus the projected defined benefit obligation. Plan assets are the investments of the pension fund. These may include investment in the company's stock, other stocks listed on any stock exchange, exchange-traded funds, bonds, real estate, etc.

Projected defined benefit obligations (also known as present value of defined benefit plan) is the present value of expected pension payments which the employees are entitled to receive based on the service they have accumulated to date. Under US GAAP, when the fair value of plan assets exceeds the projected defined benefit obligation, a net pension asset equal to the excess of fair value of plan assets over the projected benefit obligation is reported on the balance sheet. On the other hand, if the projected defined benefit obligation exceeds the fair value of plan assets, a net liability equal to the excess of defined benefit obligation over the fair value of plan assets is reported on the balance sheet.

## Example

FS Ltd. has a defined benefit plan. As at December 31, 2016, its plan assets had a book value of $140 million and fair value of $160 million. The PBO at the time was $150 million. During the year, the company contributed an amount of $20 million to the fund, the fund paid out $15 million while the return on plan assets was $10 million. Service costs were $30 million, interest cost amounted to $12 million while actuarial gains were $3 million.

## Solution

The funded status = fair value of plan assets − projected defined benefit obligation
   As at December 31, 2016, the funded status was $10 million (calculated as $160 of fair value of plan assets minus $150 million of projected defined benefit obligation) and it would be reported as an asset on the balance sheet.
   After one year, i.e., as at December 31, 2017, new fair value of plan assets is:

| | |
|---|---|
| Opening fair value of plan assets | 160 |
| Contributions received | 20 |
| Benefits paid | (15) |
| Actual return on plan assets | 10 |
| Closing fair value of plan assets | 175 |

The projected defined benefit obligation as at December 31, 2017 will equal $180 million as calculated below:

| Opening PBO | 150 |
|---|---|
| Service cost | 35 |
| Interest cost | 12 |
| Benefits paid | (15) |
| Actuarial gain | (2) |
| Closing PBO | 180 |

Funded status as at December 31, 2017 would be −$5 million which represents a net pension liability of $5 million to be reported on the balance sheet.

## 10.8    POSTRETIREMENT BENEFITS OTHER THAN PENSIONS

The determination of the costs and obligations for postretirement benefits is based on the calculation of the actuarial present value of the postretirement benefits that are expected to be paid to or on behalf of current and future retirees under the terms of the plan and the attribution of such present value to periods of service. In general, the attribution period is from the date of hire to the date the employee gains full eligibility for benefits. Benefits are generally allocated equally to each year of service.

USA GAAP rules require that the cost of these benefits be recorded throughout the period starting with the employee's date of hire until the date the employee is fully eligible for the benefit (attribution period). The postretirement benefit obligation (PBO) expense is reported on the income statement throughout the employee's attribution period and it is calculated by determining the values of six variables that make up the expense amount.

### Example

For example, an actuary's calculations indicate that Ariel Corporation postretirement costs will average $10,000 per year for the 30 years that an employee is expected to live following retirement. Thus, the postretirement cost would be $300,000 ($10,000 times 30 years).

# CHAPTER 11

# Shareholders' Equity

## 11.1 GENERAL

A firm can finance its activities either through debt or equity instruments. Each option has its drawbacks in terms of control of the firm, earnings, and various financial ratios. The choice between equity and debt depends on a firm's individual circumstances one firm may prefer issuing equity, while another may prefer the debt financing.

The traditional distinction between equity and debt is blurred through the use of instruments with characteristics of both. These hybrid instruments raise the question of whether they should be recorded as a liability or equity for the issuing firm. The GAAP treatment of convertible debt depends on the specific terms involved. Traditional convertible debt is classified entirely as a liability, and upon conversion, the carrying amount of the liability is reclassified as equity.[1] However, in circumstances in which debt contains a conversion option that is in the money at the date of issue, or if the debt can be settled wholly or partly in cash, GAAP generally require the issuer of the instrument to split the instrument into its separate debt and equity components.[2] In other cases, GAAP require

---

[1] ASC 470-20-05—Liabilities.

[2] FASB Emerging Issues Task Force, Income Tax Consequences of Issuing Convertible Debt with a Beneficial Conversion Feature (Issue No. 5–8), August 29, 2005, and FASB Staff Position APB 14-1, Accounting for Convertible Debt Instruments That May Be Settled in Cash upon Conversion (Including Partial Cash Settlement), May 9, 2008.

© The Author(s) 2018
F. I. Lessambo, *Financial Statements*,
https://doi.org/10.1007/978-3-319-99984-5_11

financial instruments labeled as equity that have characteristics of both debt and equity to be classified as a liability on the balance sheet.

Preferred stock is classified as equity when settlement requires delivery of an ownership interest. However, some instruments labeled as preferred stock are instead classified as liabilities (i.e., mandatorily redeemable preferred stock is classified as a liability).[3] These instruments are structured such that they embody an unconditional obligation requiring the issuer of the instrument to redeem it by transferring assets at a specified or determinable date (or dates) or upon an event that is certain to occur.

Stock is an instrument representing an equity or ownership interest in a corporation. It is a risk capital entirely subject to the fortunes of the corporate venture. The holder of stock may receive a share of the corporation's profits in the form of dividends. Appreciation or depreciation in value of the corporation's business is reflected in the price of the stock. Stock may be acquired directly upon issuance by the corporation of the stock or in the market from another holder of the stock.[4] If an instrument is treated as stock for Federal income tax purposes, gain or loss with respect to the stock is recognized at the time of a taxable sale or exchange in accordance with the holder's method of accounting.[5]

Shareholders' equity represents the interest of a company's shareholders in the net assets of the company. According to the accounting equation:

Shareholders' equity = Assets − Liabilities

On a balance sheet, there is separate section for shareholders' equity which includes its components such as common stock, preferred stock, additional paid-up capital, accumulated other comprehensive income, treasury stock, and retained earnings.

---

[3] ASC 480-10-25-4—Distinguishing Liabilities from Equity provides that a mandatorily redeemable financial instrument is classified as a liability unless the redemption is required to occur only upon the liquidation or termination of the reporting entity.

[4] US Congress (2011): Present Law and Issues Related to the Taxation of Financial Instrument and Products—A Report to the Joint Committee on Taxation, p. 24.

[5] US Congress (2011): Present Law and Issues Related to the Taxation of Financial Instrument and Products—A Report to the Joint Committee on Taxation, p. 25.

- Common stock represents the legal capital of the company.
- Preferred stock is a sort of share capital which has a preferred right to dividends.
- Additional paid-up capital represents the cash contributed by the shareholders of the company in excess of the legal capital of the company, i.e., the common stock.

Accumulated other comprehensive income represents the credits or debits in shareholders' equity which are other than those related to transactions with shareholders, for example, credit for revaluation surplus, credits and debits related to translation reserve, and changes in fair value of available for sale investments.

- Treasury stock is contra-equity account which means that it appears as a deduction from other shareholders' equity accounts and it represents the cost of the company's investment in its own share stock.
- Retained earnings represent the total earnings of the company retained by the company for reinvestment. It equals the retained earnings of last period plus net income for the period minus dividends paid during the period.

## 11.2   COMMON STOCK

Common stock is a component of shareholder equity on a company's balance sheet which represents the interest of the company's owners.

Unlike a sole proprietorship or a partnership (in which the capital is contributed by one or a limited number of people), companies are normally owned by hundreds and thousands of people. The share capital of companies is divided into large numbers of shares called common shares. A common share is evidence of ownership in a company and represents a right to its net assets. It makes transfer of ownership easy and is the prime reason for the popularity of companies as a form of business. The common characteristics of common shares are[6]:

---

[6]Anthony Saunders, Marcia M. Cornett (2009): Financial Markets & Institutions, Irwin/McGraw-Hill, p. 224.

- Discretionary dividend payments;
- Residual claims status;
- Limited liability; and
- Voting rights (or political rights).

### 11.2.1    Par Value of Common Stock

A company normally assigns a value called par value to a share of its common stock and mentions it in the legal document. The figure might be $1 or $10 or $100 or just trivial. For example, the par value of a share of Microsoft is $0.00000625. However, it is not mandatory for a company to assign a par value. For example, Apple Inc. has no par value assigned to its shares.

### 11.2.2    Stated Value of a Common Stock

Stated value is a value attached to a share of common stock with no par value. Stated value per share is used to determine the legal capital of the company for accounting purposes.

### 11.2.3    Authorized Capital

A company has to obtain authorization from the relevant securities regularly regarding issue of share capital. Authorized capital is the number of shares which the company is authorized to issue.

### 11.2.4    Issued Capital

Issued capital is the number of shares which the company has issued. It is lower or equal to the authorized capital.

### 11.2.5    Outstanding Capital

Outstanding capital is the issued capital of the company minus its treasury stock.

### Comprehensive Example

The common stock portion of the equity section of Apple Inc. balance sheet as at September 24, 2011, is given below:
Common stock (no par value):
Shares authorized 1,800,000
Shares issued and outstanding 929,277
Value in million Dollars 13,331
It provides the following information:

- The company has no par value stock.
- There is no stated value disclosed.
- Authorized share capital is 1.8 million shares.
- The company has issued roughly half of its authorized share capital as at September 24, 2011.
- The company has no treasury stock that is why shares issued and shares outstanding are equal.

## 11.3   ISSUANCE OF SHARES OF STOCK

When companies need more capital, they issue new shares to investors. Usually, the shares are issued in exchange of cash or cash equivalents but they may be issued in exchange of other assets such as property, plant, and equipment. The investor receives share certificates as evidence of contribution toward the capital of the company.

The journal entries to record the issuance of stocks depend on whether the shares have been issued at par value, at stated value, or not.

### 11.3.1   Issuance of Par Value Stock

Par value shares are those which have a face value assigned to them. Such shares may be issued at par, above par or below par.

When par value shares are issued exactly at par, cash is debited and common stock or preferred stock account is credited.

> ## Example
>
> - Kimberley Inc. is a US-based business located in the state of South Dakota, which requires that businesses issue their shares at $15 par value.
> - Kimberley Inc. issued 10,000 shares at $15 per share. Journal Recording:
>
> |  |  |  |
> |---|---|---|
> | (DR) Cash | 150,000 | |
> | (CR) Common Stock | | 150,000 |

In case of issuance above par, cash account is debited for the total cash received by the company, common stock or preferred stock is credited for the par value multiplied by number shares issued, and additional paid-in capital account is credited for the excess of cash received over the par value multiplied by number of shares issued.

When par value shares are issued below par, cash is debited for the actual amount received, common stock or preferred stock is credited for the total par value, and discount on capital is debited for the excess of total par value over cash received. The discount on capital is part of shareholders' equity and it appears as a deduction from other equity accounts on balance sheet.

### 11.3.2    Issuance of No Par Stock

Issuance of shares having no par value is recorded by debiting cash and crediting common stock or preferred stock. However, if board of directors of the company assigns a value to share orally, such value is called stated value and the journal entries will be similar to par value stock.

> ## Example
>
> A company received $34,000 for issuing 10,000 shares of common stock of $3 par value. Pass the journal entry to record the issuance of shares.

Journal Entry

| | | |
|---|---|---|
| (DR) Cash | 34,000 | |
| (CR) Common Stock | | 30,000 |
| (CR) Additional Paid-In Capital | | 4000 |

## 11.4   ISSUANCE OF SHARES FOR NON-CASH ITEMS

Corporations usually issue shares in exchange of cash or cash equivalents since cash can be used to purchase other assets or services. However, shares may be issued in exchange of non-cash assets or services if the company actually needs them. For example, shares may be issued to the supplier of machinery as purchase price and to attorneys as legal fee.

Generally, such transactions of share issuance are recorded at the fair market value of the shares or the non-cash assets/services whichever can be determined more reliably. The determination of fair market value is the right of the board of directors of the company, and they may obtain services of professional appraisers to determine the fair market value.

### Example

A company issued 1000 shares of common stock of $10 par value to its attorney as a consideration for legal services received by the company. The total fair market value of the shares, which was $10,200 at the time of issuance of shares, is to be used as the basis for valuation of the legal services.

Pass a journal entry to record the issuance of shares for non-cash consideration.

Journal Entry

| | | |
|---|---|---|
| (DR) Legal Expense | 10,200 | |
| (CR) Common Stock | | 10,000 |
| (CR) Additional Paid-In Capital | | 200 |

## 11.5    Lump-Sum Stock Issuance

A corporation may issue different types of stocks in a single transaction in exchange of a lump-sum of cash or other assets or services. For example, common stock and preferred stock may be issued in exchange of a single sum of cash or machinery. To record such transactions, it is necessary to determine the portion of lump-sum cash or the value of property obtained to be allocated to each class of stock.

Usually, the lump-sum amount is apportioned to each class of stock issued on the basis of the market values of each class of stock. This method is called the apportionment method. It uses the following formula to calculate the amount of lump-sum to be allocated to each class of stock:

$$\text{Apportionment} = A/B \times C$$

Where

A is the market value of a particular class of stock issued for lump-sum;
B is the total market value of all the stocks issued for lump-sum; and
C is the lump-sum cash received or, in case of some other asset or service, its fair market value.

When two classes of stocks have been issued for a lump-sum and the market value of one class is known and that of the other is unknown, then the incremental method should be employed. According to incremental method, the portion of lump-sum equal to the stock's market value would be allocated to that class of stock and rest will be allocated to the other class. Once the amount to be apportioned to each class of stock is calculated, the issuance of stocks is recorded via separate journal entries for each class of stock in such a way as if there had been separate transactions for each class of stock. This is illustrated in the following example:

### Example

A company issued 3000 shares of $6 par value common stock and 1000 shares of $10 par value preferred stock for a lump-sum of $56,000. On the day of issuance of the stocks for lump-sum, the market values per share of common stock and preferred stock were $10 and $20, respectively.

Apportion the lump-sum to common stock and preferred stock.

### Solution

- Market Value
- Common Stock $30,000 3/7 × $56,000 = $24,000
- Preferred Stock $40,000 4/7 × $56,000 = $32,000
- Journal Entries:

| | | |
|---|---|---|
| (DR) Cash | 24,000 | |
| (CR) Common Stock | | 18,000 |
| (CR) Additional Paid-In Capital | | 6000 |
| (DR) Cash | 32,000 | |
| (CR) Preferred Stock | | 20,000 |
| (CR) Additional Paid-In Capital | | 12,000 |

## 11.6   TREASURY STOCK—COST METHOD

Cost method is one of the two methods of accounting for treasury stock, the stock which has been bought back by the issuing company itself. The other method is called the par value method. Under the cost method, the purchase of treasury stock is recorded by debiting treasury stock account by the actual cost of purchase. The cost method ignores the par value of the shares and the amount received from investors when the shares were originally issued. When treasury shares are later reissued, the treasury stock account is credited for the cost at which they were purchased, cash account is debited for the amount actually received, and if the amount received on reissuance of treasury stock is:

- More than the cost of treasury stock, the difference between the amount received and the cost of the treasury stock is credited to additional paid-in capital.
- Less than the cost of treasury stock, the excess of cost of treasury stock over the amount received is debited to discount on capital account.

## Example

A company issued 10,000 shares of common stock of $5 par value and received $53,000 cash. The company then purchased back 900 shares out of those at $6 per share. The company then resold 500 shares from treasury stock at $6.50 per share.
Task: Pass journal entries to record the above transactions.

## Solution

- Issuance of Common Stock:

| | | |
|---|---|---|
| (DR) Cash | 53,000 | |
| (CR) Common Stock | | 50,000 |
| (CR) Additional Paid-In Capital | 3000 | |

- Purchase of Treasury Stock (Cost Method):

| | | |
|---|---|---|
| (DR) Treasury Stock | 5400 | |
| (CR) Cash | | 5400 |

- Resale of Treasury Stock (Cost Method):

| | | |
|---|---|---|
| (DR) Cash | 3250 | |
| (CR) Treasury Stock | | 3000 |
| (CR) Additional Paid-In Capital | | 250 |

## 11.7    TREASURY STOCK—PAR VALUE METHOD

Par value method of accounting for treasury stock is one of the two techniques of accounting to record the purchase and resale of treasury stock. Under par value method, purchase of treasury stock is recorded by debiting treasury stock by the total par value of the shares. Cash account is credited for the actual amount paid to purchase the treasury stock. Any additional paid-in capital or discount on capital relating to treasury shares is cancelled by a debit or credit, respectively. At this point, if the sum of credit side of the journal entry is less than the sum of debit side, additional paid-in capital account will be credited for the difference. Alternatively, if the sum of credit side exceeds the sum of debit side of the journal entry, the difference will be debited to additional paid-in capital account up to the available balance and the rest, if any, will be debited to retained earnings account.

The resale of treasury stock is recorded by debiting cash account for the actual amount received, crediting treasury stock for the par value of the treasury shares, and if the cash received on resale is:

- More than the total par value of treasury shares, the excess is credited to additional paid-in capital account.
- Less than the total par value of treasury shares, the difference is debited to additional paid-in capital from treasury stock provided it has sufficient credit balance; otherwise, retained earnings account is debited.

The following example shows the journal entries to record the purchase and resale of treasury stock under par value method.

## Example

A corporation issued 12,000 shares of common stock of $4 par value and received $57,000 from investors. It then bought back 1000 of the shares and paid a sum of $4500 for the purchase. Later, it resold 500 of the treasury shares at a price of $5 per share.

Journalize the above transactions according to the par value method of accounting for treasury stock.

## Solution

- Issuance of Common Stock:

| | | |
|---|---|---|
| (DR) Cash | 57,000 | |
| (CR) Common Stock | | 48,000 |
| (CR) Additional Paid-In Capital | | 9000 |

- Purchase of Treasury Stock (Par Value Method):

| | | |
|---|---|---|
| (DR) Treasury Stock | 4000 | |
| (DR) Additional Paid-In Capital | 750 | |
| (CR) Cash | | 4500 |
| (CR) Add. Paid-In Capital from TS | | 250 |

1: 9000 × (1000 ÷ 12,000)
2: 4000 + 750 − 4500

- Resale of Treasury Stock (Par Value Method):

| | | |
|---|---|---|
| (DR) Cash | 2500 | |
| (CR) Treasury Stock | | 2000 |
| (CR) Additional Paid-In Capital | | 500 |

## 11.8   STOCK DIVIDENDS

Stock dividends (also called bonus shares) represent the distribution of retained earnings to investors in the form of additional shares in the company instead of cash.

When companies have high retained earning but they do not have necessary excess cash, they resort to issuing stock dividends. Another motivation to issue stock dividends is to bring down the stock price in the market. Introduction of additional shares in the market without any increase in the company's value reduces the company's share price. Companies want to reduce their share price in order to bring down their price to earnings ratio and encourage investors to hold the company's shares.

When the board of directors of a company declares a 10% stock dividend, it means that additional shares equivalent to 10% of the current shares are to be issued to the shareholders. The accounting for stock dividend depends on whether it is considered to be a large stock dividend of a small one.

### 11.8.1   Small Stock Dividend

If the stock dividend is less than 20–25%, it is a small stock dividend and is accounted for by the journal entries explained below:

- At the time of declaration, retained earnings are debited by the amount equal to the product of the share's market price, the stock dividend percentage, and the current number of shares outstanding; and stock dividends distributable are credited by the same amount.
- At the time of issuance of stock, the stock dividends distributable are debited by the full amount, and common stock is credited by amount equal to the product of par value per share, stock dividend percentage, and the number of current shares outstanding. Any excess of stock dividends distributable over the amount credited to common stock are credit to additional paid-in capital.

### 11.8.2   Large Stock Dividend

If the stock dividend declared is more than 20–25%, it is a large stock dividend and is more like a stock split. In this case, declaration is recorded by debiting retained earnings by the product of par value per share, percentage of stock dividend, and number of outstanding shares; and crediting stock dividends distributable. At the time of issuance, the stock dividends distributable are debited and common stock is credited.

## Example

A company has 200,000 outstanding shares of common stock of $10 par value. It declares 10% stock dividend. The market price per share of common stock was $15 on the date of declaration.

Task: Record the declaration and payment of the stock dividend using journal entries.

## Solution

- Journal entry on the date of declaration

| | | |
|---|---|---|
| (DR) Retained Earnings | 300,000 | |
| (CR) Stock Dividends Distributable | | 300,000 |

- Journal entry on the date of distribution

| | | |
|---|---|---|
| (DR) Stock Dividends Distributable | 300,000 | |
| (CR) Common Stock | | 200,000 |
| (CR) Addition Paid-In Capital | | 100,000 |

## 11.9    EMPLOYEE STOCK OPTIONS

### 11.9.1    Legal Understanding

ESOs are offers to sell stock at a stated price (i.e., the exercise price) for a stated period of time. ESOs are used by many companies to attract, retain, and motivate employees and align employee and employer goals. There are basically three types of ESOs: (i) statutory or incentive stock options (ISOs), (ii) non-statutory stock options (NSOs), and (iii) purchase rights issued pursuant to an employee stock purchase plan (ESPP purchase rights). ISOs and NSOs allow employees to purchase stock at a fixed price for a specified period of time. ESPP purchase rights allow employees to purchase stock at a discount through the use of payroll deductions. ISOs and ESPP purchase rights receive special tax treatment and are typically not subject to tax when they are granted or exercised, but the stock acquired pursuant to the exercise of these options is subject to tax when such stock is sold. NSOs, however, are, pursuant to section 83, Property Transferred in Connection with the Performance of Services, subject to tax upon exercise unless the option has a readily ascertainable fair market value. If an NSO has a readily ascertainable fair market value, income is recognized on the grant date, and the issuer is entitled to a deduction. NSOs, when granted, may be "in-the-money," "out-of-the-money," or "at-the-money." ISOs, however, may only be "at-the-money" or "out-of-the-money." An option is deemed in-the-money when the exercise price on the grant date is below the stock's market price. Conversely, an option is out-of-the-money when the exercise price on the grant date is above the stock's market price. An option that has an exercise price equal to the stock's market price on the grant date is considered at-the-money.

An employee typically cannot exercise options, until the employee has a vested right (i.e., a legal right that is not contingent on the performance of additional services) in the option pursuant to the stock option plan's terms. Some companies permit immediate vesting upon issuance of an option, while others delay vesting several years or allow incremental vesting over a period of years.

### 11.9.2    Statement of Financial Accounting Standard No. 123

The original pronouncement regarding accounting for stock options, Accounting Principles Board Opinion (APB) No. 25, was issued in 1972. APB No. 25 employed the "Intrinsic Value Method," under which firms were required to report compensation expense due to stock options in an amount equal to the excess of the stock price at the grant date over the exercise price.

In October 1995, FASB issued SFAS 123, which is effective for fiscal years ending after December 15, 1995. SFAS 123 added the "fair value method" (FVM) as the preferred method for valuing ESOs. The value of an ESO is composed of two components: the intrinsic value and the call premium. While the intrinsic value is equal to the stock's market price on the grant date over the exercise price, the call premium is the amount, in excess of an ESO's intrinsic value, that a purchaser would be willing to pay for the ESO. An ESO's call premium is difficult to measure because it, unlike the call premium of a publicly traded option, cannot be valued daily based on market transactions. Pursuant to the FVM, a corporation must measure the amount of the expense as equal to the fair value of the ESO on the grant date and amortize such expense over the vesting period. Under SFAS 123, fair value is measured using option pricing models that consider the following six attributes of equity-based instruments: (1) the exercise price, (2) the expected life of the option, (3) the current price of the underlying stock, (4) the expected price volatility of the underlying stock, (5) expected dividends, and (6) the risk-free interest rate for the expected life of the option.

The FVM utilizes option pricing models, such as the Black–Scholes model (BS model), for purposes of measuring the value of ESOs. In general, a company recognizes compensation expense in the periods in which its employees perform the service—the "service period." Unless otherwise specified, the service period is the VESTING period—the time between the grant date and the vesting date. Thus, the company determines total compensation cost at the grant date and allocates it to the periods benefited by its employees' services.

### 11.9.3 Illustration

Assume that the Board of Directors of Alexandra Company approves a plan that grants the company's five executive options to purchase 2000 shares each of the company's $1 par value common stock. The company grants the options on January 1, 2006. The executives may exercise the options at any time over the next 10 years. The option price per share is $60 and the market price of the stock is $70 per share on the grant date.

#### Solution

Under the fair value method, Alexandra co. computes the total compensation expense by applying an acceptable fair value option-pricing model. Assume that the option pricing model determines Alexandra co.'s total compensation expense to be $220,000.

## Basic Entries

(i)   At date of grant (January 1, 2006): no entry

(ii)  On December 31, 2006: To record compensation expense for 2006, assuming
      that the company recognizes the value of the options as an expense in the peri-
      ods in which the employee performs services, which in this case is 2 years
      (DR) Compensation Expense (Income statement)    110,000
      (CR) Paid-In Capital—Stock Options                          110,000

(iii) On December 31, 2007: To record compensation expense for 2007:
      (DR) Compensation Expense (Income statement)    110,000
      (CR) Paid-In Capital—Stock Options (Balance                 110,000
      sheet)

(iv)  Exercise: Assume that the executives exercise the options on June 1, 2009:
      (DR) Cash (10,000 options × $60)                            600,000
      (DR) Paid-In Capital—Stock Options              220,000
      (CR) Common Stock (10,000 × $1 par value)                    10,000
      (CR) Paid-In Capital in excess of par                       810,000

## 11.10   Stock Splits

Stock split is the issuance of additional shares by a company to its shareholders without receiving any related contribution from them. Such an
issue increases the number of shares issued and outstanding without
increasing the total balance of common stock and market capitalization
of the company. The effect of stock split is to split the par value and
market price per share. In fact, the sole purpose of the stock split is to
reduce the market price per share so as to make it more attractive for
investors.

Stock splits are designed by companies in regard to their intended
effect on the market price. If a company wants to reduce its market price
to half, it will issue 2-for-1 stock split which means the company shall
issue in addition 1 share per 1 share currently issued and outstanding
thereby doubling the total number of shares. There might be a 3-for-2
stock split, for example, which means that 3 shares are to be issued for
every 2 shares of currently issued shares.

Stock split has no effect on balance of any equity account. It just
increases the number of shares and reduces par value.

## Example

Z Ltd. has 2 million of $10 par value common stock issued and outstanding which is currently trading at $300 per share. The management believes that the share price is too high and it intends to reduce it to 1/3.

The company would need to issue a 3-for-1 stock split which means that for each of the currently issued common shares the company shall issue 3 shares. It will increase the total number of shares issued and outstanding to 6 million (2 million × 3) resulting in a par value of $3.33 ($10 ÷ 3) and a market price of $100 ($300 ÷ 33).

It will not affect balance in any of the accounts.

## 11.11   RETAINED EARNINGS

A company either pays out its earnings for a period or it retains it to fuel internal growth. Retained earnings are the equity account which holds those accumulated retained earnings. Retained earnings are affected by net income for the period, dividends paid out during the period, etc. Other adjustments to retained earnings include adjustment related to changes in accounting policies and estimates, etc.

## Example

IG Plc. has a balance in retained earnings as at January 1, 2011, of $102 million. It earned a net income of $40 million for the year and declared dividends of $45 million in the year.

The statement of retained earnings would look like as follows:

| | |
|---|---|
| Retained earnings as at January 1, 2011 | $102 million |
| Plus: net income for the period | $40 million |
| Less: dividends declared | −$45 million |
| Retained earnings as at December 31, 2011 | $97 million |

# PART II

# The Statement of Income

Income statement (also referred to as (a) statement of income and expense or (b) statement of profit or loss or (c) profit and loss account) is a financial statement that summarizes the results of a company's operations for a period. It presents a picture of a company's revenues, expenses, gains, losses, net income, and earnings per share (EPS).

Together with balance sheet, statement of cash flows, and statement of changes in shareholders' equity, income statement forms a complete set of financial statements.

- Format

A typical income statement is in report form. The header identifies the company, the statement, and the period to which the statement relates, the reporting currency, and the level of rounding-off. The header is followed by revenue and cost of goods sold and calculation of gross profit. Further down the statement, there is a detail of operating expenses, non-operating expenses, and taxes and eventually, the statement presents net income differentiating between income earned from continuing operations and total net income. In case of a consolidated income statement, a distribution of net income between the equity holders of the parent and non-controlling interest holders is also presented. The statement normally ends with a presentation of earnings per share, both basic and diluted. Important line items such as revenue and cost of sales are cross-referred to the relevant detailed schedules and notes.

- Types

There are two types of income statements: single-step income statement, in which there are no subtotals such as gross profit, operating income, and earnings before taxes, and multi-step income statement, in which similar expenses are grouped together and intermediate figures such as gross profit, operating income, and EBIT are calculated.

Another classification of income statement depends on whether the expenses are grouped by their nature or function. Income statement by nature classifies expenses according to their nature, i.e., without allocating them to different business activities, while income statement by function classifies expenses according to the business operations that they support. For example, income statement by nature shows line items such as salaries, depreciation, and rent, while income statement by function allocates salaries, depreciation, rent, etc., between cost of goods sold, selling expense, general and admin expenses, etc.

- Components

Following are key line items that appear on a typical income statement:

– Revenue: represents the amount earned by the company in exchange for goods it supplied and services it provided. The price paid by customers for the goods or services sold by a company is known as revenues. When a company sells these goods or services to a customer, they receive money in the form of cash or book credit sales to accounts receivable, which is money to be collected in the near future. When there are few sources of revenue, a breakup may appear on the face of the income statement; otherwise, a separate note provides a complete picture.

– Cost of sales: represents the cost of goods sold and services provided. It includes all such costs that can be traced or assigned to goods sold or services provided. Examples include raw materials, salaries of factory or service shop employees, manufacturing facility rent, depreciation of manufacturing equipment, lease rentals on equipment used in manufacturing or service delivery, indirect materials needed for production, etc. Typically, a separate note provides a complete breakup of cost of sales.

– Gross profit = revenue – cost of sales; it represents the profit earned on the goods and services of the company before any selling, general, and administrative expenses and finance costs are accounted for.

– Operating expenses: mainly include selling and distribution expenses and general and administrative expenses. Examples include salary of the CEO, marketing expenses, office rent, salaries of administrative staff, fuel for delivery vehicles, etc.

– Operating profit: (equivalent to earnings before interest and taxes (EBIT)) = gross profit – operating expenses; as the name suggests, it is the profit after cost of sales and all operating expenses have been charged to revenue. It is before any adjustment for interest or investment income and interest expense and taxes.

– Income from continuing operations = EBIT – taxes; it represents the net income (i.e., after-tax income) earned from business components that the company intends to own in the future. It excludes any income earned during the year from business components that are treated as discontinued operations. Income from continuing operations provides a picture of the company's continuing earning capacity.

– Income from discontinued operations: is the after-tax income of business components which the company has disposed off during the year or has classified as held-for-sale at the year-end.

– Net income = income from continued operations + after-tax income from discontinued operations; a company's total net income includes income from both continued operations and discontinued operations. It represents the income earned during the year after accounting for all expenses. It is carried to statement of changes in shareholders' equity where it is added to opening balance of the retained earnings component of equity.

– Distribution of income: a consolidated income statement provides a statement of how the income is distributed between parent and minority shareholders.

– Earnings per share (EPS): is a critical part of income statement for companies that are required to calculate and present their EPS (mainly companies listed on a stock exchange). Both basic EPS and diluted EPS are reported, where basic EPS = (net income – preferred dividends)/ weighted-average number of common shares.

# CHAPTER 12

# Analysis of the Statement of Income

## 12.1 GENERAL

The income statement is one of the major financial statements required by the FASB. The income statement is sometimes referred to as the profit and loss statement (P&L), statement of operations, or statement of income. The income statement is important because it shows the profitability of a company during the time interval specified in its heading. There are two types of income statement: (i) the single-step income statement and (ii) the multiple-step income statement.

## 12.2 THE SINGLE-STEP INCOME STATEMENT

A single-step income statement uses just one subtraction. This is done by subtotaling all the revenues and gains together at the top of income statement and subtotaling all the expenses and losses together below revenues. The sum of expenses and losses is then subtracted from the sum of revenues and gains to arrive at net income. Thus:

$$(\text{Revenues} + \text{Gains}) - (\text{Expenses} + \text{Losses}) = \text{Net Income}$$

The net income calculated using the single-step income statement must equal to that calculated using a multi-step income statement.

© The Author(s) 2018                                                            149
F. I. Lessambo, *Financial Statements*,
https://doi.org/10.1007/978-3-319-99984-5_12

## Example and Format

The following example shows the format of a single-step income statement.

Company A
Income statement
For the month ended December 31, 2010

*Revenues:*

| | |
|---|---|
| Sales revenues | $64,510 |
| Interest revenues | 1650 |
| Gain on sale of investments | 5000 |
| Total revenues | $71,160 |

*Expenses:*

| | |
|---|---|
| Cost of goods sold | $31,400 |
| Depreciation expense | 7980 |
| Rent expense | 8000 |
| Advertising expense | 1000 |
| Salaries expense | 13,500 |
| Utilities expense | 1360 |
| Loss due to theft | 300 |
| Total expenses | $63,540 |
| Net income | $7620 |

The major drawback of single-step income statement is that it does not calculate the gross profit of the business. To calculate gross profit, revenues and expenses must be classified. This is why most businesses use the other format of income statement called multi-step income statement.

## 12.3   MULTIPLE-STEP INCOME STATEMENT

Multi-step income statement involves more than one subtraction to arrive at net income, and it provides more information than a single step. The most important of which are the gross profit and the operating profit figures.

Multi-step income statement is divided into two main sections: the operating section and the non-operating sections.

The operating section contains information about revenues and expenses of the principal business activities. The gross profit and the operating profit figures are calculated in the operating section of a multi-step income statement. All operating revenues are grouped at the top of the income statement. The operating expenses are sub-classified into cost of goods sold, selling expenses, and administrative expenses.

Selling expenses are those which are incurred directly on making sales. Examples are: sales commissions, sales salaries, advertising expense, delivery expense, and depreciation expense of sales equipment. The administrative expenses are those relating to general administrative activities (i.e., depreciation expense on office building, office salaries, office supplies expense, and office utilities expense).

The non-operating section of a multi-step income statement, usually labeled as "other incomes and expenses," contains those revenues and expenses which are not earned directly through principle business activities but are incidental to them, for example, gains/losses on sales of investments or fixed assets, and interest revenue/expense. It also includes extraordinary items of revenues and expenses which are infrequent and unusual such as loss due to natural calamity.

### 12.3.1   Analysis of the Multiple-Step Components

– Sales and Revenue
  GAAP has complex, detailed, and disparate revenue recognition requirements for specific transactions and industries including, for example, software and real estate. As a result, different industries use different accounting for economically similar transactions. However, on May 28, 2014, the FASB and the International Accounting Standards Board (IASB) issued converged guidance on recognizing revenue in contracts with customers. The new guidance is a major achievement in the Boards' joint efforts to improve this important area of financial reporting. A company would apply the following five steps to achieve the core principle (Fig. 12.1):

– Cost of goods sold
  Cost of goods sold is the cost of the merchandise that was sold to customers. The cost of goods sold is reported on the income statement when the sales revenues of the goods sold are reported. Cost

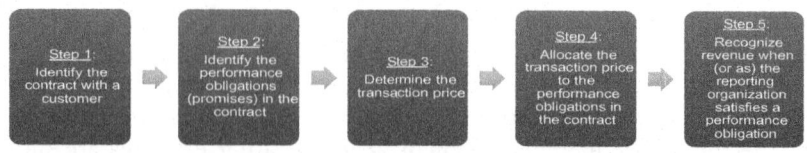

**Fig. 12.1** Revenue—Multiple steps recognition process (*Source* Author)

of goods sold is usually the largest expense on the income statement of a company selling products or goods. Cost of goods sold is a general ledger account under the perpetual inventory system. Under the periodic inventory system, there will not be an account entitled cost of goods sold. Rather, the cost of goods sold is computed as follows: cost of beginning inventory + cost of goods purchased (net of any returns or allowances) + freight-in – cost of ending inventory.

– Gross profit

The statement of income gross profit is the difference between the net sales and the cost of goods sold. Gross profit is distinct from the gross profit margin, which is the ratio of gross profit to total revenue expressed as a percentage. Gross profit margin is a ratio that provides quick comparison between the company and its competitors within the same industry.

– Operating expenses

Operating expenses are costs associated with running a business's core operations on a daily basis.

- Selling expenses
- Administrative expenses

– Non-operating revenues and expenses

Non-operating expenses and losses include expense and loss accounts that are due to the transactions other than the primary operations of the company. Most commonly found are: interest expense, loss on sale of securities, loss on sale of buildings, loss on sale of machinery, loss on sale of equipment.

- Other revenues and gains
- Others expenses and losses

– EBIT

Earnings before interest and taxes (EBIT) measures the profitability of a company without taking into account its cost of capital or tax implications. EBIT focuses solely on a company's ability to generate earnings from operations, ignoring variables such as the tax burden and capital structure. EBIT enables one to analyze operating profitability as a singular measure of performance. Such analysis is particularly important when comparing similar companies across a single industry where those companies may have varying capital structures or tax environments. EBIT is calculated by taking the net income figure from the income statement and adding the income tax expense and interest expense back in.

> ### Example
>
> Zhifan Corp. has sales of $500,000 with operating costs of $400,000, interest paid of $5000, and a tax rate of 30%.
>
> Task: Calculate the EBIT.
>
> $$EBIT = R - E = \$500,000 - \$400,000 = \$100,000$$

– EBITDA

EBITDA is a financial number that measures a company's profitability before deductions that are considered somewhat superfluous to the business decision-making process. These deductions are interest, taxes, depreciation, and amortization, which are not part of a company's operating costs and although important, should be dealt with separately.

• Benefits of the EBITDA margin

Calculating the EBITDA margin allows people to compare and contrast companies of different sizes in different industries because it breaks down operating profit as a percentage of revenue. This means that an investor, owner, or analyst can understand how much operating cash is generated for each dollar of revenue earned and use the margin as a comparative benchmark.

EBITDA effectively removes the profit-distorting effects of taxes, interest income, and expense and eliminates the effects of making capital investments in the firm. Because EBITDA helps measure the company's underlying profit, banks and other sources of capital tend to use EBITDA when determining how much money they can lend. These institutions measure that amount in turns; one turn is equal to the business's EBITDA.

### Example

Zhifan Corp. is generating $3 million in EBITDA; one turn of EBITDA is $3 million. If a Zhifan Corp is being sold for $15 million, the Buyer needs to come up with five turns of EBITDA.

### 12.3.2    Format and Example

## Lina corporation

### Income statement (sample)

| | | |
|---|---:|---:|
| Sales | | $200,000 |
| Cost of goods sold | | (120,000) |
| Gross profit | | 80,000 |
| Operating expenses | | |
| Selling expenses | 10,000 | |
| Administrative expenses | 2500 | |
| Total operating expenses | | (12,500) |
| Operating income | | 67,500 |
| Non-operating revenues and expenses | | |
| Interest revenue | 4500 | |
| Interest expense | (2000) | |
| Total non-operating | | 2500 |
| Net income | | 70,000 |

## 12.4   HOLDING EQUITY

The financial accounting for equity instruments is based on the extent to which the firm's total investment in another entity allows it to influence or control the other entity. Equity investments are separated into three categories: investments that do not give rise to influence, investments giving rise to influence, and investments giving rise to control.

- Investments that do not give rise to influence

An investment of less than 20% in an entity is presumed not to enable the firm to exert a significant influence, unless such ability can be demonstrated. If a firm holds equity instruments for the short term, they are classified as trading securities and marked to fair value with gains and losses recorded in earnings. If an equity instrument does not meet the criteria to be classified as a trading security, it is treated as an available-for-sale security and valued at fair value with gains and losses recorded in OCI.[1]

- Investments giving rise to influence: between 20 and 50%

An investment giving rise to influence is a 50% or less interest that gives the firm the ability to exercise significant influence over operating and financial policies of an entity. The equity method is generally used to account for this type of equity investment. This category of equity investment is commonly used to report investments in corporate joint ventures where a firm holds less than a controlling interest. Under the equity method, the equity investment is recorded on the firm's balance sheet at its historical cost. Thus, the proportional share of the net assets (equal to assets minus liabilities) is included as an asset (or liability) in the firm's financial statements. Over time, the value of the investment is increased by the firm's proportional share of the equity investment's earnings and is reduced by any dividends received. The proportional share of the equity investment's earnings is included in the firm's earnings for the current period.

---

[1] US Congress (2011): Present Law and Issues Related to the Taxation of Financial Instrument and Products—A Report to the Joint Committee on Taxation, p. 54.

## Example

On January 2013, Alexandra Inc. purchased 40% of Fuji LLC for $500,000. On December 31, Fuji LLC had a net income of $800,000. Fuji LLC distributed dividends of $400,000.

Alexandra Inc. records the receipt of the dividends as follows:

| | | |
|---|---|---|
| (DR) Cash | $160,000 | |
| (CR) Investment—Fuji LLC | | $160,000 |

- Investments giving rise to control

An investment giving rise to control is a more than 50% interest in another entity. The assets and liabilities of the entity must be consolidated with those of the firm. If entities are consolidated, the gross values of the assets, liabilities, revenues, and expenses of the investment (subsidiary) are included in the firm's financial report, even though the firm (the parent) may own less than a 100% interest. The firm's income statement and balance sheet contain a single line item subtracting proportional net income and net assets attributable to any minority ownership interests in the entity.

## Example

On January 2013, Kusuba Inc. purchased 60% of Fuji LLC for $500,000.

- On December 31, Fuji LLC had a net income of $800,000
- Fuji LLC distributed dividends of $400,000

## Solution

Kusuba Inc. records the receipt of the dividends as follows:

| | | |
|---|---|---|
| (DR) Cash | $240,000 | |
| (CR) Investment—Fuji LLC | | $240,000 |

- Kusuba Inc. and Fuju LLC must file consolidated statement.

## 12.5    INCOME FROM DISCONTINUED OPERATIONS

Income (or loss) from discontinued operations is a line item on an income statement of a company below income from continuing operations and before net income. It represents the after-tax gain or loss on sale of a segment of business and the after-tax effect of the operations of the discontinued segment for the period.

Income from discontinued operations is distinguished from income from continuing operations in order to communicate to users that the company has disposed-off assets that generated this much income and that only income from continuing operations should be expected to be earned next year unless the proceeds from disposal are used in more profitable way.

### Example

Company C has income from continuing operations of US $700 million. During the year, it disposed-off one of its segments Segment A for US$ 120 million. The segment earned revenue of US$ 200 million and incurred costs of US$ 150 million. Its book value was US$ 100 million. Tax rate applicable to the company overall and the segment is 35%. Present net income for the period for the company.

### Solution

Company C—Income statement for the year ended 31 December 2011(in millions)

| | |
|---|---|
| Income from continuing operations | $700.0 |
| Income from discontinued operations: | |
| Income from operations of segment A (net of tax) $(0.65 \times (200 - 150)) =$ | 32.5 |
| Income from disposal of segment A (net of tax) $(0.65 \times (120 - 100)) =$ | 13.0 |
| Net effect of income from discontinued operations | 45.5 |
| Net income for the period | 739.5 |

# CHAPTER 13

# Other Comprehensive Income

## 13.1   GENERAL

Other comprehensive income contains all changes that are not permitted to be included in profit or loss. It is particularly valuable for understanding ongoing changes in the fair value of a company's assets. Items reported in other comprehensive income include:

- Available-for-sale securities fair value changes that were previously written down as impaired.
- Available-for-sale securities unrealized gains and losses.
- Cash flow hedge derivative instrument gains and losses.
- Debt security unrealized gains and losses arising from a transfer from the available-for-sale category to the held-to-maturity category.
- Foreign currency gains and losses on intra-entity currency transactions where settlement is not planned or anticipated in the foreseeable future.
- Foreign currency transaction gains and losses that are hedges of an investment in a foreign entity.
- Foreign currency translation adjustments.
- Pension or postretirement benefit plan gains or losses.
- Pension or postretirement benefit plan prior service costs or credits.
- Pension or postretirement benefit plan transition assets or obligations that are not recognized as a component of the net periodic benefit or cost.

© The Author(s) 2018
F. I. Lessambo, *Financial Statements*,
https://doi.org/10.1007/978-3-319-99984-5_13

## 13.2    PRESENTATION OF THE OCI

Under ASC 220, companies have been required to disclose, either on the face of the financial statements or as a separate disclosure in the notes, the changes in the accumulated balances for each component of other comprehensive income included in that separate component of equity. It is acceptable to either report components of other comprehensive income net of related tax effects, or before related tax effects with a single aggregate income tax expense or benefit shown that relates to all of the other comprehensive income items.

The items to be included in this classification may be only rarely encountered by a smaller business, so this type of organization may only occasionally report other comprehensive income.

### Example

The shareholders' equity of Company OCI as of January 1, 2014, comprised of the following:

- Common stock $100,000
- Additional paid-in capital 200,000
- Accumulated other comprehensive income 100,000

During the year, the company issued share capital with face value of $20,000 (leading to $10,000 of additional capital), revalued its properties up by $20,000 but incurred an unrealized loss of $10,000 on available-for-sale securities, earned a net income of $50,000, and paid dividends of $25,000.

### Solution

Accumulated comprehensive income as of December 31, 2014 = accumulated OCI as at January 1, 2012 of $100,000 + net income of $50,000 + revaluation gain of $20,000 − loss on available-for-sale securities of $10,000 = $160,000.

Change in comprehensive income during the year = net income ($50,000) + gain on revaluation ($20,000) − loss on available-for-sale-securities ($10,000) = $60,000.

Accumulated other comprehensive income for the year = accumulated comprehensive income for the year ($60,000) − net income ($50,000) = $10,000.

## 13.3 ACCUMULATED OCI

The total of other comprehensive income for a period shall be transferred to a component of equity that is presented separately from retained earnings and additional paid-in capital in a statement of financial position at the end of an accounting period. A descriptive title such as accumulated other comprehensive income shall be used for that component of equity (Table 13.1).

**Table 13.1** Walmart (2014): Currency translation

| (Amounts in millions and net of income taxes) | Currency Translation and Other | Derivative Instruments | Minimum Pension Liability | Total |
|---|---|---|---|---|
| Balances as of January 31, 2011 | $ 1,226 | $ 60 | $(640) | $ 646 |
| Other comprehensive income (loss) | (2,032) | (67) | 43 | (2,056) |
| Balances as of January 31, 2012 | (806) | (7) | (597) | (1,410) |
| Other comprehensive income (loss) | 853 | 136 | (166) | 823 |
| Balances as of January 31, 2013 | 47 | 129 | (763) | (587) |
| Other comprehensive income (loss) before reclassifications | (2,769) | 194 | 149 | (2,426) |
| Amounts reclassified from accumulated other comprehensive income (loss) | — | 13 | 4 | 17 |
| Balances as of January 31, 2014 | $(2,722) | $336 | $(610) | $(2,996) |

*Source* SEC—Walmart (2014)

### 13.3.1 Foreign Currency Accounting

Many US corporations are conducting the business/trade overseas and making the bulk of their profits outside the USA. However, the reporting of their financial statements need to be presented in US dollar. FASB ASC 830-10-20 defines foreign currency transactions as transactions whose terms are denominated in a currency other than the entity's functional currency.

## 13.3.2    Discontinued Operations

Under ASC 205-20-05-2, the required disclosures about discontinued operations vary depending on the nature of the discontinued operation. For example, if a discontinued operation includes a component or group of components of an entity that is not an equity method investment, a more comprehensive set of disclosures about the discontinued operation is required. If the discontinued operation includes an equity method investment, or a business or nonprofit activity that is classified as held for sale on acquisition, a more limited set of disclosures is required.

A disposal of a component of an entity or a group of components of an entity[1] shall be reported in discontinued operations if the disposal represents a strategic shift that has (or will have) a major effect on an entity's operations and financial results when any of the following occurs:

a. The component of an entity or group of components of an entity meets the criteria in paragraph 205-20-45-1E to be classified as held for sale.
b. The component of an entity or group of components of an entity is disposed of by sale.
c. The component of an entity or group of components of an entity is disposed of other than by sale in accordance with paragraph 360-10-45-15 (e.g., by abandonment or in a distribution to owners in a spinoff).

However, a business or nonprofit activity that, on acquisition, meets the below criteria shall also be classified as held for sale is a discontinued operation:

• Management, having the authority to approve the action, commits to a plan to sell the entity to be sold.
• The entity to be sold is available for immediate sale in its present condition subject only to terms that are usual and customary for sales of such entities to be sold.

---

[1] ASC 205-20-45-1B.

- An active program to locate a buyer or buyers and other actions required to complete the plan to sell the entity to be sold have been initiated.
- The sale of the entity to be sold is probable, and transfer of the entity to be sold is expected to qualify for recognition as a completed sale, within one year.
- The entity to be sold is being actively marketed for sale at a price that is reasonable in relation to its current fair value. The price at which an entity to be sold is being marketed is indicative of whether the entity currently has the intent and ability to sell the entity to be sold. A market price that is reasonable in relation to fair value indicates that the entity to be sold is available for immediate sale, whereas a market price in excess of fair value indicates that the entity to be sold is not available for immediate sale.
- Actions required to complete the plan indicate that it is unlikely that significant changes to the plan will be made or that the plan will be withdrawn.

The results of all discontinued operations, less applicable income taxes (benefit), shall be reported as a separate component of income before extraordinary items (if applicable). The reporting of the discontinued component in the income statement would depend whether the component has been disposed of before the end of the reporting period or after it. If the disposition of the discontinued component occurred before the end of the reporting, the income to report must reflect to elements: (i) the income or loss from operations of that component from the beginning of the reporting period to the date of the sale or disposal and (ii) the gain or loss on disposal of that component's assets. However, if the disposal of the component is not yet consumed by the end of the reporting period, the firm must consider the component as held for sale. Thus, the firm must report the two elements of the "held for sale" to reflect: (i) the income or loss from operations of that component from the beginning of the reporting period to the close of the reporting period and (ii) an impairment loss, if any.

## Example 1

The Discontinued Component Has Been Sold During the Reporting Period

- On August 15, 2018, the management of Arline Inc. decided to sell off one of its business segment running excessive losses.
- The transaction was completed by November 30, 2018.
- From January 1, 2018 to November 30, 2018, the business segment (or division) had a pretax loss from operations of $10,000,000.
- The assets of that business segment have a net selling price of $25,000,000 and book value of $20,000,000.
- Arline Inc. income statement for 2018 after-tax income from continuing operations of $40,000,000.

Task: Report the income from the discontinued operation within Arline Inc. income statement for FY 2018 (tax rate 21%).

Solution

- Income from continuing operations $40,000,000
- Discontinued operations:
  - Loss from operations of the discontinued segment: ($5,000,000)
    ($10,000,000 of loss minus $5,000,000 of gain on disposal)
  - Income tax benefit ($5,000,000 × 21%) 1,050,000
  - Loss on discontinued operations (3,950,000)
- **Net income 36,050,000**

## Example 2

The Discontinued Component Is Held for Sale

- On August 15, 2018, the management of Arline Inc. decided to sell off one of its business segment running excessive losses.
- The transaction was completed by February 28, 2019.
- From January 1, 2018 to December 31, 2018, the business segment (or division) had a pretax loss from operations of $10,000,000.

– The assets of that business segment have a book value of $22,000,000, and a fair value (minus all selling costs) of $20,000,000.
– Arline Inc. income statement for 2018 after-tax income from continuing operations of $40,000,000.

Task: Report the income from the discontinued operation within Arline Inc. income statement for FY 2018 (tax rate 21%).

Solution

• Income from continuing operations $40,000,000
• Discontinued operations:
  – Loss from operations of the discontinued segment: ($12,000,000)
    ($10,000,000 plus the impairment loss of ($20 million–22 million)
  – Income tax benefit (12,000,000 × 21%) 2,520,000
  – Loss on discontinued operations (9,480,000)
• **Net income 30,520,000**

## 13.4    RECLASSIFICATION OUT
OF ACCUMULATED OTHER COMPREHENSIVE INCOME

On February 5, 2013, the FASB issued Accounting Standards Update No. 2013-02, Reporting of Amounts Reclassified out of Accumulated Other Comprehensive Income. The standard is effective for public entities for annual periods, and interim periods within those periods, beginning after December 15, 2012.

An entity shall separately provide information about the effects on net income of significant amounts reclassified out of each component of accumulated other comprehensive income if those amounts all are required under other Topics to be reclassified to net income in their entirety in the same reporting period. An entity shall provide this information together, in one location, in either of the following ways:

(a) on the face of the statement where net income is presented;
(b) as a separate disclosure in the notes to the financial statements.

ASU No. 2013-02 applies to all public and nonpublic entities that report items of other comprehensive income except for not-for-profit entities that report under Subtopic 958-205, not-for-profit entities—presentation of financial statements. The ASU requires an entity to report the effect of those reclassifications on line items of net income only if the amounts are required to be reclassified in their entirety to net income under USA generally accepted accounting principles (GAAP). The ASU is intended to improve reporting of such reclassifications by requiring that information about significant reclassifications out of accumulated other comprehensive income be presented in one place in the financial statements, either on the face of the statement where net income is presented or as a separate disclosure in the notes to the financial statements.

### 13.4.1    Presentation
### on the Face of the Statement—In Net Income

If an entity chooses to present information about the effects of significant amounts reclassified out of accumulated other comprehensive income on net income, on the face of the statement where net income is presented, the entity shall present parenthetically by component of other comprehensive income the effect of significant reclassification amounts on the respective line items of net income. An entity also shall present parenthetically the aggregate tax effect of all significant reclassifications on the line item for income tax benefit or expense in the statement where net income is presented.

| John Aristotle Corporation<br>Statement of Income<br>For the Period Ended December 31, 2017 | |
| --- | --- |
| • Revenues (includes $4000 accumulated other comprehensive income reclassifications for net gains on cash flow hedges) | $ 150,000 |
| • Expenses (includes (41,000) accumulated other comprehensive income reclassifications for net losses on cash flow hedges) | (52,000) |
| • Other gains and losses | 15,000 |

| | |
|---|---:|
| • Gain on sale of securities (includes $4000 accumulated other comprehensive income reclassifications for unrealized net gains on available-for-sale securities) | <u>4000</u> |
| • Income from operations before tax | 117,000 |
| • Income tax expense (includes (1750) income tax expense from reclassification items) | (36,550) |
| • Net income | **$ 81,450** |

### 13.4.2  Presentation as a Separate Disclosure in the Notes

If an entity chooses to present information about significant amounts reclassified out of accumulated other comprehensive income in the notes to the financial statements or is required to do so by, it shall present the significant amounts by each component of accumulated other comprehensive income and provide a subtotal of each component of comprehensive income. The subtotals for each component shall agree with the requirements in paragraph 220-10-45-14A.[2] Both before-tax and net-of-tax presentations are permitted provided the entity complies with the requirements in paragraph 220-10-45-12. For each significant reclassification amount, the entity shall identify, for those amounts that are required under other Topics to be reclassified to net income in their entirety in the same reporting period, each line item affected by the reclassification on the statement where net income is presented. For any significant reclassification for which other Topics do not require that reclassification to net income in its entirety in the same reporting period, the entity shall cross-reference to the note where additional details about the effect of the reclassifications are disclosed.

[2] In addition to the presentation of changes in accumulated balances, an entity shall present separately for each component of other comprehensive income, current period reclassifications out of accumulated other comprehensive income, and other amounts of current period other comprehensive income.

**John Aristotle Corporation**
**Notes to Financial Statements**
**Reclassifications Out of Accumulated Other Comprehensive Income**
**For the Period Ended December 31, 2017**

| Details about accumulated other comprehensive income components | Amount reclassified from accumulated other comprehensive income | Affected line item in the statement where net income is presented |
|---|---|---|
| *Gains and losses on cash flow hedges* | | |
| • Interest rate contracts | 1000 | Interest income (expense) |
| • Credit derivative | (500) | Other income (expense) |
| • Foreign exchange contracts | 2500 | Sales/revenue |
| • Commodity contracts | (2000) | Cost of sales |
| | 1000 | Total before tax |
| | (300) | Tax (expense) or benefit |
| | 700 | Net of tax |
| *Unrealized gains or losses on available-for-sale securities* | | |
| • Insignificant items | 2300 | Realized gain (loss) on sale of securities |
| | (285) | Impairment expense |
| | (15) | |
| | 2000 | Total before tax |
| | (600) | 30% Tax expense/benefit |
| | 1400 | Net of tax |
| *Amortization of defined benefit pension items* | | |
| • Prior service cost | (2000) | |
| • Transition obligation | (2500) | |
| • Actuarial G/Losses | (1500) | |
| | (6000) | Total before tax |
| | 2000 | Tax (expense) or benefit |
| | (4000) | Net of tax |
| Total reclassifications for the period | (1900) | Net of tax |

ASU 2018-02 provides financial statement preparers with an option to reclassify stranded tax effects from AOCI to retained earnings in each period in which the effect of change in the US federal corporate tax rate included in Tax Cut and Job Act is recorded. ASU 2018-02 has the following additional financial statement disclosure requirements:

• the company's accounting policy for releasing income tax effects from AOCI into retained earnings,

- whether the company has elected to reclassify the stranded income tax effects resulting from TCJA, and
- information about the other income tax effects that are reclassified from AOCI by the company.

If a company does not elect to reclassify stranded tax effects of TCJA, ASU 2018-02 requires the company to disclose that the election was not made.

## 13.5 EARNINGS PER SHARE

Most income statements include a calculation of earnings per share or EPS. This calculation tells readers of financial statements how much money shareholders would receive for each share of stock they own if the company distributed all of its net income for the period. Often businesses reported two types of EPS: the simple EPS and the diluted EPS.

### 13.5.1 The Computation of the Simple EPS

Basic earnings per share is computed by dividing profit or loss attributable to ordinary equity holders of the parent entity (the numerator) by the weighted average number of ordinary shares outstanding (the denominator) during the period.

$$\text{Basic EPS} = \frac{\text{Net income} - \text{Preferred dividends}}{\text{Weighted average number of common stock outstanding}}$$

### Example 1

- Daxa Inc. has net income of $500,000 in FY 2016.
- Daxa Inc. has no preferred shares outstanding.
- Daxa Inc. has 5000 weighted average shares outstanding during the FY year 2016.

Task: EPS (Basic) = 500,000 − 0/5000
      EPS (Basic) = $100

## Example 2

- Chintan Inc. earned a profit of $1,000,000 net of taxes in FY 2016.
- Chintan Inc. owes $250,000 in dividends to the holders of its cumulative preferred stock.
- Chintan Inc. has 50,000 weighted average shares outstanding during the FY year 2016

Task: Calculate the basic earnings per share
EPS (Basic) = (1,000,000 − 250,000)/50,000
EPS (Basic) = $15 per share

## Example 3

Computation of the average weighted common stock.

The weighted average number of common shares is the number of shares outstanding; during the year weighted by the portion of the year, they were outstanding. There are steps to consider in the computation of the weighted average number of common shares outstanding:

Step 1: Identify the beginning balance of common shares and changes in the common shares during the year.
Step 2: For each change in the common shares:

(a) compute the number of shares outstanding after each change in the common shares,
(b) weight the shares outstanding by the portion of the year between this change and next change (weight = days outstanding/365 = months outstanding/12), and
(c) sum up to compute the weighted average number of common shares outstanding.

Let us assume the following for Chintan Inc. shares outstanding in 2016:

| Dates | Share changes | Shares outstanding | Portion of the year outstanding | Weighted average |
|---|---|---|---|---|
| 01/01–03/31 | Beginning balance | 100,000 | 3/12 | 25,000 |
| 04/01–05/31 | 20,000 shares issued | 120,000 | 2/12 | 20,000 |
| 06/01–09/30 | 30,000 shares redeemed | 90,000 | 4/12 | 30,000 |
| 10/01–12/31 | 50,000 shares issued | 140,000 | 3/12 | 35,000 |

Using the same facts in Example 2:

(a) Chintan Inc. earned a profit of $1,000,000 net of taxes in FY 2016.
(b) Chintan Inc. owes $250,000 in dividends to the holders of its cumulative preferred stock.

Task: Calculate the EPS (Basic)
EPS (Basic) = (1,000,000–250,000)/110,000

### 13.5.2   The Computation of the Diluted EPS

SFAS No. 128 requires companies with complex capital structures to compute another measure called diluted earnings per share.

$$\text{Diluted EPS} = \frac{\text{Net income} - \text{Preferred dividends} + \begin{array}{c}\text{Income adjustments due to}\\\text{dilutive financial instruments}\end{array}}{\begin{array}{c}\text{Weighted average number of}\\\text{common shares outstanding}\end{array} + \begin{array}{c}\text{Newly issuable shares due to}\\\text{dilutive financial instruments}\end{array}}$$

The dilutive effect of financial instruments (i.e., options warrants and convertible bonds) on EPS is calculated starting with the instrument with the lowest conversion rate (most dilutive) and working up to the instrument with the highest conversion rate (least dilutive).

### 13.5.2.1 Dilution Through the Issuance of Stock Options

Diluted shares can be tricky to calculate, especially when it comes to stock options, which are the most common obligation to issue shares that companies face. Basically, when a company issues stock options at a certain exercise (strike) price, it must account for the intrinsic value of the options and how much stock could be purchased with that amount of money.

Several steps must be considered in order to get the diluted shares:

Step 1: multiply the number of issued stock options by the exercise price in order to determine how much would be paid in order to exercise the options

Step 2: divide that result from step 1 by the current market price of the stock to determine how many shares could be purchased for the exercise price of the options

Step 3: subtract the figure from step 2 from the number of options outstanding to determine the excess shares that would need to be issued to meet these obligations.

---

### Example

Diluted Earnings per Share

- Patel Corp. reported a net profit of $400,000.
- Patel Corp. has 5,000,000 common shares outstanding that sell at $40 per share.
- In addition, Patel Corp. has issued 100,000 options outstanding that can be converted to Patel Corp's common stock at $35 each.

Task: Compute Patel Corp. diluted earnings per share?

## Solution

To compute the diluted earnings per share, Patel Corp. comptroller must follow the below steps:

i. Calculate the number of shares that would have been issued at market price:
   100,000 options @ $35 = $3,500,000 paid to exercise the option by the option-holders

ii. Divide the amount paid to exercise the options by the market price to determine the number of shares that could be purchased:
   $3,500,000 paid to exercise the option by 40 (the market price per share) or
   $3,500,000/40 = 87,500 shares

iii. Subtract the number of shares that could have been purchased from the number of options exercised:
   87,500 out of 100,000 = 22,500 shares

iv. Add the incremental number of shares to the shares already outstanding:
   22,500 shares + 5,000,000 = 5,022,750

Thus, the diluted EPS = Net profit/Common shares outstanding
$$= 400,000/5,022,750$$
$$= \$0.078$$

**Table 13.2**   Walmart (2014): Basic and Diluted Income per Common Share

The following table provides a reconciliation of the numerators and denominators used to determine basic and diluted income per common share from continuing operations attributable to Walmart:

| | Fiscal Years Ended January 31, | | |
|---|---|---|---|
| (Amounts in millions, except per share data) | **2014** | 2013 | 2012 |
| **Numerator** | | | |
| Income from continuing operations | **$16,551** | $17,704 | $16,408 |
| Less income from continuing operations attributable to noncontrolling interest | **(633)** | (741) | (674) |
| Income from continuing operations attributable to Walmart | **$15,918** | $16,963 | $15,734 |
| **Denominator** | | | |
| Weighted-average common shares outstanding, basic | **3,269** | 3,374 | 3,460 |
| Dilutive impact of stock options and other share-based awards | **14** | 15 | 14 |
| Weighted-average common shares outstanding, diluted | **3,283** | 3,389 | 3,474 |
| **Income per common share from continuing operations attributable to Walmart** | | | |
| Basic | **$   4.87** | $   5.03 | $   4.55 |
| Diluted | **4.85** | 5.01 | 4.53 |

Walmart 2014 Annual Report

*Source* SEC: Walmart 10-K Form

From 2012 to 2014: The trends in the numerators have gone up from 2012 to 2013, and down from 2013 to 2014, whereas the trends in the denominator have consistently gone down from 2012 to 2014. That is reflected in the trends of the basic and diluted income per common share (Table 13.2).

# CHAPTER 14

# The Sub-Statement of Retained Earnings

## 14.1    General

The statement of retained earnings is financial statement which outlines the changes in retained earnings for a specified period. The statement of retained earnings is prepared in accordance with generally accepted accounting principles (GAAP). The statement of retained earnings reconciles the beginning and ending retained earnings for the period, using information such as net income from the other financial statements. This statement can appear as a separate statement or as an inclusion on either a balance sheet or an income statement. In practice, the statement of retained earnings is the second financial statement prepared after the income statement and before the balance sheet. The statement of retained earnings explains the changes in retained earnings from net income (or loss) and from any dividends over a period of time.

## 14.2    Steps in Preparing
### the Statement of Retained Earnings

Five steps are or shall be conducted in preparing the statement of retained earnings:
  Step 1: Record the statements heading.
  The heading of the statement includes the name of the company, the name of the statement—statement of retained earnings, and the time period (i.e., year ending December 31, 2008).

© The Author(s) 2018                                                          175
F. I. Lessambo, *Financial Statements*,
https://doi.org/10.1007/978-3-319-99984-5_14

Step 2: List beginning retained earnings.

Beginning retained earnings is equal to ending retained earnings of the previous year. So, the retained earnings at December 31, 2013 is the retained earnings at January 1, 2012. For a new entity, the beginning retained earnings would always be equal to zero.

Step 3: Add net income or subtract net loss.

In step 3, we add net income as provided in the statement of income or subtract net loss from the beginning retained earnings number.

Step 4: Subtract the dividends, which represent payments or distributions to owners and decrease retained earnings. When dividends are declared in a period, they must be deducted in the statement of retained earnings of that period. It does not matter whether the payment of dividend has been made or not.

Step 5: Computation of the ending retained earnings.

## 14.3    Retained Earnings Formula

| | |
|---|---|
| | Beginning Retained Earnings |
| + | Net Income |
| − | Withdrawals by Owners |
| = | Retained Earnings |

### Example

The following example shows the format of a statement of retained earnings.

### Company A
### Statement of Retained Earnings
### For the year ended Dec 31, 2014

| | | |
|---|---|---|
| Beginning Retained Earnings | | $32,100 |
| Correction of Error in Telephone Expense | −$1000 | |
| Tax Effect @30% | 300 | |
| Net Correction | | −700 |
| Adjusted Beginning Balance | | 31,400 |
| + Net Income | | 44,950 |
| − Dividends Declared | | (7200) |
| Ending Retained Earnings | | $69,150 |

## 14.4   CHANGES IN RETAINED EARNINGS

Retained earnings are the portion of a company's income that management retains for internal operations instead of paying it to owners in form of dividends.

In general, the statement of retained earnings is affected by any transaction that affects net income and dividends. Thus, when total dividends paid out is increased or decreased, there is a definite effect on the statement of retained earnings. A change in net income may be due to accounting changes or errors corrections.

---

### Example

Change in Retained Earnings
   Yuco, Inc. had $150,000 when the reporting period (FY 2015) started and at the end of the 2015, Yuco, Inc. realized $140,000 in net income and paid out $200,000 in dividends.
   Task: Compute Yuco, Inc. Retained Earnings:

| Beginning Balance | + | Net Income | – | Dividends | = | Retained Earnings |
|---|---|---|---|---|---|---|
| $150,000 | + | $140,000 | – | $200,000 | = | $90,000 |

---

### 14.4.1   Accounting Changes and Retained Earnings

An accounting change can be a change in an accounting principle, an accounting estimate, or the reporting entity.

- Change in accounting principle

The US GAAP presumes that an accounting principle once adopted shall not be changed in accounting for events and transactions of a similar type. That is, consistent use of the same accounting principle from one accounting period to another provides better understanding of the numbers and facilitates comparisons across fiscal/accounting years.

A firm can change an accounting principle only if either of the following applies:

- The change is required by a newly issued Codification update.
- The entity can justify the use of an allowable alternative accounting principle on the basis that it is preferable.

Examples of accepted accounting changes in accounting principle include, but are not limited to, the following:

a. Change in inventory valuation method (i.e., from LIFO to FIFO, retail inventory method to weighted-average cost)
b. Change in method of amortization or depreciation method (i.e., from straight-line to accelerated)
c. Change in measurement date for conducting annual goodwill impairment test

US GAPP requires that changes in accounting principles be made retrospectively. Retrospective application of a change in accounting principle requires the following:

- The cumulative effect of the change to the new accounting principle on periods prior to those presented is reflected in the carrying amounts of assets and liabilities as of the beginning of the first period presented.
- An offsetting adjustment, if any, is made to the opening balance of retained earnings (or other appropriate components of equity or net assets in the statement of financial position) for that period.
- Financial statements for each individual prior period presented are adjusted to reflect the period-specific effects of applying the new accounting principle.

However, if the retrospective correction is impractical, the new method would be use prospectively, from now on.

Retrospective application of a change in accounting principle requires the following:

- The cumulative effect of the change to the new accounting principle on periods prior to those presented is reflected in the carrying amounts of assets and liabilities as of the beginning of the first period presented.

– An offsetting adjustment, if any, is made to the opening balance of retained earnings (or other appropriate components of equity or net assets in the statement of financial position) for that period.
– Financial statements for each individual prior period presented are adjusted to reflect the period-specific effects of applying the new accounting principle.

• Change in accounting estimates

Change in accounting estimates occurs when new information comes to light (i.e., a change in method, rate, or one-time amount adjustments for accounting for the allowance for bad debts). A change in accounting estimate shall not be accounted for by restating or retrospectively adjusting amounts reported in financial statements of prior periods or by reporting pro forma amounts for prior periods. Rather, the change is carried prospectively.

• Change in the reporting entity

A change in reporting entity occurs when two or more previously separate entities are combined into one entity for reporting purposes, or when there is a change in the mix of entities being reported. A changes in the reporting entity continue to be applied retrospectively. Companies should restate the financial statements of all prior periods presented and must include a description of the nature of the change, the reason behinds it, as well as the effect on income before extraordinary items, net income and related per-share amounts for all periods that are presented.

### 14.4.2   Accounting Errors and Retained Earnings

An accounting error is a non-fraudulent discrepancy in financial documentation. The term is used in financial reporting.

Types of accounting errors include:

• Error of omission occurs when a transaction that occurred is not recorded.
• Error of commission occurs when a transaction that is calculated incorrectly.
• Error of principle occurs when a transaction is not recorded in accordance with generally accepted accounting principles.

If a company discovers that an accounting error significantly affected a previous report, it usually issues a restatement of the original release.

It should be noted that both accounting changes and errors will often require an adjustment of the beginning retained earnings in the fiscal years that they have been discovered and corrected.

CHAPTER 15

# The Computation of the Taxable Income

## 15.1   General

US GAAP takes an asset-liability approach to accounting for income taxes and thus records deferred tax assets and liabilities. A deferred tax liability or asset generally should be recognized for the future tax effects of all temporary differences and carryforward. Deferred taxes are calculated using the asset or liability approach, which is intended to recognize, in the balance sheet, the future tax consequences of events that have been either recognized in the financial statements or the tax return. Accounting Standards Update 2015–2017 requires that deferred tax liabilities and assets be classified as non-current in a classified statement of financial position (Balance sheet). For public business entities, the amendments in this Update are effective for financial statements issued for annual periods beginning after December 15, 2016, and interim periods within those annual periods. While the update is welcome for simplicity sake, businesses should be aware that the change may have an impact on their working capital.

## 15.2   Differed Taxes and Assets

Deferred taxes are measured on an undiscounted basis. A deferred tax liability is recorded if the book basis of the underlying asset (liability) is greater (less) than the tax basis of the underlying asset (liability). US GAAP precludes recognition of a deferred tax liability for the excess of

© The Author(s) 2018
F. I. Lessambo, *Financial Statements*,
https://doi.org/10.1007/978-3-319-99984-5_15

the book basis over the tax basis of goodwill if it arises at the initial recognition of goodwill.

A deferred tax asset is recorded if the book basis of the underlying asset (liability) is less (greater) than the tax basis of the underlying asset (liability). US GAAP allows the recognition of a deferred tax liability subsequently if the goodwill is tax deductible.

### 15.2.1    Temporary Differences for Revenue and Expenses

Companies in the USA maintain two separate sets of books for financial and tax purposes. Because the rules that govern financial and tax accounting differ, temporary differences arise between the two sets of books.

Also, temporary differences arise when business income or expenses are recognized in different periods on the financial statements than on the tax returns. These differences might include revenue recognition, expenses incurred but not yet paid, or depreciation calculation differences. This can result in either deferred tax liability or deferred assets. Deferred tax liabilities and assets are measured using the applicable tax rate.

- Deferred tax liabilities

Deferred tax liability often arises when the real tax payment according to tax accounting is lower than that according to financial accounting. Deferred tax liability commonly exists when there are differences between tax and financial accounting in depreciating fixed assets, recognizing revenues, and valuing inventories.

---

### Example

- Lina Inc. is a US business subject to 30% CIT.
- In 2015, Lina Inc. sold 1000 tons of wheat to Alex Corporation for $10 million. The parties (Lina Inc. and Alex Corp.) agreed that Lina Inc. would have to receive payments from Alex Corp. on an installment basis over the next five years ($2 million per year).
- For financial accounting purposes, Lina Inc. recognizes the entire $10 million revenue at the time of the sale, while it

records only $2 million based on the installment method for tax purposes.
- This results in an $8 million temporary difference that Lina Inc. expects to liquidate within the next four years.
- Lina Inc. records $2.4 million ($8 million × 30%) in deferred tax liability on its financial statements.

- Deferred tax assets

A deferred tax asset is an asset on a company's balance sheet that may be used to reduce taxable income. Deferred tax assets are recognized without reference to offsetting, and then, an assessment is made about the need for a valuation allowance. A deferred tax asset arises when a firm recognizes an expense earlier for financial reporting than for tax reporting. For instance, business often expenses their estimates of warranty costs in the year they sell the warranted products, for book purposes, while they claim tax deductions thereof later when they make actual expenditures for warranty repairs.

### Example

- In 2015, Caroll Inc. has developed a new medicine to cure the Zika virus. Though approved by the FDA, the Zika medicine has some challenging side effects.
- Caroll Inc. expenses an estimate of warranty costs of $2 billion in the year 2015, for book purposes.
- These expenses ($2 billion) can only be deducted, for tax purposes, the years when Caroll Inc. makes actual expenditures for warranty repairs.
- In FY 2015, Caroll Inc. has made a profit of $10 billion (Net Income of $25 billion minus net expenses of $15 billion, including the warranty).
- For financial reporting (FY 2015), Caroll Inc. would have to exclude the $2 billion warranty and declare a profit of $12 billion:

$$(\$25B - (\$15B - \$2B)) = \$12B$$

- Tax rate considerations

The US tax regime is often criticized as being among the top rates in the world. Though true, the argument lacks consistency as rates alone do not depict the true reality. Comparisons between corporate tax rates in the USA and those found elsewhere in the world are made frequently.[1] Though the statutory corporate income tax rate was of 35%, the effective tax of US corporations has been estimated at less than half that much, 13%, reduced through a variety of mechanisms, including tax provisions that permit multinational corporations to defer US tax on active business earnings of their offshore subsidiaries until those earnings are brought back to the USA.[2] In 2017, the Trump administration has simplified the corporate income tax rate for US business bringing down to rate to a flat 21%. Corporations file a tax return each year and pay quarterly estimated taxes.

### Example

In FY 2018, Lupita Inc. has earnings of $3,000,000.
Task: Compute Lupita's corporate income tax.

$CIT = (3,000,000) \times 21\%$
$CIT = \$630,000$

### 15.2.2    Permanent Differences

If an item is included in the computation of taxable income but it is never included in book income, or if it is included in the computation of book income but never in taxable income, then it gives rise to a permanent difference.

---

[1] Felix I. Lessambo, International Aspects of US Taxation System, Chapter 2. Palgrave Macmillan. 2016.

[2] US Senate Permanent Subcommittee on Investigations (April 1, 2014): Caterpillar's Offshore Tax Strategy, p. 9.

Permanent differences can arise when expenses recognized on the financial statements will never be deductible on the income tax returns. For example, tax penalties on underpaid taxes and fines resulting from a violation of the law are recognized as expenses on the financial statements but are not deductible expenses on the tax return. With certain start-up costs, such as the cost of raising capital for a new business, the CPS enters them as expenses on the financial statements but he cannot deduct them on the tax return. Business entertainment and meal expenses are fully deductible on the financial statements, but the CPA can use only 50% of these expenses as allowable deductions on the tax return. Other examples of permanent differences for tax and financial statement reporting purposes include: (i) interest on municipal bonds, (ii) penalties and fines, (iii) special dividend received deduction, (iv) life insurance proceeds upon the death of an insured executive, and (v) premiums paid for life insurance policies when the payer is the beneficiary.

## Example

### Revenue from municipal bonds

- Lilian Corp. has invested $100,000 in municipal bonds issued by the municipality of Larchmont, in New York.
- By end of the FY, Lilian Corp. received $10,000 of interests from its investment.
- For financial statement purpose, Lilian Corp. must include the $10,000 as other income in its statement of income. However, for tax purposes, the $10,000 interest-income from municipal bonds should not be included in Lilian Corp. Form 1020.

## 15.3   NET OPERATING LOSSES

An asset (tax receivable or deferred tax asset) and a tax benefit are recognized in the period that a company experiences a net operating loss that it will carry back or carry forward.

In the case of a deferred tax asset recognized in conjunction with a net operating loss carryback, the asset needs to be measured and, thus, might be reduced to zero if no future benefit is expected.

## 15.4    UNDISTRIBUTED
## PROFITS OF FOREIGN SUBSIDIARIES

Undistributed earnings of foreign subsidiaries give rise to a temporary difference. However, an exception is made to this general rule if the earnings are reinvested in the subsidiary.

ASC 740-30-25-17 states:

> The presumption that all undistributed earnings will be transferred to the parent company may be overcome, and no income taxes should be accrued by the parent company, if sufficient evidence shows that the subsidiary has invested or will invest the undistributed earnings indefinitely or that the earnings will be remitted in a tax-free liquidation.

Undistributed earnings must be reinvested in the foreign subsidiary "indefinitely[3]".

ASC paragraph 740-30-25-3: It shall be presumed that all undistributed earnings of a subsidiary will be transferred to the parent entity. Accordingly, the undistributed earnings of a subsidiary included in consolidated income shall be accounted for as a temporary difference unless the tax law provides a means by which the investment in a domestic subsidiary can be recovered tax free.

ASC paragraph 740-30-25-17: The presumption in paragraph 740-30-25-3 that all undistributed earnings will be transferred to the parent entity may be overcome, and no income taxes shall be accrued by the parent entity, for entities and periods identified in the following paragraph if sufficient evidence shows that the subsidiary has invested or will invest the undistributed earnings indefinitely or that the earnings will be remitted in a tax-free liquidation. A parent entity shall have evidence of specific plans for reinvestment of undistributed earnings of a subsidiary which demonstrate that remittance of the earnings will be postponed indefinitely. These criteria required to overcome the presumption are sometimes referred to as the indefinite reversal criteria. Experience of the entities and definite future programs of operations and remittances are examples of the types of evidence required to substantiate the parent entity's representation of indefinite postponement of remittances from a subsidiary.

---

[3] "Indefinite" is typically interpreted as permanent.

Note that even though an entity may be required to recognize in its financial statements deferred US income taxes in a particular period, such taxes are not payable to the USA unless the entity actually repatriates the earnings to the USA. In other words, the recognition of deferred US income taxes in financial statements does not mean US tax law requires the entity to actually pay the income taxes in that period. This treatment reflects a policy decision of when taxes should be payable to the USA and is not a matter of accounting standards.

It also is important to note that US GAAP requires an entity to disclose in its financial statements circumstances where it has not recognized deferred US income taxes attributable to unremitted earnings of a foreign subsidiary. The following excerpts from US GAAP include such disclosure requirements.

ASC paragraph 740-30-50-2: All of the following information shall be disclosed whenever a deferred tax liability is not recognized because of the exceptions to comprehensive recognition of deferred taxes related to subsidiaries and corporate joint ventures:

a. A description of the types of temporary differences for which a deferred tax liability has not been recognized and the types of events that would cause those temporary differences to become taxable.

b. The cumulative amount of each type of temporary difference.

c. The amount of the unrecognized deferred tax liability for temporary differences related to investments in foreign subsidiaries and foreign corporate joint ventures that are essentially permanent in duration if determination of that liability is practicable or a statement that determination is not practicable. While paragraph 740-30-25-14 prohibits recognition of a tax benefit for tax deductions or favorable tax rates attributable to future dividends of undistributed earnings for which a deferred tax liability has not been recognized, favorable tax treatment would be reflected in measuring that unrecognized deferred tax liability for disclosure purposes.

d. The amount of the deferred tax liability for temporary differences other than those in (c) (that is, undistributed domestic earnings) that is not recognized in accordance with the provisions of paragraph 740-30-25-18.

## 15.5    APB 23 AND INDEFINITELY REINVESTED EARNINGS

APB 23 establishes a presumption that all undistributed earnings of a subsidiary will be transferred to the US parent company and requires companies to book both the current foreign cash tax expense and an accrual for future US tax liability. However, the presumption can be overcome, if sufficient evidence exists that: (i) the earnings have or will be invested indefinitely, (ii) the earnings will be remitted in a tax-free liquidation, and (iii) the temporary difference will not reverse in the foreseeable future consideration. The exception allows an issuer to avoid booking a deferred tax liability on such foreign earnings and requires evidence of both the intent and ability of an issuer to indefinitely reinvest foreign earnings or forgo repatriation of foreign earnings. Given the uncertainty surrounding APB 23, US parent companies have been utilizing the indefinite reversal criteria within ASC 740 to avoid paying US taxes on approximately $2.4 trillion of foreign earnings. Remittance of earnings of a subsidiary may sometimes be indefinite because of the specific long-term investment plans and objectives of the parent company. Even in the absence of long-term investment plans, the flexibility inherent in the US Internal Revenue Code may permit a parent company to postpone income taxes on the earnings of a subsidiary for an extended period or may permit the ultimate distribution to be taxed at special rates applicable to the nature of the distribution. More, the decision to repatriate foreign profits or to reverse the decision does not require a restatement of the prior years' earnings. Businesses are not even required to treat the additional tax expense (or income) as an extraordinary item in the financial statements. The only disclosure requirements surrounding APB 23 are the cumulative amount of indefinitely reinvested earnings and, if practicable, the additional tax that would be incurred on repatriation.

### Example

- GemCo, a US MNC, has a wholly owned subsidiary in Bermuda, a country with CIT at the rate of 0%.
- In 2015, the Bermudan subsidiary had an after-tax profit of $1 billion.
- GemCo decided to permanently invest the $1 billion in Bermuda.

- GemCo disclosed the cumulative amount of indefinitely reinvested earnings ($1 billion).
- GemCo did not book a deferred tax liability on its Bermudan earnings, as GemCo's management considered the exception available to the company.
- Thus, the after-tax profit from the Bermudan subsidiary would escape taxation in the USA.

## 15.6   ASC 740: Accounting for Uncertainty in Income Taxes (Formerly FIN 48)

ASC 740 (formerly known as FASB Interpretation No. 48, Accounting for Uncertainty in Income Taxes or "FIN 48") establishes a "more-likely-than-not" threshold for the reporting of uncertain tax positions on financial statements. This standard requires new disclosures in annual financial statements, including a reconciliation of total unrecognized tax benefits, classification of income tax-related interest and penalties, years which remain open to examination and unrecognized tax benefits that are expected to significantly change within 12 months of the reporting period.

Tax contingencies are reported as a liability on the balance sheet. US GAAP reports tax contingencies as a liability on the balance sheet. A contingent liability is created for an unrecognized tax benefit because it represents an enterprise's potential future obligation to the taxing authority for a tax position that was taken. An entity that presents a classified statement of financial position classifies a liability associated with an unrecognized tax benefit as a current liability, to the extent the enterprise anticipates payment (or receipt) of cash within one year or the operating cycle, if longer. The liability for unrecognized tax benefits should not be combined with deferred tax liabilities or assets.

ASC 740-10 provides extensive guidance on accounting for uncertain tax positions.

A two-step approach to uncertain tax positions:

- First is the decision whether to recognize and second is the determination of the measurement.
- Second, it must determine the level at which the tax position will be evaluated (i.e., unit of account). The evaluation can be either

qualitative or quantitative. To that end, the company should take into account the support, documentation, and law of the tax position, as well as the position the taxing authority may take upon audit.

A benefit is recognized when it is more likely than not to be sustained based on the technical merits of the position. The amount of the benefit to be recognized is based on the largest amount of tax benefit that is greater than 50% likely of being realized upon ultimate settlement. Detection risk is precluded from being considered in the analysis by the assumption that the regulators have knowledge of all relevant facts and information.

## Example 1

- In its 2015 Form 1020, Greedy Corp. takes a $100,000 tax credit for research and development.
- Greedy Corp. determines that the probability it would receive the full $100,000 credit is 35%.
- Greedy Corp. then accesses the probability that it would receive $75,000 of the credit at 55%.
- Therefore, Greedy Corp. can only recognize the tax benefit of the research and development of $75,000 and is required to set up a FIN 48 liability for the remaining $25,000.
- Greedy Corp. cannot recognize the tax benefit of the $25,000 until it is recognized, with the recognition event being either the lapsing of the statute of limitations or the acceptance under audit of the position by the taxing authority.

## Example 2

- Greedy Corp. typically writes off all its fixed assets purchased under $400.
- The IRS has audited and accepted Greedy Corp.'s position.
- No FIN 48 liability would be required, even though there is no specific guidance that allows Greedy Corp. to expense these fixed assets.

## 15.7    FINANCIAL STATEMENT REPORTING

### 15.7.1    Statement Reporting

The total income tax expense reported on the statement of income is the sum of the current tax expense and the deferred tax expense. Both the current and deferred tax expenses do not include any tax expense that is recognized directly in equity. Certain items may be accounted for directly in equity instead of going through the statement of income (e.g., excess tax benefits arising from stock compensation arrangements, available-for-sale investments, and certain transactions with shareholders). The tax effects of those items also are recognized directly in equity in the period they arise.

The effect of tax rate changes and changes in the assessment of recoverability of deferred tax assets on items that were previously recognized in equity is recognized through net income.

### 15.7.2    Presentation

In a classified balance sheet, deferred tax assets and liabilities are generally classified based on the classification of the related asset or liability, or for tax losses and credit carryforward, based on the expected timing of realization.

The net deferred current tax amount is reported on the face of the balance sheet, and the net deferred non-current tax amount is reported on the face of the balance sheet.

### 15.7.3    Disclosure

Requires disclosure of:

- The components of the deferred tax liabilities and deferred tax assets.
- The components of tax expense.
- The amounts and expiration dates of operating loss and tax credit carryforward for which tax benefits have not been recognized.
- The amounts of temporary differences that aren't recorded due to the permanent reinvestment of undistributed foreign earnings.

ASC 740-10-50-12 requires the use of "domestic federal statutory tax rates" based on the premise that those rates provide the most meaningful information for domestic users of an enterprise's financial statements. An aggregation of separate reconciliations using foreign tax rates is not permitted (Table 15.1).

The total amount of the deferred tax asset, net of valuation allowance, has decreased from 2013 ($1550.8) to $1540.1 (2014), whereas the total amount of the deferred tax liabilities has increased from $317.6 (2013) to $330.5 (2014). Also, the net deferred tax asset has decreased from $1233.2 (2013) to $1209.6 (2014).

**Table 15.1**    Starbucks (2014): Tax effect of temporary differences and carryforward

Tax effect of temporary differences and carryforwards that comprise significant portions of deferred tax assets and liabilities *(in millions):*

|  | Sep 28, 2014 | Sep 29, 2013 |
|---|---|---|
| Deferred tax assets: | | |
| Property, plant and equipment | $ 78.5 | $ 64.9 |
| Accrued occupancy costs | 58.8 | 69.0 |
| Accrued compensation and related costs | 75.3 | 77.6 |
| Other accrued liabilities | 27.6 | 22.0 |
| Asset retirement obligation asset | 18.6 | 21.0 |
| Deferred revenue | 63.4 | 49.9 |
| Asset impairments | 49.5 | 33.3 |
| Tax credits | 20.3 | 19.1 |
| Stock-based compensation | 131.5 | 120.9 |
| Net operating losses | 104.4 | 99.0 |
| Litigation charge | 1,002.0 | 1,071.9 |
| Other | 77.0 | 62.7 |
| Total | $ 1,706.9 | $ 1,711.3 |
| Valuation allowance | (166.8) | (160.5) |
| Total deferred tax asset, net of valuation allowance | $ 1,540.1 | $ 1,550.8 |
| Deferred tax liabilities: | | |
| Property, plant and equipment | (148.2) | (182.9) |
| Intangible assets and goodwill | (92.9) | (81.6) |
| Other | (89.4) | (53.1) |
| Total | (330.5) | (317.6) |
| Net deferred tax asset | $ 1,209.6 | $ 1,233.2 |
| Reported as: | | |
| Current deferred income tax assets | $ 317.4 | $ 277.3 |
| Long-term deferred income tax assets | 903.3 | 967.0 |
| Current deferred income tax liabilities (included in Accrued liabilities) | (4.2) | (1.0) |
| Long-term deferred income tax liabilities (included in Other long-term liabilities) | (6.9) | (10.1) |
| Net deferred tax asset | $ 1,209.6 | $ 1,233.2 |

*Source* SEC—Starbucks (2014)

# PART III

# The Statements of Cash Flows and Financial Ratios

Since 1987, the cash flow statement has become a mandatory part of a company's financial reports. The cash flow statement is distinct from the income statement and balance sheet because it does not include the amount of future incoming and outgoing cash that has been recorded on credit. This statement allows investors and other financial statement readers to understand how a company's operations are running, where its money is coming from, and how it is being spent. The overall statement of cash flows is made of three components:

(i) Operating cash flow;
(ii) Investing cash flow; and
(iii) Financing cash flow.

The cash flow statement is derived from the income statement and the balance sheet. However, the information provided cannot be revealed by anyone of either the statement of income or the statement of position (or balance Sheet).

# CHAPTER 16

# Analysis of the Statements of Cash Flows

## 16.1    GENERAL

FAS 95—statement of cash flows—supersedes APB Opinion No. 19, Reporting Changes in Financial Position and requires a statement of cash flows as part of a full set of financial statements for all business enterprises in place of a statement of changes in financial position. FAS 95 requires that a statement of cash flows classify cash receipts and payments according to whether they stem from operating, investing, or financing activities and provides definitions of each category.

The primary purpose of a statement of cash flows is to provide relevant information about the cash receipts and cash payments of an enterprise during a period. The information provided in a statement of cash flows, if used with related disclosures and information in the other financial statements, should help investors, creditors, and others to (a) assess the enterprise's ability to generate positive future net cash flows; (b) assess the enterprise's ability to meet its obligations, its ability to pay dividends, and its needs for external financing; (c) assess the reasons for differences between net income and associated cash receipts and payments; and (d) assess the effects on an enterprise's financial position of both its cash and noncash investing and financing transactions during the period. A statement of cash flows shall explain the change during the period in cash and cash equivalents.

© The Author(s) 2018
F. I. Lessambo, *Financial Statements*,
https://doi.org/10.1007/978-3-319-99984-5_16

## 16.2    Classification of Cash Flows

The statement of cash flows shall classify cash receipts and cash payments as resulting from investing, financing, or operating activities. However, certain cash receipts and payments may have aspects of more than one class of cash flows. For example, a cash payment may pertain to an item that could be considered either inventory or a productive asset. If so, the appropriate classification shall depend on the activity that is likely to be the predominant source of cash flows for the item. For example, the acquisition and sale of equipment to be used by the enterprise or rented to others generally are investing activities. However, equipment sometimes is acquired or produced to be used by the enterprise or rented to others for a short period and then sold. In those circumstances, the acquisition or production and subsequent sale of those assets shall be considered operating activities. Moreover, a statement of cash flows of an enterprise with foreign currency transactions or foreign operations shall report the reporting currency equivalent of foreign currency cash flows using the exchange rates in effect at the time of the cash flows. An appropriately weighted average exchange rate for the period may be used for translation if the result is substantially the same as if the rates at the dates of the cash flows were used.

### 16.2.1    Cash Flows from Operating Activities

Operating activities generally involve producing and delivering goods and providing services. Cash flows from operating activities are generally the cash effects of transactions and other events that enter into the determination of net income.

Cash inflows from operating activities are:

- Cash receipts from sales of goods or services, including receipts from collection or sale of accounts and both short- and long-term notes receivable from customers arising from those sales.
- Cash receipts from returns on loans, other debt instruments of other entities, and equity securities—interest and dividends.
- All other cash receipts that do not stem from transactions defined as investing or financing activities, such as amounts received to settle lawsuits; proceeds of insurance settlements except for those

that are directly related to investing or financing activities, such as from destruction of a building; and refunds from suppliers.

Cash outflows for operating activities are:

- Cash payments to acquire materials for manufacture or goods for resale, including principal payments on accounts and both short- and long-term notes payable to suppliers for those materials or goods.
- Cash payments to other suppliers and employees for other goods or services.
- Cash payments to governments for taxes, duties, fines, and other fees or penalties.
- Cash payments to lenders and other creditors for interest.
- All other cash payments that do not stem from transactions defined as investing or financing activities, such as payments to settle lawsuits, cash contributions to charities, and cash refunds to customers.

This section includes cash flows from the principal revenue generation activities such as sale and purchase of goods and services. Cash flows from operating activities can be computed using two methods. One is the direct method and the other indirect method.

### 16.2.2  *Cash Flows from Investing Activities*

Investing activities include making and collecting loans and acquiring and disposing of debt or equity instruments and property, plant, and equipment and other productive assets, that is, assets held for or used in the production of goods or services by the enterprise (other than materials that are part of the enterprise's inventory).

Cash inflows from investing activities are:

- Receipts from collections or sales of loans made by the enterprise and of other entities' debt instruments (other than cash equivalents) that were purchased by the enterprise.
- Receipts from sales of equity instruments of other enterprises and from returns of investment in those instruments.
- Receipts from sales of property, plant, and equipment and other productive assets.

Cash outflows for investing activities are:

- Disbursements for loans made by the enterprise and payments to acquire debt instruments of other entities (other than cash equivalents).
- Payments to acquire equity instruments of other enterprises.
- Payments at the time of purchase or soon before or after purchase to acquire property, plant, and equipment and other productive assets.

Cash flows from investing activities are cash inflows and outflows related to activities that are intended to generate income and cash flows in future. This includes cash inflows and outflows from sale and purchase of long-term assets.

### 16.2.3    Cash Flows from Financing Activities

Financing activities include obtaining resources from owners and providing them with a return on, and a return of, their investment; borrowing money and repaying amounts borrowed, or otherwise settling the obligation; and obtaining and paying for other resources obtained from creditors on long-term credit.

Cash inflows from financing activities are:

- Proceeds from issuing equity instruments.
- Proceeds from issuing bonds, mortgages, notes, and from other short- or long-term borrowing.

Cash outflows for financing activities are:

- Payments of dividends or other distributions to owners, including outlays to reacquire the enterprise's equity instruments.
- Repayments of amounts borrowed.
- Other principal payments to creditors who have extended long-term credit.

Cash flows from financing activities are the cash flows related to transactions with stockholders and creditors such as issuance of share capital, purchase of treasury stock, dividend payments (Table 16.1).

**Table 16.1**   PepsiCo (2014): Consolidated statements of cash flows

Consolidated Statement of Cash Flows
PepsiCo, Inc. and Subsidiaries
Fiscal years ended December 27, 2014, December 28, 2013 and December 29, 2012
(in millions)

| | 2014 | 2013 | 2012 |
|---|---|---|---|
| **Operating Activities** | | | |
| Net income | $   6,558 | $   6,787 | $   6,214 |
| Depreciation and amortization | 2,625 | 2,663 | 2,689 |
| Stock-based compensation expense | 297 | 303 | 278 |
| Merger and integration charges | — | 10 | 16 |
| Cash payments for merger and integration charges | — | (25) | (83) |
| Restructuring and impairment charges | 418 | 163 | 279 |
| Cash payments for restructuring charges | (266) | (133) | (343) |
| Restructuring and other charges related to the transaction with Tingyi | — | — | 176 |
| Cash payments for restructuring and other charges related to the transaction with Tingyi | — | (26) | (109) |
| Venezuela remeasurement charges | 105 | 111 | — |
| Excess tax benefits from share-based payment arrangements | (114) | (117) | (124) |
| Pension and retiree medical plan expenses | 667 | 663 | 796 |
| Pension and retiree medical plan contributions | (655) | (262) | (1,865) |
| Deferred income taxes and other tax charges and credits | (19) | (1,058) | 321 |
| Change in assets and liabilities: | | | |
|   Accounts and notes receivable | (343) | (88) | (250) |
|   Inventories | (111) | 4 | 144 |
|   Prepaid expenses and other current assets | 80 | (51) | 89 |
|   Accounts payable and other current liabilities | 1,162 | 1,007 | 548 |
|   Income taxes payable | 371 | 86 | (97) |
| Other, net | (269) | (349) | (200) |
| **Net Cash Provided by Operating Activities** | 10,506 | 9,688 | 8,479 |
| | | | |
| **Investing Activities** | | | |
| Capital spending | (2,859) | (2,795) | (2,714) |
| Sales of property, plant and equipment | 115 | 109 | 95 |
| Cash payments related to the transaction with Tingyi | — | (3) | (306) |
| Acquisitions and investments in noncontrolled affiliates | (88) | (109) | (121) |
| Divestitures | 203 | 133 | (32) |
| Short-term investments, by original maturity | | | |
|   More than three months - purchases | (6,305) | — | — |
|   More than three months - maturities | 3,891 | — | — |
|   Three months or less, net | 116 | 61 | 61 |
| Other investing, net | (10) | (21) | 12 |
| **Net Cash Used for Investing Activities** | (4,937) | (2,625) | (3,005) |

*Source* SEC—PepsiCo

The amount of the net cash provided by operating activities has consistently increased from 2012 to 2014. However, the investing activities have almost doubled from $2625 (2013) to $4937 (2014). Such an increase often reflects a pursuit of new activities by the firm.

## 16.3    Content and Form
### of the Statement of Cash Flows

A statement of cash flows for a period shall report net cash provided or used by operating, investing, and financing activities and the net effect of those flows on cash and cash equivalents during the period in a manner that reconciles beginning and ending cash and cash equivalents.

### 16.3.1    Reporting Cash Flows from Operating Activities

In reporting cash flows from operating activities, enterprises can use either the direct method or the indirect method, and each one of the two has its advantages and disadvantages. The principal advantage of the direct method is that it shows operating cash receipts and payments. The principal advantage of the indirect method is that it focuses on the differences between net income and net cash flow from operating activities. The more comprehensive and presumably more useful approach would be to use the direct method in the statement of cash flows and to provide a reconciliation of net income and net cash flow from operating activities in a separate schedule—thereby reaping the benefits of both methods while maintaining the focus of the statement of cash flows on cash receipts and payments.

#### 16.3.1.1    The Operating Cash Flows: Direct Method

Under the direct method, enterprises to report major classes of gross cash receipts and gross cash payments and their arithmetic sum—the net cash flow from operating activities. The direct method shows as its principal components operating cash receipts and payments, such as cash received from customers and cash paid to suppliers and employees, the sum of which is net cash flow from operating activities.

Enterprises that do so should, at a minimum, separately report the following classes of operating cash receipts and payments:

- Cash collected from customers, including lessees, licensees, and the like interest and dividends received.
- Other operating cash receipts, if any.
- Cash paid to employees and other suppliers of goods or services, including suppliers of insurance, advertising, and the like.
- Interest paid.

- Income taxes paid.
- Other operating cash payments, if any.

If the direct method of reporting net cash flow from operating activities is used, the reconciliation of net income to net cash flow from operating activities shall be provided in a separate schedule.

If the direct method of preparing the statement of cash flows is used, the Financial Accounting Standards Board requires companies to disclose the reconciliation of net income to the net cash provided by (used by) operating activities that would have been reported if the indirect method had been used to prepare the statement.

## Example

Carusso LLC has recorded the following transactions in its cashbook for FY 2017:

| | |
|---|---|
| Balance of as January 1/1/2017: | $10,000 |
| Collections from customers: | $12,000 |
| Proceed from equipment sale: | $8000 |
| Proceed from short-term loan: | $12,500 |
| Payments to suppliers: | $8000 |
| Payments for operating expenses: | $12,000 |
| Interests payment: | $4500 |
| Purchase of a small equipment: | $4500 |

*Task:* Prepare the statement of cash flow from operation under the direct method.

## Solution

| | |
|---|---|
| Balance of as January 1/1/2017: | $10,000 |
| Collections from customers: | $12,000 |
| Proceed from equipment sale: | $8000 |
| Proceed from short-term loan: | $12,500 |
| Payments to suppliers: | $8000 |
| Payments for operating expenses: | $12,000 |
| Interests payment: | $4500 |
| Purchase of a small equipment: | $4500 |
| Cash flow from operations | $13,500 |

### 16.3.1.2 The Operating Cash Flows: Indirect Method

Under the indirect method, determine and report the same amount for net cash flow from operating activities indirectly by adjusting net income to reconcile it to net cash flow from operating activities. The indirect method starts with net income and adjusts it for revenue and expense items that were not the result of operating cash transactions in the current period to reconcile it to net cash flow from operating activities.

That requires adjusting net income to remove (a) the effects of all deferrals of past operating cash receipts and payments, such as changes during the period in inventory, deferred income, and the like, and all accruals of expected future operating cash receipts and payments, such as changes during the period in receivables and payables, and (b) the effects of all items whose cash effects are investing or financing cash flows, such as depreciation, amortization of goodwill, and gains or losses on sales of property, plant, and equipment and discontinued operations (which relate to investing activities), and gains or losses on extinguishment of debt (which is a financing activity). If the indirect method is used, the reconciliation may be either reported within the statement of cash flows or provided in a separate schedule, with the statement of cash flows reporting only the net cash flow from operating activities.

---

### The Indirect Method in a Nutshell

Under the indirect method, the operating cash flows is computed through several steps:

- Begin with the net income as reported on the income statement
- Add back depreciation, amortization, and depletion
- Subtract any gain on disposal of fixed assets
- Add back any loss on disposal of fixed assets
- Adjust for changes in current assets and current liabilities as follows:
  - an increase in current asset is deducted from the net income
  - an increase in current liability is added to the net income
  - a decrease in current asset is added to the net income
  - a decrease in current liability is deducted from net income

### 16.3.2   Quick Analysis of the Operating Cash Flows

The cash from operating activities is compared to the company's net income. If the cash from operating activities is consistently greater than the net income, the company's net income or earnings are said to be of a "high quality". If the cash from operating activities is less than net income, a red flag is raised as to why the reported net income is not turning into cash.

## 16.4   EXAMPLES

### 16.4.1   Example of Operating Cash Flows

The following example shows the format of the cash flows from operating activities section of cash flows statement prepared using indirect method.

Use the following information to calculate net cash flow from operating activities using indirect method:

| | |
|---|---|
| Net Income | $7000 |
| Depreciation Expense | 1000 |
| Increase in Accounts Receivable | 4400 |
| Increase in Prepaid Rent | 7000 |
| Decrease in Prepaid Insurance | 1300 |
| Increase in Accounts Payable | 14,000 |
| Increase in Wages Payable | 1000 |
| Decrease in Income Tax Payable | 700 |
| Gain on Sale of Equipment | 1800 |

### Solution

| | |
|---|---|
| Cash Flows from Operating Activities: | |
| Net Income | $7000 |
| Depreciation Expense | 1000 |
| Gain on Sale of Equipment | −1800 |
| Increase in Accounts Receivable | −4400 |
| Increase in Prepaid Rent | −7000 |
| Decrease in Prepaid Insurance | 1300 |
| Increase in Accounts Payable | 14,000 |
| Increase in Wages Payable | 1000 |
| Decrease in Income Tax Payable | −700 |
| Net Cash Flow from Operating Activities | 10,400 |

## 16.4.2    Example with Investing Cash Flows

CD Ltd. is engaged in manufacture of fertilizer. For the year ended June 30, 2012, it installed a new plant worth US $800 million (50% of which is financed by issue of debt instruments). The old plant is disposed at a loss of $10 million. The closing written down value of the disposed plant was $150 million. It expended $20 million on construction on new plant building and infrastructure. The company sold off its stake of $50 million in EF Ltd., a subsidiary that was engaged in food processing and received US $10 on account of repayment of principal and $2 million on account of interest income. It received dividends of $5 million during the year. The company reports results in both US GAAP and IFRS.

### Solution

Cash flows from investing activities ($ in million)

| | |
|---|---|
| Cash paid to acquire new plant | (400) |
| Cash paid to construct new buildings | (20) |
| Cash receipt from sale of old plant | 140 |
| Cash receipt from sale of investment in EF Ltd. | 50 |
| Cash receipt from payback of loan principal | 20 |
| Net cash flows from investing activities | (210) |

Notes:

1. Only $400 million is shown as a cash outflow because 50% is paid through issue of debt instrument which is reported in schedule of noncash transactions.
2. Cash receipt from sale of plant equals written down value of the plant of $150 million minus the loss of $10 million.
3. Receipt of principal is reported as an investing cash inflow while dividend income and interest income is not included in cash flows from investing activities under US GAAP. It is reported as a cash inflow from operating activities.

If the company is reporting its performance globally, it would most likely prepare the financial statements in accordance with IFRS. Under IFRS, net cash flows from investing activities would increase by $7 million ($5 million on account of dividend income plus $2 million on account of interest income earned). The corresponding net cash flows from operating activities would be lower by $7 million. The net cash flows are same under both US GAAP and IFRS.

### 16.4.3 Example with Financing Cash Flow Activities

CD Fertilizer had the following transactions in fiscal year 2015:
CD obtained a $20,000 loan from Wells Fargo Bank; it issued common stock for $125,000; redeemed its pre-issued stock for $32,000; paid $10,000 dividends to its shareholders.

#### Solution

| | |
|---|---|
| Loan Obtained | $20,000 |
| Issuance of Common Stock | 125,000 |
| Treasury Stock Purchased | 32,000 |
| Dividends Paid | 10,000 |
| Net Cash Flow from Financing Activities | $103,000 |

## 16.5 NONCASH INVESTING AND FINANCING ACTIVITIES

All information about investing and financing activities of an enterprise during a period that affect recognized assets or liabilities but that do not result in cash receipts or cash payments in the period shall be reported in related disclosures. Those disclosures may be either narrative or summarized in a schedule, and they shall clearly relate the cash and noncash aspects of transactions involving similar items. Examples of noncash investing and financing transactions are converting debt to equity; acquiring assets by assuming directly related liabilities, such as purchasing a building by incurring a mortgage to the seller; obtaining an asset by entering into a capital lease; and exchanging noncash assets or liabilities for other noncash assets or liabilities. Some transactions are part cash and part noncash; only the cash portion shall be reported in the statement of cash flows.

Example of supplemental schedule on noncash and financing investing

- The company purchased all of the capital stock of Company S for $950. In conjunction with the acquisition, liabilities were assumed as follows:

| | |
|---|---|
| Fair value of assets acquired | $1580 |
| Cash paid for the capital stock | (950) |
| Liabilities assumed | $630 |

- A capital lease obligation of $850 was incurred when the company entered into a lease for new equipment.
- Additional common stock was issued upon the conversion of $500 of long-term debt.

CHAPTER 17

# Financial Ratios Analysis

## 17.1 GENERAL

When it comes to investing, analyzing financial statement information (also known as quantitative analysis) is one of, if not, the most important elements in the fundamental analysis process. At the same time, the massive amount of numbers in a company's financial statements can be bewildering and intimidating to many investors. However, through financial ratio analysis, one may be able to work with these numbers in an organized fashion. Ratio analysis is a diagnostic tool that helps to identify problem areas and opportunities within a company.

Among the dozens of financial ratios available, we've chosen the measurements that are the most relevant to the investing process and organized them into ten main categories as per the following list:

## 17.2 LIQUIDITY MEASUREMENT RATIOS

Liquidity ratios analyze the ability of a company to pay off both its current liabilities as they become due and their long-term liabilities as they become current. In other words, these ratios show the cash levels of a company and the ability to turn other assets into cash to pay off liabilities and other current obligations. Liquidity is not only a measure of how much cash a business has. It is also a measure of how easy it will be for the company to raise enough cash or convert assets into cash. Assets like accounts receivable, trading securities, and inventory are relatively easy

© The Author(s) 2018
F. I. Lessambo, *Financial Statements*,
https://doi.org/10.1007/978-3-319-99984-5_17

for many companies to convert into cash in the short term. Thus, all of these assets go into the liquidity calculation of a company.

Below are the most common liquidity ratios:

- Current Ratio

The current ratio is a liquidity and efficiency ratio that measures a firm's ability to pay off its short-term liabilities with its current assets. The current ratio is an important measure of liquidity because short-term liabilities are due within the next year. This means that a company has a limited amount of time in order to raise the funds to pay for these liabilities. Current assets like cash, cash equivalents, and marketable securities can easily be converted into cash in the short term. This means that companies with larger amounts of current assets will more easily be able to pay off current liabilities when they become due without having to sell off long-term, revenue-generating assets.

$$\text{Current ratio} = \frac{\text{Total Current Assets}}{\text{Total Current Liabilities}}$$

The current ratio is calculated by dividing current assets by current liabilities. This ratio is stated in numeric format rather than in decimal format.

### Example 1

On December 31, 2014, Xiao Corporation had current assets of $100,000 and current liabilities of $50,000. Calculate its current ratio.

### Solution

| Current Assets | ÷ | Current Liabilities | = | Current Ratio |
|---|---|---|---|---|
| $100,000 | | $50,000 | | 2.00 |

### Example 2

On December 31, 2014, Zhifan Corporation had total asset of $350,000, equity of $150,000, non-current assets of $50,000, and non-current liabilities of $50,000. Calculate the current ratio.

| i. | Total Asset | − | Non-current Assets | = | Current Assets |
|----|-------------|---|--------------------|---|----------------|
| | $350,000 | | $50,000 | | $300,000 |
| ii. | Total Assets | − | Total Equity | = | Total Liabilities |
| | $350,000 | | $150,000 | | $200,000 |
| iii. | Total liabilities | − | Non-current liabilities | = | Current Liabilities |
| | $200,000 | | $50,000 | | $150,000 |
| iv. | Current Assets | ÷ | Current Liabilities | = | Current Ratio |
| | $300,000 | | $150,000 | | 2.00 |

- Quick Ratio

The quick ratio or acid test ratio is a liquidity ratio that measures the ability of a company to pay its current liabilities when they come due with only quick assets. Quick assets are current assets that can be converted to cash within 90 days or in the short term. Cash, cash equivalents, short-term investments or marketable securities, and current accounts receivable are considered quick assets.

Short-term investments or marketable securities include trading securities and available for sale securities that can easily be converted into cash within the next 90 days. Marketable securities are traded on an open market with a known price and readily available buyers. Any stock on the New York Stock Exchange would be considered a marketable security because they can easily be sold to any investor when the market is open. The quick ratio is often called the acid test ratio in reference to the historical use of acid to test metals for gold by the early miners. If the metal passed the acid test, it was pure gold. If metal failed the acid test by corroding from the acid, it was a base metal and of no value.

The acid test of finance shows how well a company can quickly convert its assets into cash in order to pay off its current liabilities. It also shows the level of quick assets to current liabilities.

$$Quick\ ratio = \frac{Cash + Cash\ equivalents + Short\ term\ investment + Current\ receivables}{Total\ Current\ Liabilities}$$

The quick ratio is calculated by adding cash, cash equivalents, short-term investments, and current receivables together and then dividing them by current liabilities.

## Example

Yin Corp. balance sheet provides the following information:

| | |
|---|---|
| Cash in hand | $25,000 |
| Cash at bank | $50,000 |
| Receivables: | $45,000 |
| Marketable securities | $100,000 |
| Total current liabilities | $160,000 |

$$Quick\ ratio = \frac{25,000 + 50,000 + 45,000 + 100,000}{160,000} = \frac{220,000}{160,000} = 1.375$$

- Cash Ratio

The cash ratio or cash coverage ratio is a liquidity ratio that measures a firm's ability to pay off its current liabilities with only cash and cash equivalents. The cash ratio is much more restrictive than the current ratio or quick ratio because no other current assets can be used to pay off current debt—only cash. This is why many creditors look at the cash ratio. They want to see if a company maintains adequate cash balances to pay off all of their current debts as they come due. Creditors also like the fact that inventory and accounts receivable are left out of the equation because both of these accounts are not guaranteed to be available for debt servicing. Inventory could take months or years to sell and receivables could take weeks to collect. Cash is guaranteed to be available for creditors.

$$Formula = \frac{Cash + Cash\ equivalents}{Total\ Current\ Liabilities}$$

The cash coverage ratio is calculated by adding cash and cash equivalents and dividing by the total current liabilities of a company.

## Example

Chang LLP is a beauty salon with the below balance sheet. On January 1, 2015, Chang LLP got a $100,000 loan from Wells Fargo. Calculate Chang LLP cash ratio?

| | |
|---|---|
| Cash | $10,000 |
| Cash Equivalents | $2000 |
| Accounts Payable | $3000 |
| Current Taxes Payable | $1000 |
| Current Long-term Liabilities | $10,000 |

$$Formula = \frac{Cash + Cash\ equivalents}{Total\ Current\ Liabilities}$$

$$Cash\ ratio = \frac{10,000 + 2000}{3000 + 1000 + 10,000} = 0.85$$

This stands to say that Chang LLP only has enough cash and equivalents to pay off 75% of her current liabilities. This is a fairly high ratio which means Chang LLP maintains a relatively high cash balance during the year.

- Cash Conversion Cycle

The cash conversion cycle is a cash flow calculation that attempts to measure the time it takes a company to convert its investment in inventory and other resource inputs into cash. In other words, the cash conversion cycle calculation measures how long cash is tied up in inventory before the inventory is sold and cash is collected from customers.

The cash cycle has three distinct parts. The first part of the cycle represents the current inventory level and how long it will take the company to sell this inventory. This stage is calculated by using the days inventory outstanding calculation.

The second stage of the cash cycle represents the current sales and the amount of time it takes to collect the cash from these sales. This is calculated by using the days sales outstanding calculation.

The third stage represents the current outstanding payables. In other words, this represents how much a company owes its current vendors for inventory and goods purchases and when the company will have to pay off its vendors. This is calculated by using the days payables outstanding calculation.

*Formula* = Days of inventory outstanding − Days payable outstanding

The cash conversion cycle is calculated by adding the days inventory outstanding to the days sales outstanding and subtracting the days payable outstanding.

---

### Example

Yin Corp. has receivables turnover ratio of 12, inventory turnover ratio of 10, and payable turnover ratio of 8.
Compute Yin Corp. cash conversion cycle.

### Solution

First, convert the turnover measures to number of days measures.

$$Days\,sales\,outstanding\,(DSO) = \frac{365}{Receivables\,turnover\,ratio}$$
$$= \frac{365}{12} = 30.42\,days$$

$$Days\,inventory\,outstanding\,(DIO) = \frac{365}{Inventory\,turnover\,ratio}$$
$$= \frac{365}{10} = 36.5\,days$$

$$Days\,payables\,outstanding\,(DPO) = \frac{365}{Payables\,turnover\,ratio}$$
$$= \frac{365}{8} = 45.62\,days$$

Second, calculate the cash conversion cycle

$$Cash\,conversion\,cycle = DSO + DIO - DPO$$
$$= 30.42 + 36.5 - 45.62 = 21.30$$

- Working Capital Ratio

The working capital ratio, also called the current ratio, is a liquidity ratio that measures a firm's ability to pay off its current liabilities with current assets. The working capital ratio is important to creditors because it shows the liquidity of the company.

Current liabilities are best paid with current assets like cash, cash equivalents, and marketable securities because these assets can be converted into cash much quicker than fixed assets. The faster the assets can be converted into cash, the more likely the company will have the cash in time to pay its debts.

The reason this ratio is called the working capital ratio comes from the working capital calculation. When current assets exceed current liabilities, the firm has enough capital to run its day-to-day operations. In other words, it has even capital to work. The working capital ratio transforms the working capital calculation into a comparison between current assets and current liabilities.

$$Working\ capital\ ratio = \frac{Current\ assets}{Current\ liabilities}$$

The working capital ratio is calculated by dividing current assets by current liabilities.

**Example**

Yin Corp. provides the following information from its balance sheet:

| Total current assets | $150,000 |
| Total current liabilities | $75,000 |

$$Working\ capital\ ratio = \frac{\$150,000}{\$75,000} = 2$$

- Times Interest Earned Ratio

The times interest earned ratio, sometimes called the interest coverage ratio (ICR), is a coverage ratio that measures the proportionate amount of income that can be used to cover interest expenses in the future.

In some respects, the times interest ratio is considered a solvency ratio because it measures a firm's ability to make interest and debt service payments. Since these interest payments are usually made on a long-term basis, they are often treated as an ongoing, fixed expense. As with most fixed expenses, if the company can't make the payments, it could go bankrupt and cease to exist. Thus, this ratio could be considered a solvency ratio.

$$\text{Times interest earned ratio} = \frac{\text{Income before interest and income taxes}}{\text{Interest expense}}$$

The times interest earned ratio is calculated by dividing income before interest and income taxes by the interest expense.

### Example

Yin Corp. has interest expense and earnings before interest and tax for the year ended Dec 31, 2014, of $250,000 and $5,000,000, respectively.

$$\text{Times interest earned ratio} = \frac{\$5,000,000}{\$250,000} = 20$$

## 17.3    SOLVENCY RATIOS

Solvency ratios, also called leverage ratios, measure a company's ability to sustain operations indefinitely by comparing debt levels with equity, assets, and earnings. In other words, solvency ratios identify going concern issues and a firm's ability to pay its bills in the long term. Many people confuse solvency ratios with liquidity ratios. Although they both measure the ability of a company to pay off its obligations, solvency ratios focus more on the long-term sustainability of a company instead of the current liability payments. Solvency ratios show a company's ability to make payments and pay off its long-term obligations to creditors, bondholders, and banks. Better solvency ratios indicate a more creditworthy and financially sound company in the long term.

The most common solvency ratios include:

- Debt-to-Equity Ratio

The debt-to-equity ratio is a financial, liquidity ratio that compares a company's total debt to total equity. The debt-to-equity ratio shows the percentage of company financing that comes from creditors and investors. A higher debt-to-equity ratio indicates that more creditor financing (bank loans) is used than investor financing (shareholders).

$$\text{Debt-to-equity ratio} = \frac{\text{Total liability}}{\text{Total equity}}$$

The debt-to-equity ratio is calculated by dividing total liabilities by total equity. The debt-to-equity ratio is considered a balance sheet ratio because all of the elements are reported on the balance sheet.

### Example

Yin Corp. provides the following information from its balance sheet:

| Total liability | $2,500,000 |
|---|---|
| Total equity | $10,000,000 |

$$\text{Debt-to-equity ratio} = \frac{\$2,500,000}{\$10,000,000} = 0.025$$

- Equity Ratio

The equity ratio is an investment leverage or solvency ratio that measures the amount of assets that are financed by owners' investments by comparing the total equity in the company to the total assets.

The equity ratio highlights two important financial concepts of a solvent and sustainable business. The first component shows how much of the total company assets are owned outright by the investors. In other words, after all of the liabilities are paid off, the investors will end up with the remaining assets.

The second component inversely shows how leveraged the company is with debt. The equity ratio measures how much of a firm's assets were financed by investors. In other words, this is the investors' stake in the company. This is what they are on the hook for. The inverse of this calculation shows the amount of assets that were financed by debt. Companies with higher equity ratios show new investors and creditors that investors believe in the company and are willing to finance it with their investments.

$$\text{Equity ratio} = \frac{\text{Total equity}}{\text{Total assets}}$$

The equity ratio is calculated by dividing total equity by total assets. Both of these numbers truly include all of the accounts in that category. In other words, all of the assets and equity reported on the balance sheet are included in the equity ratio calculation.

**Example**

Yin Corp. provides the following information from its balance sheet

| Total assets | $5,000,000 |
| Total equity | $10,000,000 |

$$\text{Equity ratio} = \frac{\$10,000,000}{\$5,000,000} = 2$$

- Debt Ratio

Debt ratio is a solvency ratio that measures a firm's total liabilities as a percentage of its total assets. In a sense, the debt ratio shows a company's ability to pay off its liabilities with its assets. In other words, this shows how many assets the company must sell in order to pay off all of its liabilities. This ratio measures the financial leverage of a company. Companies with higher levels of liabilities compared with assets are considered highly leveraged and more risky for lenders.

This helps investors and creditors to analyze the overall debt burden on the company as well as the firm's ability to pay off the debt in future, uncertain economic times.

$$Debt\ ratio = \frac{\text{Total liabilities}}{\text{Total assets}}$$

The debt ratio is calculated by dividing total liabilities by total assets. Both of these numbers can easily be found in the balance sheet.

### Example

Yin Corp. provides the following information from its balance sheet

| Total liability | $5,000,000 |
|---|---|
| Total assets | $5,000,000 |

$$Debt\ ratio = \frac{\$5,000,000}{\$5,000,000} = 1$$

## 17.4   PROFITABILITY INDICATOR RATIOS

Profitability ratios compare income statement accounts and categories to show a company's ability to generate profits from its operations. Profitability ratios focus on a company's return on investment in inventory and other assets. These ratios basically show how well companies can achieve profits from their operations. Investors and creditors can use profitability ratios to judge a company's return on investment based on its relative level of resources and assets. In other words, profitability ratios can be used to judge whether companies are making enough operational profit from their assets. In this sense, profitability ratios relate to efficiency ratios because they show how well companies are using their assets to generate profits. Profitability is also important to the concept of solvency and going concern.

Here are some of the key ratios that investors and creditors consider when judging how profitable a company should be:

- Profit Margin Analysis

The profit margin ratio, also called the return on sales (ROS) ratio or gross profit ratio, is a profitability ratio that measures the amount of net income earned with each dollar of sales generated by comparing the net income and net sales of a company. In other words, the profit margin ratio shows what percentage of sales are left over after all expenses are paid by the business. Creditors and investors use this ratio to measure how effectively a company can convert sales into net income. Investors want to make sure profits are high enough to distribute dividends while creditors want to make sure the company has enough profits to pay back its loans. In other words, outside users want to know that the company is running efficiently. An extremely low profit margin would indicate the expenses are too high and the management needs to budget and cut expenses.

The ROS ratio is often used by internal management to set performance goals for the future.

$$Profit\ margin\ ratio = \frac{Net\ income}{Net\ sales}$$

The profit margin ratio formula can be calculated by dividing net income by net sales.

---

### Example

Yin Corp. provides the following information from its statement of income:

| | |
|---|---|
| Net income | $100,000 |
| Net sales | $1,000,000 |

$$Profit\ margin\ ratio = \frac{\$100,000}{\$1,000,000} = 10\%$$

---

- Effective Tax Rate

The effective tax rate is the average rate at which an individual is taxed on earned income or the average rate at which a corporation is taxed on pre-tax profits. The formulas for effective tax rate are as follows:

$$Individual: \frac{Total\ tax\ expense}{Taxable\ income}$$

$$Corporation: \frac{Total\ tax\ expense}{Earnings\ before\ Taxes}$$

Effective tax rates simplify comparisons among companies or taxpayers. This is especially true where a progressive or tiered tax system is in place. Those subject to progressive taxes will see different levels of income taxed at different rates.

### Example

If a company earned $100,000 and paid $25,000 in taxes, the effective tax rate is equal to 25,000/100,000 or 0.25.

- Return on Assets

The return on assets ratio, often called the return on total assets, is a profitability ratio that measures the net income produced by total assets during a period by comparing net income to the average total assets. In other words, the return on assets ratio or ROA measures how efficiently a company can manage its assets to produce profits during a period. Since company assets' sole purpose is to generate revenues and produce profits, this ratio helps both management and investors see how well the company can convert its investments in assets into profits. You can look at ROA as a return on investment for the company since capital assets are often the biggest investment for most companies. In this case, the company invests money into capital assets and the return is measured in profits.

In short, this ratio measures how profitable a company's assets are.

$$Return\ on\ assets\ ratio = \frac{\text{Net income}}{\text{Average total assets}}$$

The return on assets ratio formula is calculated by dividing net income by average total assets.

### Example

The following information provides the financial statements of Yuco Inc.:

- July 1, 2013, and June 30, 2014, were $2,000,000 and $3,000,000, respectively.

- During the year ended June 30, 2014, it earned net income of $250,000.

$$Average\ Total\ Assets = \frac{\$2,000,000 + \$3,000,000}{2} = \$2,500,000$$

$$Return\ on\ Assets = \frac{\$250,000}{\$2,500,000} = 0.10\ or\ 10\%.$$

- Return on Sales

The ROS ratio (also known as a firm's operating profit margin) is a ratio used to evaluate a company's operational efficiency. It provides insight into how much profit is being produced per dollar of sales. Put differently, it measures a company's performance by analyzing what percentage of total company revenues are actually converted into company profits.

$$Return\ on\ sales\ (ROS)\ ratio = \frac{Operating\ profits}{Net\ sales}$$

### Example

Allison LLC generates $400,000 of business each year and shows operating profit of $100,000 before any taxes or interest expenses are accounted for.

$$ROS = \frac{\$100,000}{\$400,000} = 25\%$$

- Return on Operating Expenses (Berry Ratio)

Operating expenses are costs associated with running a business's core operations on a daily basis. In general, the lower a business's operating expenses are, the more profitable it is. The operating expense ratio (OER) is equal to a company's operating expenses divided by its revenues.

$$Operating\ expense\ ratio\ (OER) = \frac{Operating\ expenses}{Revenues}$$

**Example**

In 2016, Yudelka Inc. operating expenses were $5,000,000 and its revenues were $20,000,000.

$$OER = \frac{\$5,000,000}{\$20,000,000} = 25\%$$

- Return on Total Costs

The return on total costs (ROC) ratio refers to the ratio of the total costs to the sales of a business. Some analysts consider the ROC as an additional indicator of the ROS. The lower the indicator value, the better the enterprise has a financial result.

$$Return\ on\ total\ costs\ (ROC) = \frac{Total\ costs}{Sales}$$

**Example**

In 2016, Polanco Inc. total costs were $5,000,000 and its net sales $20,000,000.

$$ROC = \frac{\$5,000,000}{\$20,000,000} = 25\%$$

- Return on Equity

The return on equity ratio or ROE is a profitability ratio that measures the ability of a firm to generate profits from its shareholders' investments in the company. In other words, the return on equity ratio shows how much profit each dollar of common stock holders' equity generates.

So a return on 1 means that every dollar of common stock holders' equity generates 1 dollar of net income. This is an important measurement for potential investors because they want to see how efficiently a company will use their money to generate net income.

ROE is also an indicator of how effective management is at using equity financing to fund operations and grow the company.

$$Return\ on\ equity\ (ROE)\ ratio = \frac{Net\ income}{Shareholder\prime s\ equity}$$

The return on equity ratio formula is calculated by dividing net income by shareholder's equity.

### Example

Yuco Inc. generated $10 million net income in 2014. If Yuco Inc. shareholders' equity equaled $20 million in 2014, its ROE is computed as follows:

$$ROE = \frac{\$10,000,000}{\$20,000,000} = 50\%$$

- Return on Capital Employed

Return on capital employed or ROCE is a profitability ratio that measures how efficiently a company can generate profits from its capital employed by comparing net operating profit to capital employed. In other words, return on capital employed shows investors how many dollars in profits each dollar of capital employed generates. ROCE is a long-term profitability ratio because it shows how effectively assets are performing while taking into consideration long-term financing. This is why ROCE is a more useful ratio than return on equity to evaluate the longevity of a company. This ratio is based on two important calculations: operating profit and capital employed. Net operating profit is often called EBIT or earnings before interest and taxes. EBIT is often reported on the income statement because it shows the company profits generated from operations. EBIT can be calculated by adding interest and taxes back into net income if needed.

Capital employed is a fairly convoluted term because it can be used to refer to many different financial ratios. Most often capital employed refers to the total assets of a company less than all current liabilities. This could also be looked at as stockholders' equity less than long-term liabilities. Both convey the same figure.

$$Return\ on\ capital\ employed\ (ROCE) = \frac{Net\ operating\ profit}{Employed\ capital}$$

Return on capital employed formula is calculated by dividing net operating profit or EBIT by the employed capital.

### Example

Wally Inc. has a net profit of $150,000 in 2014 and an average capital employed of $3,000,000.

$$ROCE = \frac{\$150,000}{\$3,000,000} = 0.05\ or\ 5\%$$

## 17.5    EFFICIENCY RATIOS

Efficiency ratios also called activity ratios measure how well companies utilize their assets to generate income. Efficiency ratios often look at the time it takes companies to collect cash from customer or the time it takes companies to convert inventory into cash—in other words, make sales. These ratios are used by management to help improve the company as well as outside investors and creditors looking at the operations of profitability of the company. Efficiency ratios go hand in hand with profitability ratios. Most often when companies are efficient with their resources, they become profitable. WalMart is a good example. WalMart is extremely good at selling low margin products at high volumes. In other words, they are efficient at turning their assets. Even though they don't make much profit per sale, they make a ton of sales. Each little sale adds up. The most common efficiency ratios include:

• Account Receivable Turnover Ratio

It measures how many times a business can turn its accounts receivable into cash during a period. In other words, the accounts receivable turnover ratio measures how many times a business can collect its average accounts receivable during the year.

This ratio shows how efficient a company is at collecting its credit sales from customers. Some companies collect their receivables from customers in 90 days while others take up to 6 months to collect from customers.

In some ways, the receivables turnover ratio can be viewed as a liquidity ratio as well. Companies are more liquid the faster they can convert their receivables into cash.

$$\text{Account receivable turnover ratio} = \frac{\text{Net credit sales}}{\text{Average Account Receivables}}$$

Accounts receivable turnover is calculated by dividing net credit sales by the average accounts receivable for that period.

### Example

Wally Inc. had $20,000 of average receivables during FY 2014 and collected $40,000 of receivables during the same fiscal year.

$$\text{Account receivable turnover ratio} = \frac{\$40,000}{\$20,000} = 2$$

- Working Capital Ratio

The working capital ratio, also called the current ratio, is a liquidity ratio that measures a firm's ability to pay off its current liabilities with current assets. The working capital ratio is important to creditors because it shows the liquidity of the company.

Current liabilities are best paid with current assets like cash, cash equivalents, and marketable securities because these assets can be converted into cash much quicker than fixed assets. The faster the assets can be converted into cash, the more likely the company will have the cash in time to pay its debts.

The reason this ratio is called the working capital ratio comes from the working capital calculation. When current assets exceed current liabilities, the firm has enough capital to run its day-to-day operations. In other words, it has even capital to work. The working capital ratio transforms the working capital calculation into a comparison between current assets and current liabilities.

$$\text{Working capital ratio} = \frac{\text{Current assets}}{\text{Current liabilities}}$$

The working capital ratio is calculated by dividing current assets by current liabilities.

- Asset Turnover Ratio

The asset turnover ratio is an efficiency ratio that measures a company's ability to generate sales from its assets by comparing net sales with average total assets. In other words, this ratio shows how efficiently a company can use its assets to generate sales.

The total asset turnover ratio calculates net sales as a percentage of assets to show how many sales are generated from each dollar of company assets. For instance, a ratio of .5 means that each dollar of assets generates 50 cents of sales.

$$\text{Asset turnover ratio} = \frac{\text{Net sales}}{\text{Average total assets}}$$

The asset turnover ratio is calculated by dividing net sales by average total assets.

- Inventory Turnover Ratio

The inventory turnover ratio is an efficiency ratio that shows how effectively inventory is managed by comparing cost of goods sold with average inventory for a period. This measures how many times average inventory is "turned" or sold during a period. In other words, it measures how many times a company sold its total average inventory dollar amount during the year. A company with $1000 of average inventory and sales of $10,000 effectively sold its 10 times over.

This ratio is important because total turnover depends on two main components of performance. The first component is stock purchasing. If larger amounts of inventory are purchased during the year, the company will have to sell greater amounts of inventory to improve its turnover. If the company can't sell these greater amounts of inventory, it will incur storage costs and other holding costs.

The second component is sales. Sales have to match inventory purchases; otherwise, the inventory will not turn effectively. That's why the purchasing and sales departments must be in tune with each other.

$$\text{Inventory turnover ratio} = \frac{\text{COGS}}{\text{Average inventory}}$$

The inventory turnover ratio is calculated by dividing the cost of goods sold for a period by the average inventory for that period.

• Days Sale to Inventory

The inventory turnover ratio is an efficiency ratio that shows how effectively inventory is managed by comparing cost of goods sold with average inventory for a period. This measures how many times average inventory is "turned" or sold during a period. In other words, it measures how many times a company sold its total average inventory dollar amount during the year. A company with $1000 of average inventory and sales of $10,000 effectively sold its 10 times over.

This ratio is important because total turnover depends on two main components of performance. The first component is stock purchasing. If larger amounts of inventory are purchased during the year, the company will have to sell greater amounts of inventory to improve its turnover. If the company can't sell these greater amounts of inventory, it will incur storage costs and other holding costs.

The second component is sales. Sales have to match inventory purchases; otherwise, the inventory will not turn effectively. That's why the purchasing and sales departments must be in tune with each other.

$$\text{Days sale to Inventory} = \frac{\text{Ending inventory}}{\text{COGS}} \times 365$$

### Example

At the end of FY 2016, Mignon Corporation financial statements show an ending inventory of $100,000.

The COGS as reported in the Income Statement: $300,000

*Task*: Compute Mignon Corporation Days sale to inventory in FY 2016

### Solution

$$\text{Days sale to inventory} = \left( \frac{\$100,000}{\$300,000} \right) \times 365 = 122$$

## 17.6 DEBT RATIOS

• Debt Ratio

Debt ratio is a solvency ratio that measures a firm's total liabilities as a percentage of its total assets. In a sense, the debt ratio shows a company's ability to pay off its liabilities with its assets. In other words, this shows how many assets the company must sell in order to pay off all of its liabilities.

This ratio measures the financial leverage of a company. Companies with higher levels of liabilities compared with assets are considered highly leveraged and more risky for lenders.

This helps investors and creditors to analyze the overall debt burden on the company as well as the firm's ability to pay off the debt in future, uncertain economic times.

$$\text{Debt Ratio} = \frac{\text{Total liabilities}}{\text{Total assets}}$$

The debt ratio is calculated by dividing total liabilities by total assets. Both of these numbers can easily be found in the balance sheet. Here is the calculation

• Debt-to-Equity Ratio

The debt-to-equity ratio is a measure of the relationship between the capital contributed by creditors and the capital contributed by shareholders. It also shows the extent to which shareholders' equity can fulfill a company's obligations to creditors in the event of a liquidation.

$$\text{Debt-Equity Ratio} = \frac{\text{Total liabilities}}{\text{Shareholders equity}}$$

Both total liabilities and shareholders' equity figures in the above formula can be obtained from the balance sheet of a business. A variation of the above formula uses only the interest-bearing long-term liabilities in the numerator.

• Capitalization Ratio

The capitalization ratio compares total debt to total capitalization (capital structure). The capitalization ratio reflects the extent to which a company is operating on its equity.

Capitalization ratio is also known as the financial leverage ratio. It tells the investors about the extent to which the company is using its equity to support its operations and growth. This ratio helps in the assessment of risk. The companies with high capitalization ratio are considered to be risky because they are at a risk of insolvency if they fail to repay their debt on time. Companies with a high capitalization ratio may also find it difficult to get more loans in the future.

A high capitalization ratio is not always bad; however, higher financial leverage can increase the return on a shareholder's investment because usually there are tax advantages associated with the borrowings. The capitalization ratio is calculated by dividing the long-term debt by the total shareholder's equity and long-term debt. This can be expressed as:

$$\text{Capitalization Ratio} = \frac{\text{Long-term debt}}{\text{Long-term debt} + \text{Shareholders equity}}$$

The capitalization ratio is a very meaningful debt ratio because it gives an important insight into the use of financial leverage by a company. It focuses on the relationship of long-term debt as a component of the company's total capital base. The total capital is the capital raised by the shareholders and the lenders.

The company's capitalization, which should not be confused with the market capitalization, explains the makeup of the long-term capital of the company. Capitalization is also known as capital structure. A company's long-term capital consists of long-term borrowings and shareholder's equity.

- Interest Coverage Ratio

The ICR is a measure of a company's ability to meet its interest payments. ICR is equal to EBIT for a time period, often one year, divided by interest expenses for the same time period. The ICR is a measure of the number of times a company could make the interest payments on its debt with its EBIT. It determines how easily a company can pay interest expenses on outstanding debt. ICR is also known as interest coverage, debt service ratio or debt service coverage ratio.

$$\text{Interest coverage ratio (ICR)} = \frac{\text{Earnings before interest and taxes (EBIT)}}{\text{Interest expenses}}$$

The ICR is calculated by dividing a company's EBIT by the company's interest expenses for the same period.

Interest coverage ratio = EBIT/Interest expenses

The lower the ICR, the higher the company's debt burden and the greater the possibility of bankruptcy or default. A lower ICR means less earnings are available to meet interest payments and that the business is more vulnerable to increases in interest rates. When a company's ICR is only 1.5 or lower, its ability to meet interest expenses may be questionable. An ICR below 1.0 indicates the business is having difficulties generating the cash necessary to pay its interest obligations (i.e., interest payments exceed its earnings [EBIT]).

A higher ratio indicates a better financial health as it means that the company is more capable to meeting its interest obligations from operating earnings. On the other hand, a high ICR may suggest a company is "too safe" and is neglecting opportunities to magnify earnings through leverage.

- Cash Flow to Debt Ratio

This coverage ratio compares a company's operating cash flow to its total debt, which, for purposes of this ratio, is defined as the sum of short-term borrowings, the current portion of long-term debt and long-term debt. This ratio provides an indication of a company's ability to cover total debt with its yearly cash flow from operations. The higher the percentage ratio, the better the company's ability to carry its total debt.

$$\text{Cash flow to Debt ratio} = \frac{\text{Operating cash flow}}{\text{Total debt}}$$

## 17.7   Operating Performance Ratios

Operational performance ratios measure how different aspects of a company's finances are performing. The fixed-asset turnover ratio, operating cycle ratio, and revenue per employee ratio each provide a different look into how a company is bringing in revenue, if the business is spending its money well and how efficiently it is using its assets and resources. Analyzing these ratios provides deeper insight into the company's finances than simply studying accounting or other financial records.

- Fixed-Asset Turnover

The fixed-asset turnover ratio is a measure of whether the money a company spends on the equipment and buildings the company owns, often referred to as property, plant and equipment, or PP&E, actually adds value to the company. To find the fixed-asset turnover ratio, divide the company's net revenue by the current value of the fixed assets.

$$\text{Fixed-asset turnover} = \frac{\text{Net annual sales}}{\text{Gross fixed assets} - \text{Accumulated depreciation}}$$

A high ratio generally indicates that the company is generating adequate revenue with its assets and that the fixed assets are a wise investment of the company's resources. However, companies that don't require much investment in PP&E, such as consulting firms or IT companies, often have lower fixed-asset turnover ratios than companies that rely more on equipment to make money, such as manufacturers. This means that you must analyze the fixed-asset turnover ratio within the norms of the industry. Analysts also compare the current fixed-asset turnover ratio to historical fixed-asset turnover ratio figures to determine if the ratio is increasing or decreasing. A declining ratio may indicate that the company has too much money tied up in its equipment or property. An increasing ratio often indicates that the company is making better use of its property and equipment or has upgraded effectively

### Example

Yin Company has gross fixed assets of $6,000,000 and accumulated depreciation of $2,000,000. Sales over the last 12 months totaled $12,000,000. Yin Company fixed-asset turnover ratio is:

$$\text{Turnover per year} = \frac{\$12,000,000}{\$6,000,000 - \$2,000,000} = 3.0$$

- Sales/Revenue per Employee

The revenue per employee ratio indicates how much revenue each employee is producing for the company. To find the revenue per employee ratio, divide the annual revenue the company earns by the number of employees it has. This ratio is expressed as a dollar amount.

$$\text{Revenue per employee ratio} = \frac{\text{Annual revenue}}{\text{Number of employee (average)}}$$

A high revenue per employee ratio means that employees are generating adequate sales or revenue for the company, while a low ratio is often a sign of low productivity. This is especially true for labor-heavy industries, such as retail and manufacturing. However, businesses that do not rely as much on employee productivity, such as technology fields, may have lower revenue per employee ratios, even if the company's employees are producing adequate revenue. For this reason, analysts must compare the revenue per employee ratio to other companies in the same industry to get an accurate idea of what is normal.

**Example**

As of December 31, 2015, Zian LLC generated $1.2 billion in sales with an average personnel of 6000 employees.

$$\text{Revenue per employee} = \frac{\$1.2\,billion}{6000} = \$200,000$$

- Operating Cycle

The operating cycle ratio shows if a company is managing its accounts payable, accounts receivable, and inventory efficiently. The operating cycle ratio involves three aspects of the company's finances: the days inventory outstanding, the days sales outstanding, and the days payable outstanding. These aspects all are calculated the same way. Divide the cost of processing the accounts payable, accounts receivable, or inventory by 365, the number of days in a year, to get the daily cost. Add the beginning and ending balances of the accounts payable, accounts receivable, or inventory account and divide the answer by two to get the average amount for each account. Divide the average amount by the cost per day to find the days inventory outstanding, days sales outstanding, or days payable outstanding. Calculate the operating cycle ratio by adding the days inventory outstanding and the days sales outstanding and then subtracting the days payable outstanding. The resulting figure is expressed as a number of days.

$$\text{Operating cycle ratio} = \text{Days sales of inventory} + \text{Days sales outstanding}$$

Note that each component of the above formula is computed under its own formula:

$$(i)\ \text{Days sales of inventory} = \text{Average inventories} \times \left(\frac{365}{\text{Purchases}}\right)$$

$$(ii)\ \text{Days sales outstanding} = \text{Average account receivables} \times \left(\frac{365}{\text{Credit sales}}\right)$$

A shorter operating cycle means that a company collects money from customers efficiently, has good payment terms with businesses and other entities to which it owes money, and is moving inventory at a pace that keeps up with average production ability and customer demand. A longer operating cycle indicates that the business has too much money tied up in unsold inventory, uncollected payments, and unpaid operating expenses. To perform an accurate analysis, the operating cycle ratio should be compared against industry standards, competitor operating cycle data, and the company's own historical operating cycle information.

## 17.8   Cash Flow Indicator Ratios

These ratios can give users another look at the financial health and performance of a company.

- Operating Cash Flow/Sales Ratio

This ratio, which is expressed as a percentage, compares a company's operating cash flow (OCF) to its net sales or revenues, which gives investors an idea of the company's ability to turn sales into cash. It would be worrisome to see a company's sales grow without a parallel growth in OFC. Positive and negative changes in a company's terms of sale and/or the collection experience of its accounts receivable will show up in this indicator.

$$\text{Operating cash flow/sales ratio} = \frac{\text{Operating cash flow}}{\text{Net sales (revenue)}}$$

- Free Cash Flow/Operating Cash Flow (FCF/OCF) Ratio

The free cash flow/operating cash flow (FCF/OCF) ratio measures the relationship between FCF and OFC. Free cash flow is most often defined as OFC minus capital expenditures, which, in analytical terms, are considered to be an essential outflow of funds to maintain a company's competitiveness and efficiency. The cash flow remaining after this deduction is considered "free" cash flow, which becomes available to a company to use for expansion, acquisitions, and/or financial stability to weather difficult market conditions. The higher the percentage of FCF embedded in a company's OFC, the greater the financial strength of the company.

$$\text{FCF/OCF ratio} = \frac{\text{Free cash flow} \times (\text{Operating cash flow} - \text{Capital expenditures})}{\text{Operating cash flow}}$$

- Cash Flow Coverage Ratio

This ratio measures the ability of the company's OFC to meet its obligations—including its liabilities or ongoing concern costs.

The OFC is simply the amount of cash generated by the company from its main operations, which are used to keep the business funded. The larger the OFC coverage for these items, the greater the company's ability to meet its obligations, along with giving the company more cash flow to expand its business, withstand hard times, and not be burdened by debt servicing and the restrictions typically included in credit agreements. Two formulas are available for the computation of this ratio:

$$(1) \ \frac{\text{Operating cash flow}}{\text{Total debt}}$$

$$(2) \ \frac{(\text{Net earnings} + \text{Depreciation} + \text{Amortization})}{\text{Total debt}}$$

- Dividend Payout Ratio

This ratio identifies the percentage of earnings (net income) per common share allocated to paying cash dividends to shareholders. The dividend payout ratio is an indicator of how well earnings support the dividend payment.

Here's how dividends "start" and "end." During a fiscal year quarter, a company's board of directors declares a dividend. This event triggers the posting of a current liability for "dividends payable." At the end of the quarter, net income is credited to a company's retained earnings, and assuming there's sufficient cash on hand and/or from current OFC, the dividend is paid out. This reduces cash, and the dividends payable liability is eliminated.

The payment of a cash dividend is recorded in the statement of cash flows under the "financing activities" section.

$$\text{Dividend payout ratio} = \frac{\text{Dividends per common share}}{\text{Earnings per share}}$$

## 17.9    Investment Valuation Ratios

- Price Earnings Ratio

The investment valuation ratios price/earnings ratio (P/E) is the best known of the investment valuation indicators. The P/E ratio has its imperfections, but it is nevertheless the most widely reported and used valuation by investment professionals and the investing public. The financial reporting of both companies and investment research services use a basic earnings per share (EPS) figure divided into the current stock price to calculate the P/E multiple (i.e., how many times a stock is trading [its price] per each dollar of EPS).

It's not surprising that estimated EPS figures are often very optimistic during bull markets, while reflecting pessimism during bear markets. Also, as a matter of historical record, it's no secret that the accuracy of stock analyst earnings estimates should be looked at skeptically by investors. Nevertheless, analyst estimates and opinions based on forward-looking projections of a company's earnings do play a role in Wall Street's stock-pricing considerations.

Historically, the average P/E ratio for the broad market has been around 15, although it can fluctuate significantly depending on economic and market conditions. The ratio will also vary widely among different companies and industries.

$$\text{Price earnings ratio} = \frac{\text{Market value price per share}}{\text{Earnings per share}}$$

### Example

Chan Corporation stock is currently trading at $90 a share and its earnings per share for the year is $10. Chan's P/E ratio would be:

$$\text{Price earnings ratio} = \frac{\$90}{\$10} = \$9$$

- Price/Book Value Ratio

A valuation ratio used by investors compares a stock's per share price (market value) to its book value (shareholders' equity). The price-to-book value ratio, expressed as a multiple (i.e., how many times a company's stock is trading per share compared to the company's book value per share), is an indication of how much shareholders are paying for the net assets of a company.

The book value of a company is the value of a company's assets expressed on the balance sheet. It is the difference between the balance sheet assets and balance sheet liabilities and is an estimation of the value if it were to be liquidated.

The price/book value ratio, often expressed simply as "price-to-book," provides investors a way to compare the market value, or what they are paying for each share, to a conservative measure of the value of the firm.

$$\text{Price/book value ratio} = \frac{\text{Stock price per share}}{\text{Shareholders equity per share}}$$

- Price/Earnings to Growth Ratio

The price/earnings to growth (PEG) ratio is used to determine a stock's value while taking the company's earnings growth into account, and is considered to provide a more complete picture than the P/E ratio. While a high P/E ratio may make a stock look like a good buy, factoring in the company's growth rate to get the stock's PEG ratio can tell a different story. The lower the PEG ratio, the more the stock may be undervalued given its earnings performance. The calculation is as follows:

$$\text{Price/Earnings to growth ratio (PEG)} = \frac{\text{P/E ratio}}{\text{Annual EPS growth}}$$

The ratio is based on projected EPS growth. Projections are not always accurate—just ask Cubs fans: "This is our year…" PEG ratios are considered less useful in assessing cyclical stocks. Profits and share prices of cyclical companies tend to follow the ups and downs of the economy. Earnings of these companies can be extremely erratic.

- Price/Sales Ratio

The price-to-sales ratio is an indicator of the value placed on each dollar of a company's sales or revenues. It can be calculated either by dividing the company's market capitalization by its total sales over a 12-month period or on a per share basis by dividing the stock price by sales per share for a 12-month period. Like all ratios, the price-to-sales ratio is most relevant when used to compare companies in the same sector. A low ratio may indicate possible undervaluation, while a ratio that is significantly above the average may suggest overvaluation. Abbreviated as the P/S ratio or PSR, this ratio is also known as a "sales multiple" or "revenue multiple."

$$\text{Price/Sales ratio} = \frac{\text{Share price}}{\text{Sales per share}}$$

- Dividend Yield

Dividend yield is the ratio of dividend per share to current share price. It is a measure of what percentage an investor is earning in the form of dividends.

$$\text{Dividend yield} = \frac{\text{Dividend per share}}{\text{Current share price}}$$

Dividend yield is a measure of investor return. While dividend payout ratio judges the amount of dividend in relation to the company's earnings for the period, dividend yield ratio provides a comparison of amount of dividend in relation to investment needed to purchase its share.

- Enterprise Value Multiple

Enterprise value multiple is the comparison of enterprise value and earnings before interest, taxes, depreciation, and amortization. This is a very commonly used metric for estimating the business valuations. It compares the value of a company, inclusive of debt and other liabilities, to the actual cash earnings exclusive of the non-cash expenses.

This ratio is also known as "EV/EBITDA ratio" and "EBITDA multiple." Enterprise multiple can be used to compare the value of one company to the value of another company within the same industry. A lower enterprise multiple can be indicative of undervaluation of a company.

Enterprise value multiple is calculated by dividing the enterprise value (EV) by the earnings before interest, taxes, depreciation, and amortization (EBITDA).

$$\text{Enterprise value multiple} = \frac{\text{Enterprise value}}{EBITDA}$$

Enterprise value multiple is a better measure than the P/E ratio because it is not affected by the changes in the capital structure. Consider a scenario in which a company raises equity finance and uses these funds to repay the loans. This will usually result in lower EPS and therefore a higher P/E ratio. But the enterprise value multiple will not be affected by this change in capital structure. This means that enterprise value multiple cannot be manipulated by the changes in capital structure. Another benefit of enterprise value multiple is that it makes possible fair comparison of companies with different capital structures.

Another positive point about the enterprise value multiple is that it removes the effects of non-cash expenses such as depreciation and amortization. These non-cash items are of less significance to the investors because they are ultimately interested in the cash flows. Enterprise value multiple is not usually appropriate for comparison of companies in different industries. Capital requirements of other industries are different. Therefore, enterprise value multiple may not give reliable conclusions when comparing different industries.

## 17.10    STRATEGIC FINANCIAL RATIOS

The study of financial ratios would not be complete without exploring some key strategic financial ratios. Managers are expected to develop deeper understanding of multiple financial ratios over time and across companies, and include them in the overall business strategy in order to create value for their organizations and its shareholders.

The most considered strategic ratios are: (i) the sustainable growth rate, (ii) the ROI decomposition, (iii) the financial leverage, (iv) the segment data analysis, and (v) the operational gearing.

- The Sustainable Growth Rate

The sustainable growth rate (SGR) is a company's maximum growth rate in sales using internal financial resources, while not having to increase debt or issue new equity. In order to improve sales in sustainable growth, a firm would need new or additional assets, which can be financed through an increase in owners' equity, mainly through the firm's retained earnings.

Formula: Sustainable Growth Rate = (1− Dividend payout ratio) × ROE

The dividend payout ratio itself is obtained by dividing the dividend by the profit attributable to shareholders (dividend / profit attributable to shareholders).

The determination of the sustainable economic growth rate of a firm is important because it tells the management the level of growth the firm has to maintain in order to prevent against unknown economic troubles in the years ahead. It is used as a benchmark in comparing the firm growth within the industry and its competitors. It is often considered that a firm with a higher SGR would be able to increase its market share.

• The Decomposition of ROI and ROA

A decomposition of the ROI measure improves the information content of the return ratio by breaking it down into a variety of components to express managerial decisions and other conditions that contribute to the return.

The ratio can be decomposed into various financial subcomponents from the income statement and balance sheet to isolate on changes in financial performance that are most directly contributing to changes in ROI.

For example: Total Investment is made up of working capital plus equity in the business. If the owners reduced their equity even as earnings and working capital remained the same, the ROI of the enterprise would reflect an increase.

• The DuPont Model for the ROI and ROA

The DuPont Model is a valuable tool for business owners to use in order to analyze their return on investment (ROI) or return on assets (ROA). The name comes from the DuPont Corporation that started using this formula in the 1920s. DuPont explosives salesman Donaldson Brown invented this formula in an internal efficiency report in 1912.

Using the DuPont Model allows the business owner to break the firm's profitability down into component parts to see where it actually comes from. There are steps to consider in the breaking-down analysis of the ROI and the ROA:

*Step1*: Consider the firm ROI and ROA financial ratios
The financial ratio of the ROI formula is: ROI = Net income / Total assets. As studied above, this ratio tells how efficient a firm has used its assets to generate sales.

*Step 2*: Dissecting the number obtained under the ROI ratio

When a firm finds itself in the position where its financial ROI is below the industry average, a decomposition is the ratio that would assist the management to understand the component of the ratio which needs more attention, or which is causing the underperformance. Under the DuPont Model, the ROI (ROA) is decomposed as follows:

ROI = (Net Income / Sales) × (Sales / Total Assets)

where

Net Income / Sales = Net profit margin

Sales / Total Assets = Total asset turnover

In other words, ROI is made of two parts: the firm's profit margin and the firm's asset turnover ratio.

---

### Example

- Caroll Inc. a Connecticut computer business has reported $113.5 million in sales and has total assets of $2000 million
- ROI (ROA) = $113.5 / 2000 = 5.7%
- Assuming that the industry average ROI (ROA) is of 9%
- It is clear that Caroll Inc. is underperforming relative to its industry. Without the decomposition, we will not be able to tell which one of the two components of the ROI (ROA) is causing the underperformance. Only the decomposition of the ROI (ROA) will provide that explanation.
- Further let us assume that Caroll Inc. net profit margin was 3.8% and its total asset turnover ratio was of 1.5% (3.8% × 1.5% = 5.7%)
- Assuming that the industry average net profit margin and total asset turnover ratio are respectively of 5 and 1.8%.
- The decomposition of the ROI (ROA) tells that Caroll Inc. is underperforming on both components of the ROI (ROA), but the underperformance is significant on the net profit margin.
- Therefore, Caroll Inc. management would have to develop strategy to improve its profit margin.

- The Decomposition of the ROE

The ROE can be decomposed either through the extended DuPont model or by linking the ROA with the introduction of the financial leverage.

- The Extended DuPont Model for the ROE

The extended DuPont Model allows for a breakdown analysis of return on equity.

The ROE financial ratio is the measure of the wealth of the shareholders of the company.

$$ROE = ROI \times (Total\ Assets\ /\ Common\ Equity)$$

However, the extended DuPont equation for the ROE is as follows:

$$ROE = (Net\ Income\ /\ Sales) \times (Sales\ /\ Total\ Asset\ turnover) \times (Total\ Assets\ /\ Com.\ equity).$$

ROE is made of three components: (i) the net profit margin, (ii) the total asset turnover, and (iii) the effect of debt on equity

### Example

- Caroll Inc. a Connecticut computer business has reported $113.5 million in sales and has total assets of $2000 million
- Caroll Inc. has a total common equity of $896 million
- $ROE = (5.7\% \times 2000)\ /\ 896 = 12.7\%$
- Assuming that the industry average ROE is 15%
- The management would have to figure out, which component of the ROE is underperforming.

• The Financial Leverage

We have seen that the financial structure of most firms consists of a mixture of short-term and long-term debts and equity. Thus, linking the ROA and financial leverage explains to readers of financial statements how the assets of a firm were financed. A firm that uses debt to finance its assets acquisition can increase its profits with the infusion of liquidity, assuming that the cost of the borrowing does not outweigh the benefit. This is known as financial leverage coefficient.[1]

$$ROE = ROA \times \text{Financial leverage}$$

Or

$$ROE = \text{Net Profit Margin} \times \text{Asset Turnover} \times \text{Financial Leverage}$$

Where

$$ROA = \text{Net Income} / \text{Total Assets}$$
$$\text{Financial Leverage} = \text{Total Debt} / \text{Total Asset}$$

Therefore, both ROA and financial leverage are drivers of the ROE. The decomposition of the ROE would assist the management in determining which driver of the return to shareholders is contributing more.

• The Segment Data Analysis

Segment reporting is intended to give information to investors and creditors regarding the financial results and position of the most important operating units of a firm, which they can use as the basis for decisions related to the firm.[2] Likewise, the management can use these segment

---

[1] The financial leverage coefficient ratio is: ROE% / ROA%. A coefficient of more than 1 is considered positive.

[2] Segment reporting is required for publicly held entities and is not required for privately held ones.

ratios through time and across segments to enhance its understanding of the factors that contribute to the overall performance of the firm. Some of the most used segment ratios are:

- Segment Profit Margin

Segment profit margin = Segment Result / Segment Revenue

- Segment Asset Turnover

Segment asset turnover = Segment Revenue / Segment Assets

- Segment Return on Assets

Segment return on assets = Segment profit margin × Segment asset turnover

- The Operating Gearing

Another way of measuring a firm competitive position is through operational gearing. Operational gearing, also known as operating leverage, is based on the mix of fixed and variable costs. When comparing two companies within the same industry, the one with high fixed cost structure would not be able to react to economic shock, downturn than a competitor with high variable cost structure. The managerial accounting concept of operating gearing refers to the volatility of profit as a function of changes in sales, taking into account the firms' cost structure. It can be determined by considering the level of contribution earned in relation to sales. Managers must be aware of the impact of operational gearing on profits and risk to make good business decisions. Investors also require information about operational risk to allow them to make informed investment decisions.[3]

---

[3] Grahame Steven (2006): Financial Management, September 2006, Papers P1, P2, and P3.

## 17.11    BANKRUPTCY RATIOS

### 17.11.1    Working Capital/Total Assets

Net working capital to total asset ratio is a liquidity ratio that expresses the net current assets or working capital of a company as a percentage of its total assets. The working capital/total assets ratio, frequently found in studies of corporate problems, is a measure of the net liquid assets of the firm relative to the total capitalization. Working capital is defined as the difference between current assets and current liabilities. Liquidity and size characteristics are explicitly considered. Ordinarily, a firm experiencing consistent operating losses will have shrinking current assets in relation to total assets.

### Example

Assume a company's balance sheet has the following line entries

- Cash: $6000
- Marketable Securities: $800
- Accounts Receivables: $3500
- Inventory: $40,000
- Land: $100,000
- Accounts Payable: $3000
- Accrued Expenses $1800
- Notes Payable: $500
- Current Position Long-Term Debt: $10,000
  - The total current assets from the given information are (items 1 to 4) $50,300, and the total current liabilities (items 6 to 9) are $15,300.
  - The company's working capital is $50,300−$15,300= $35,000.
  - The company's net total assets are (Items 1 to 5) $60,300.
  - The working capital to total assets ratio is (35,000/60,300)* 100=58.04%.

### 17.11.2    Retained Earnings/Total Assets

It measures the extent to which a company relies on debt or leverage. The lower the ratio, the more a company is funding assets by borrowing instead of through retained earnings which, again, increases the risk of bankruptcy if the firm cannot meet its debt obligations. The age of a firm is implicitly considered in this ratio. For example, a relatively young firm will probably show a low RE/TA ratio because it has not had time to build up its cumulative profits. Therefore, it may be argued that the young firm is somewhat discriminated against in this analysis, and its chance of being classified as bankrupt is relatively higher than another, older firm, ceteris paribus. But, this is precisely the situation in the real world. The incidence of failure is much higher in a firm's earlier years. Unlike other financial ratios, this one is often subject to "manipulation" via corporate quasi-reorganizations.

### Example

Assume a retained earnings amount of $100,000 and a total assets amount of $250,000. When you divide $100,000 by $250,000, you get a ratio of 2:5 or 40%. This means that profits have financed 40% of your company's assets in the most recent balance sheet reporting period. While you need both your industry's standard and your company's trend to thoroughly interpret this ratio, 40% is generally solid.

### 17.11.3    Earnings Before Interest and Taxes/Total Assets

It measures a company's EBIT against its total net assets. This ratio is considered to be an indicator of how effectively a company is using its assets to generate earnings before contractual obligations must be paid.

It is calculated by dividing the total assets of a firm into its earnings before interest and tax reductions. In essence, it is a measure of the true productivity of the firm's assets, abstracting from any tax or leverage factors. Since a firm's ultimate existence is based on the earning power of its assets, this ratio appears to be particularly appropriate for studies dealing with corporate failure. Furthermore, insolvency in a bankruptcy sense occurs when the total liabilities exceed a fair valuation of the firm's assets with value determined by the earning power of the assets.

### 17.11.4    Market Value of Equity/Book Value of Total Debt

Equity is measured by the combined market value of all shares of stock, preferred and common, while debt includes both current and long term. The measure shows how much the firm's assets can decline in value (measured by market value of equity plus debt) before the liabilities exceed the assets and the firm becomes insolvent.

### Example

A company with a market value of its equity of $1000 and debt of $500 could experience a two-third drop in asset value before insolvency. However, the same firm with $250 in equity will be insolvent if its drop is only one-third in value. This ratio adds a market value dimension which other failure studies did not consider. It also appears to be a more effective predictor of bankruptcy than a similar, more commonly used ratio: Net worth/Total debt (book values).

### 17.11.5    Sales/Total Assets

It measures the ability of a business to generate sales on as small a base of assets as possible. When the ratio is quite high, it implies that management is able to wring the most possible use out of a small investment in assets. The capital-turnover ratio is a standard financial ratio illustrating the sales generating ability of the firm's assets. It is one measure of management's capability in dealing with competitive conditions. This final ratio is quite important because, as indicated below, it is the least significant ratio on an individual basis. In fact, based on the statistical significance measure, it would not have appeared at all. However, because of its unique relationship to other variables in the model, the sales/total assets ratio ranks second in its contribution to the overall discriminating ability of the model.

### Example

For example, a business has annual sales of $1,000,000 after all sales allowances have been deducted, as well as receivables of $150,000, inventory of $200,000, and fixed assets of $450,000. Its sales to total assets ratio is:

$1,000,000 Net sales ÷ $800,000 Aggregate of all assets
= 1.25 × Sales to total assets ratio

## 17.12   LIMITATIONS

Financial expert shall use ratios with caution, as there is considerable subjectivity involved, in their computation. Also, ratios may not be strictly comparable for different firms due to a variety of factors such as different accounting practices, policies, and the level of risks accepted by the management. Furthermore, if a firm is engaged in diverse product lines, it may be difficult to identify the industry category to which the firm belongs. Finally, keep in mind that ratios are based on financial statements that reflect the past and not the future. Unless the ratios are stable, it may be difficult to make reasonable projections about future trends.

# PART IV

# Pro-Forma Financial Statements

The objective of pro forma financial information is to show what the significant effects on historical financial information might have been had a consummated or proposed transaction (or event) occurred at an earlier date. Pro forma financial information is commonly used to show the effects of transactions such as the following:

- Business combination
- Change in capitalization
- Disposition of a significant portion of the business
- Change in the form of business organization or status as an autonomous entity
- Proposed sale of securities and the application of the proceeds.

*Pro-forma Financial Statements*, also known as projected or future financial statements, are elaborated based upon a firm expectations. The idea is to write down a sequence of financial statements that represent expectations of what the results of actions and policies will be on the future financial status of the firm.

---

The term 'pro forma' is a Latin term which literally means "as a matter of form". In our modern language, 'pro forma' financial statements refer to data which are hypothetical.

*Pro-forma Financial Statements* include: (i) the income statements, (ii) the balance sheets, and (iii) the resulting statements of cash flows.

The standard approach is called "percent of sales forecasting." Then, the management projects variables that have a stable relation to sales using forecasted sales and the estimated relations:

COGS will generally vary directly with sales.

Calculate the COGS/Sales ratio for the last few years. Multiply a forecast for this ratio times the forecast for sales to find a forecast for COGS.

How do we forecast the COGS/Sales ratio?

We then require estimates of the components of expenses that does not vary directly (and in a stable way) with sales to complete the income statement.

- Other Expenses
- Other Income
- Depreciation
- Taxes
- Net Income
- Dividends

# CHAPTER 18

# Forecasting Financial Statements' Analysis

## 18.1 General

When a new corporation is envisioned, its founders will prepare pro forma financial statements for the information of prospective investors. Likewise, lenders and investors also require such statements to structure or confirm compliance with debt covenants, such as debt service reserve coverage and debt to equity ratios. They are also vital for any valuation exercises one might do in investment analysis or M&A evaluation/planning. The standard approach used in the compilation of financial statements is known as the "percent of sales forecasting."

## 18.2 The Forecasted Statement of Income

Pro forma income statement is an estimate for the profits or losses of a company. In computing Pro forma income, companies usually exclude items they deem inappropriate for measuring their performance. However, many analysts and investors have raised concerns about the quality of the pro forma income, as providing managements a tool to boost their real performance. Pro forma Income statement includes revenue, COGS, operational expenses, and non-operational expenses.

© The Author(s) 2018
F. I. Lessambo, *Financial Statements*,
https://doi.org/10.1007/978-3-319-99984-5_18

251

252 F. I. LESSAMBO

### 18.2.1 Sales Forecasting

In order to forecast sales, a firm manager often starts by asserting the dollar profit he wants to attain, and then figures out what sales levels will be required to reach it. Target volume is the unit sales quantity required to meet an earnings goal. Target revenue is the corresponding figure for dollar sales. Both of these metrics can be viewed as extensions of break-even analysis. As the market leads, the manager is also required to revise sales targets. The purpose of profit-based sales target metrics is to ensure that marketing and sales objectives mesh with profit targets.

### 18.2.2 Production and COGS Forecasting

Cost of goods sold (COGS) refers to the inventory costs of the goods a business has sold during a particular period. Costs include all costs of purchase, costs of conversion, and other costs incurred in bringing the inventories to their present location and condition. The COGS in a given accounting period is recorded on a company's income statement. In general, the COGS will vary directly with sales. If not, it is likely that something has gone very wrong. To attain the COGS forecasting figure, the firm management uses the COGS/Sales ratio for the last few years, and multiply a forecast of this ratio times the forecast of sales to forecast COGS.

### 18.2.3 Expenses' Forecasting

To complete the income statement forecasting, the firm management adds the estimates of the components of the income statement that don't vary in a stable way with sales, such as other expenses, other income, depreciation, taxes, dividends.

## 18.3 THE FORECASTED STATEMENT OF POSITION

A projected balance sheet communicates expected changes in future asset investments, outstanding liabilities, and equity financing. A projected balance sheet provides the most relevant financial information needed in the business planning process. Therefore, forecasting balance sheet is a useful tool for business planning in general, and it particularly benefits those individuals responsible for arranging and bringing in additional financing. From the completed ("forecasting") income statement, and the firm's expected dividend, the firm management determines the change in retained earnings and transfers it to the balance sheet.

### 18.3.1 Making Assumptions

To prepare a projected balance sheet, a business makes certain assumptions about how individual balance sheet items may change over time in the future. Business plans often focus on anticipated future sales. Thus, a projected balance sheet also starts with forecasting sales revenues. Certain balance sheet items, such as inventory, accounts receivable and accounts payable are closely related to sales, and projections on those items can be made based on sales' projections. Other balance sheet items, particularly fixed assets, debt and equity, change only in accordance with a business's policies and management decisions, independent of future sales.

- Projecting Asset Items

The most relevant asset items commonly used in a projected balance sheet include cash, accounts receivable, inventory, and fixed assets. While the amount of cash expected to be generated from the forecast sales increase may accumulate at a comparable rate, cash balance shown on the balance sheet may not be necessarily in proportion to the sales increase. A business may choose to reinvest part of the cash received, allowing cash holdings to grow at a lower projected rate. Both accounts receivable and inventory generally change in proportion to sales increase because more sales can leave more customers on account and require more inventory in stocks. On the contrary, future changes in fixed assets are not likely to be in proportion to sales and their projections would depend on a managerial decision about future capital investments.

- Liabilities' Projections

Major liability items in a projected balance sheet include: (i) accounts payable, (ii) short-term debt, and (iii) long-term debt. Accounts payable often are the result of accepting trade financing on inventory purchases. If more sales require more inventory, the increase in inventory likely leads to an increase in outstanding accounts payable. Thus, accounts payable likely change in proportion to sales. Projection on short-term debt, such as notes payable, often depends on a business's financing policy. To accommodate a sales increase, a business may choose to increase short-term financing at a certain rate each year. Long-term debt usually is left unchanged in initial projections and may change later if additional financing is needed.

• Equity's Projections

Owners' equity and retained earnings are the two common sources of equity financing. Similar to projecting long-term debt, owners' equity is also left unchanged in initial balance sheet projections. Whether or not a business expects to issue additional equity depends on future financing situations. If a shortfall in asset financing through other means exists, a business needs to project an increase in either owners' equity or long-term debt to make up the deficit. Projecting retained earnings essentially relies on the net-income projection in a projected income statement for the same future period.

• Discretionary Projections

Discretionary projections would be needed to correct the imbalance in the forecasting statement of position, either as a shortage or a surplus. If the total projected assets exceed the total projected liabilities and equity, the forecasting statement of position would express a shortage in future financing. On the other hand, if total the projected assets are less than the total projected liabilities and equity, the forecasting statement of position has a fund surplus, which needs to be re-affected. A fund deficit or surplus in projected financing must be balanced out through discretionary financing by adjusting projections on long-term debt or equity. A projected balance sheet becomes balanced when the projected increase in long-term debt or equity equals the amount of fund deficit in initial financing projections. A projected balance sheet can also become balanced if a business uses the projected fund surplus to further increase asset investments or reduce initial financing projections.

The cash balance is usually determined by a policy decision via some inventory (of liquidity) model. Alternatively, this account may be used as a "plug."

Changes in Gross PP&E are also the result of policy decisions as are changes in preferred or common stock. Often short-term (bank loan or line of credit) or long-term debt is used as a residual to determine the required new financing (a plug to make it balance). But don't forget that these can't be chosen in isolation.

## 18.4   THE FORECASTED STATEMENTS OF CASH FLOWS

The first step in any cash flow forecast is the estimation of the sales figure. A great way to come up with these estimates is to reference the firm's previous sales history. However, as the sales figures would not always be consistent, it is good practice to take into consideration patterns that are the same each year (seasons and holidays, for example) and factors that could change each year, such as trade shows or promotions, when making the projections. For a new business with no sales history, an estimate by looking at industry standards, considering performance of similar businesses, or even a customer survey, would be needed. As often businesses sale at credit, it's crucial when doing a cash flow forecast to consider the span of expected payment from sales. Finally, a sound cash flow forecasting would include the business expenses (fixed and variables). Where variable costs are associated with the sale of the product or service, referring back to the forecasted sales to help estimate some of these variable costs.

### 18.4.1   Forecasting Operating Cash Flows

A cash flow forecast is an estimate of the amount of money a business expects to flow in and out. It includes all the business projected income and expenses. Usually, a forecast covers the next 12 months, however, it can also cover a short-term period such as a week or month. Cash flow forecasting helps in tax preparation, planning new equipment purchases or identifying financial needs.

A good place to start when forecasting operating costs is to look at the company's historic operating cost margins. The operating margin is the operating costs expressed as a proportion of revenues.

### 18.4.2    Forecasting Financing Cash Flow

Accurate cash forecasting remains a challenge for treasurers in multinational or domestic undertakings. Cash flow forecast is an important management process, similar to preparing business budgets. External stakeholders (i.e., banks) may require a regular cash flow forecast as a monitor to their loans. Thus, cash flow forecasting is crucial for several reasons:

- Identify potential shortfalls in cash balances in advance.
- Make sure that the business can afford to pay duly its suppliers and employees.
- Spot problems with customer.

By and large financing cash, flow can be forecast using either the direct or the indirect methods.

(a) The Direct Method

Under the direct method of financing cash flow forecasting a company considers its cash receipts and disbursements (R&D). Cash receipts refer to are the collection of accounts receivable from recent sales. It but also include sales of other assets, proceeds of financing, etc. Cash disbursements include payroll, payment of accounts payable from recent purchases, dividends, and interest on debt. This direct R&D method is best suited to the short-term forecasting horizon of 30 days or so because this is the period for which actual, as opposed to projected, data is available.

(b) The Indirect Methods

There are three indirect methods of forecasting financing cash flow based on the company's projected income statements and balance sheets: (i) the adjusted net income method (ANI); (ii) the pro forma balance sheet (PBS) method; and (iii) the accrual reversal method (ARM).

(i) The Adjusted Net Income

The ANI method starts with operating income (EBIT or EBITDA) and adds or subtracts changes in balance sheet accounts such as receivables, payables, and inventories to project cash flow.

## (ii) The Pro forma Balance Sheet (PBS) Method

The pro forma balance sheet (PBS) method looks straight at the projected book cash account; if all the other balance sheet accounts have been correctly forecast, cash will be correct, too.

### Example

Both the ANI and PBS methods are best suited to the medium-term (up to one year) and long-term (multiple years) forecasting horizons. Both are limited to the monthly or quarterly intervals of the financial plan and need to be adjusted for the difference between accrual accounting book cash and the often-significantly different bank balances.

## (iii) The Accrual Reversal Method (ARM)

The accrual reversal method is similar to the ANI method. But instead of using projected balance sheet accounts, large accruals are reversed and cash effects are calculated based on statistical distributions and algorithms. This allows the forecasting period to be weekly or even daily. It also eliminates the cumulative errors inherent in the direct, R&D method when it is extended beyond the short-term horizon. But because the ARM allocates both accrual reversals and cash effects to weeks or days, it is more complicated than the ANI or PBS indirect methods. The ARM is best suited to the medium-term forecasting. Typical ARM components include most of the elements of a company's R&D forecast, plus EBITDA and the accrual reversal of sales, major payables, payroll, retirement, and non-income taxes. An ARM model usually has a 5-year monthly simulation and forecast (3 prior, the current and next years) that feeds data to three 1-year daily templates (prior, current, and next).

### 18.4.3    Forecasting Investing Cash Flow

As a rule of tomb, it pays to be conservative when projecting cash sources and liberal when projecting cash uses. A pro forma cash flow is an accounting document created to predict inflow and outflow of cash to your business. Although companies prepare their quarterly and annually cash flow statements, a monthly cash flow projection often provides more accurate and more useful cash flow projection.

The first step in creating a cash flow projection starts with the knowledge of the exact cash position, then monthly breaking down of the computation of the COGS, the operating expenses, and taxes.

### Example

- Whole Inc. a US retailer had $100,000 in its checking account.
- Whole Inc. customers send their Checks within thirty days after delivery and receipt of their orders. Assuming that the delivery and receipt of the order started in January 2015. Thus, Whole Inc. would not receive any cash from sales made in January, but will be collecting on sales made in December 2014. Those sales totaled $30,000, so that amount is entered in the January sales column of the cash flow.
- In January 2015, and further, Whole Inc. purchased raw materials for $15,000 each month. And Whole Inc. pays immediately for receipt of these purchases ($15,000) which it records as the cost of goods.
- The operating expenses for Whole Inc. are $10,000 per month.
- Whole Inc. paid its estimated tax installments in December 2014 and doesn't have any tax payments due in January 2015.
- In the month of January, 2015, the total from COGS and operating expenses equaled the amounts of $25,000.
- The difference between the estimated cash used ($15,000+$10,000) or $25,000 from the estimated cash sources ($30,000) lives Whole Inc. with a net change in cash position of +$5000.
- Thus, Whole Inc. will begin its February 2015 with a projected cash flow of $95,000.

PART V

# Consolidated Financial Statements

*Consolidated Financial Statements* are the combined financial statements of a company and all of its subsidiaries, divisions, or sub-organizations. *Consolidated Financial Statements* provide a comprehensive overview of a company's operations. In the absence of consolidated statement, investors would not be able to properly assess the performance of a business as a group.

US GAAP provides specific rules as to when and how financial statements should be consolidated, and whether only certain entities would need to be consolidated. For instance, a company that only owns a minority interest (stake) in another entity usually do not need to consolidate them on its financial statements. As a matter of practice, companies commonly break out their consolidated statements by division or subsidiary so that investors can see the relative performance of each, but in many cases this is not required, especially if the company owns 100% of the division or subsidiary.

# CHAPTER 19

# Foreign Currency Accounting

## 19.1 General

ASC 830 (aka FAS 52) provides the accounting and reporting requirements for foreign currency transactions and the translation of financial
statements from a foreign currency to the reporting currency. Foreign
currency translation is used to convert the results of a parent company's
foreign subsidiaries to its reporting currency. This is a key step in the
consolidation of financial statement. The steps in this translation process
are as follows:

## 19.2 Determination of the Functional Currency of the Foreign Entity

An entity's functional currency is the currency of the primary economic
environment in which that entity operates. The functional currency can
be the dollar or a foreign currency depending on the facts. Normally, it
will be the currency of the economic environment in which cash is generated and expended by the entity.[1] A currency in a highly inflationary environment (3-year inflation rate of approximately 100% or more)
is not considered stable enough to serve as a functional currency and
the more stable currency of the reporting parent is to be used instead.

---

[1] FASB Statement 52.

© The Author(s) 2018
F. I. Lessambo, *Financial Statements*,
https://doi.org/10.1007/978-3-319-99984-5_19

The functional currency in which a business reports its financial results should rarely change. A shift to a different functional currency should be used only when there is a significant change in the economic facts and circumstances.

Note that the determination of the functional currency is not always an easy task.

### 19.2.1   Factors to Be Considered

ASC 830-10-55-5 states the following economic factors, and possibly others, should be considered both individually and collectively when determining the functional currency:

- Cash flow indicators

  (a) *Foreign currency.* Cash flows related to the foreign entity's individual assets and liabilities are primarily in the foreign currency and do not directly affect the parent entity's cash flows.
  (b) *Parent's currency.* Cash flows related to the foreign entity's individual assets and liabilities directly affect the parent's cash flows currently and are readily available for remittance to the parent entity.

- Sales price indicators

  (a) *Foreign currency.* Sales prices for the foreign entity's products are not primarily responsive on a short-term basis to changes in exchange rates but are determined more by local competition or local government regulation.
  (b) *Parent's currency.* Sales prices for the foreign entity's products are primarily responsive on a short-term basis to changes in exchange rates; for example, sales prices are determined more by worldwide competition or by international prices.

- Sales market indicators

  (a) *Foreign currency.* There is an active local sales market for the foreign entity's products, although there also might be significant amounts of exports.

(b) *Parent's currency.* The sales market is mostly in the parent's country or sales contracts are denominated in the parent's currency.

- Expense indicators

  (a) *Foreign currency.* Labor, materials, and other costs for the foreign entity's products or services are primarily local costs, even though there also might be imports from other countries.
  (b) *Parent's currency.* Labor, materials, and other costs for the foreign entity's products or services continually are primarily costs for components obtained from the country in which the parent entity is located.

- Financing indicators

  (a) *Foreign currency.* Financing is primarily denominated in foreign currency, and funds generated by the foreign entity's operations are sufficient to service existing and normally expected debt obligations.
  (b) *Parent's currency.* Financing is primarily from the parent or other dollar-denominated obligations, or funds generated by the foreign entity's operations are not sufficient to service existing and normally expected debt obligations without the infusion of additional funds from the parent entity.

- Intra-entity transactions and arrangements indicators

  (a) *Foreign currency.* There is a low volume of intra-entity transactions and there is not an extensive interrelationship between the operations of the foreign entity and the parent entity. However, the foreign entity's operations may rely on the parent's or affiliates' competitive advantages, such as patents and trademarks.
  (b) *Parent's currency.* There is a high volume of intra-entity transactions and there is an extensive interrelationship between the operations of the foreign entity and the parent entity.

These factors should be considered individually and collectively in order to identify the functional currency. No single one is determinative. Also, note that the functional currency may be one other than that of the foreign entity or the parent.

### 19.2.2   Changing the Functional Currency

Under ASC 830-10-45-7, once the functional currency for a foreign entity is determined, that determination must be used consistently unless significant changes in economic facts and circumstances indicate clearly that the functional currency has changed. Previously issued financial statements would not be restated for any change in the functional currency.

## 19.3   TRANSLATION METHODS

Re-measure the financial statements of the foreign entity into the reporting currency of the parent company. The exchange rates that are used in accounting for foreign operations and transactions (other than forward contracts) are spot rates, current exchange rates, historical exchange rates, and average rates. When translating the financial statements of an entity for consolidation purposes into the reporting currency of a business, translate the financial statements using the following methods:

### 19.3.1   Current/Noncurrent Method

Under ASC 830-30-45-3, all elements of financial statements shall be translated by using a current exchange rate as follows:

Assets and liabilities:

- All assets and liabilities are translated at the current exchange rate at the date of translation.
- Elements of income are translated at the current exchange rates that existed at the time that the revenues and expense were recognized. Income elements are normally translated at a weighted average exchange rate.

- Equity accounts other than retained earnings are translated at historical exchange rates.
- Translated retained earnings generally is equal to:

  (a) The translated retained earnings at the end of the prior period plus.
  (b) The translated income less.
  (c) The value of the dividends translated at the appropriate historical exchange rates at the date of declaration.

- Components of the statement of cash flows are translated at the exchange rates in effect at the time of the cash flows.

### 19.3.2    Monetary/Nonmonetary Method

- Monetary assets and liabilities are translated at the current exchange rate. Usually, this results in net liability exposure or translation gain, included in current income.
- Nonmonetary assets and liabilities and stockholders' equity accounts are translated at historical exchange rates.
- The translation adjustment measures the net foreign exchange gain or loss on current assets and liabilities as if these items were carried on the parent's books.

### 19.3.3    Temporal Method

The temporal method aims to translate financial statements as if the subsidiary had been using the parent's currency. Accounts measured by the foreign entity at current values will be translated using the current spot rate at the date of the financial statement. Balance sheet accounts that are measured by the foreign entity at historical cost are to be translated at the spot rates that existed at the date of the original transaction. Income statement accounts that do not represent the amortization of historical costs are translated at the spot rate that existed at the date of the revenue or expense transaction. However, revenues and expenses that result from the amortization of assets or liabilities are translated at the historical spot rates used to translate the underlying historical costs being amortized.

When functional currency is US Dollar, the temporal method is required.

## Temporal Methods

- Items carried on subsidiary's books at historical cost, including all stockholders' equity items, are translated at historical exchange rates.
- Items carried on subsidiary's books at current value are translated at current exchange rates.
- Income statement items are translated at the exchange rate in effect at the time of the transaction.

Note that under the temporal method, the gain or loss from FX translation is included as a component of net income.

### 19.3.4    Current Rate Method

The current rate method objective is to reflect that the parent's entire investment in a foreign subsidiary is exposed to exchange risk. When functional currency is foreign currency, current rate method is required.

- All assets and liabilities are translated at the current exchange rate.
- Stockholders' equity accounts are translated at historical exchange rates.
- Income statement items are translated at the exchange rate in effect at the time of the transaction.

## 19.4    RE-MEASUREMENT
### INTO THE FUNCTIONAL CURRENCY

In the aforementioned developments, we have assumed that the currency of the foreign entity was the functional currency. However, there are certain instances when the functional currency is not the currency of the foreign entity. In these instances, the financial statements of the foreign entity must be re-measured into the functional currency before the financial statements can be translated. Generally, the re-measurement process is based on the same temporal method originally adopted by FASB Statement No. 8. The re-measurement process is encountered in two situations:

### 19.4.1    The Foreign Entity
### Does Not Book or Record in Functional Currency

For example, assume a German subsidiary of an American company buys materials from British vendors with amounts due payable in British pounds. The materials are assembled in Germany and then returned to the UK for sale. Sales revenues are collected in pounds. The pound would be the functional currency. However, the German company maintains its books in Euros.

The financial statements prepared in Euros would have to be re-measured into pounds before they could be translated into dollars.

The re-measurement process requires that both current and historical (i.e., inventory, marketable securities) exchange rates be used.

### 19.4.2    Highly Inflationary Economies—US GAAP

Under ASC 830-10-45-11, the financial statements of a foreign entity in a highly inflationary economy must be re-measured as if the functional currency were the reporting currency. For the purposes of this requirement, a highly inflationary economy is one that has cumulative inflation of approximately 100 percent or more over a 3-year period. US GAAP defines such economies as those with cumulative 100% inflation over a period of three years (with compounding—average of 26% per year for three years in a row). Dealing with highly inflationary economies, the temporal method required. That is, translation gains/losses are reported in income.

### Example

- On January 1, 2016, Chintan Corp., a London subsidiary of Daxa, Inc. acquired a PPE for £10 million. The spot rate at the time of the purchase was: 1 £UK for 2 $US = $20 million.
- The PPE has a life expectancy of 10 years, depreciable on a straight-line basis (or 1 million UK£ per year).

- On December 31, 2016, the cost of the PPE is UK£ 9 million.
- Assume further than on December 31, 2016, the spot rate being: 1 UK£ for 2.5 US$
- Therefore, the PPE with the cost of UK£ 9 million translates into US$ 22.5 million using the current rate method. Had the exchange rate remained the same as that of the beginning of the year, the cost would have been US$ 18 million.

Pursuant to ASC 830-10-45-11, the financial statements of a foreign entity in a highly inflationary economy should be re-measured as if the functional currency were the reporting currency. The re-measurement process is intended to produce the same results as if the entity's books of record had been maintained in the reporting currency. Because the new functional currency will be the same as the reporting currency of the parent, translation of the financial statements into the reporting currency will no longer be necessary.

## 19.5    Hedging Balance
### Sheet and Forecasted Exposure

The most commonly balance sheet items hedge are: foreign-denominated payables, receivables, cash or other short-term assets or obligations. Under Accounting Standards Codification 830, changes in the value of the hedge contract shall be recognized on the income statement just as changes to the underlying hedged item are. Further, more businesses are trying to hedge their anticipated cash flows. The financial success of such a hedging depends on the company's ability to forecast reasonably accurately their anticipated cash flows. Businesses hedge against gains and losses by using foreign currency forward contracts, futures contracts, and options. Under ASC 830, the change in value of the hedge is recognized in the current period income statement. However, ASC 815 allows businesses to defer the mark to market changes until the forecasted item is recorded on the income statement. Only highly effective hedges qualify for the accounting deferral. To qualify for hedge accounting under ASC 815, at the inception of the hedge, businesses must document the specifics of the hedge relationship.

# CHAPTER 20

# Consolidated Financial Statements

## 20.1 OVERVIEW

ASC 810-10 provides guidance for consolidations under the US GAAP. Consolidated financial statements are required when consolidation criteria are met with some exception, such as for employee benefit plans. Combined financial statements are permitted under US GAAP if the entities being combined are under common control or management. Control is presumed to exist if the parent owns more than 50% of the voting stock. Combined financial statements would also be acceptable under US GAAP for businesses under common control and common management.

More, under the SEC's definition, control exists when one entity possesses the power to direct policies of another entity, either by ownership of voting shares, by contract, or by other means.

### Example

Zen Corporation owns 45% of the voting stock of Wang Corporation. Currently, Zen Corp. has an exercisable option to purchase an additional 6% of the voting stock at a cost of $50 per share. The shares are currently valued at $10.

© The Author(s) 2018                                              269
F. I. Lessambo, *Financial Statements*,
https://doi.org/10.1007/978-3-319-99984-5_20

*Solution*: Under the US GAAP Zen Corp. would not be allowed to consolidate with Wang Corp. since under US GAAP potential voting rights are not considered.

The consolidated financial statements include the Company's majority-owned entity, a wholly owned corporate subsidiary. All significant intercompany transactions are eliminated. Non-controlling interest is reported on the equity method.

Consolidated financial statements present the financial position and results of operations for a parent (controlling entity) and one or more subsidiaries (controlled entities) as if the individual entities actually were a single company or entity. Consolidated financial statements often represent the only means of obtaining a clear picture of the total resources of the combined entity that are under the control of the parent company.

Whether the subsidiary is acquired or created, each individual company maintains its own accounting records, but consolidated financial statements are needed to present the companies together as a single economic entity for general-purpose financial reporting. While consolidated financial statements are useful, their limitations also must be kept in mind. Some information is lost any time data sets are aggregated; this is particularly true when the information involves an aggregation across companies that have substantially different operating characteristics. Further, consolidated financial statements usually are of little use to those interested in obtaining information about the assets, capital, or income of individual subsidiaries.

Consolidation is required when a corporation owns a majority of another corporation's outstanding common stock. Two companies are considered to be related companies when one controls the other company.

## 20.2    Purpose of Consolidation

What is the purpose of financial consolidation?

- *Publically traded companies:* Regulatory authorities such as the SEC have made it a compliance requirement for publically traded companies to report consolidated results. In addition to obeying accounting standards (such as GAAP or IFRS), these types of consolidations also require an audit trail or a report that explains how source data from subsidiaries has been adjusted to give the consolidated results.

- *Private companies:* Depending on the jurisdiction, there may be no formal government or otherwise mandated requirement to produce or file consolidated financial statements; provided each legal entity pays its taxes, the government is satisfied. For private companies, reporting on consolidated numbers is either management reporting or non-legislated reporting to the shareholders.

Usually, financial consolidation is concerned with reporting historical, actual data. Some companies also want to perform a formal consolidation of planning data. For example, after all subsidiaries have formulated an annual budget, these are then consolidated and adjusted for intercompany eliminations to produce budgeted figures for the entire company. The requirements for consolidating planning data are usually a lot less rigorous than for historical data.

## 20.3   Consolidation Methods

The professional guidance regarding consolidated financial statements is provided in ARB 51 and FASB 94. Under current standards, consolidated financial statements must be prepared if one corporation owns a majority of another corporation's outstanding common stock. Although majority ownership is the most common means of acquiring control, a company may be able to direct the operating and financing policies of another with less than majority ownership, such as when the remainder of the stock is widely held. FASB 94 does not preclude consolidation with less than majority ownership, but such consolidations have seldom been found in practice. A difference in the fiscal periods of a parent and subsidiary should not preclude consolidation of that subsidiary.

US GAPP allows up to a three-month difference between the year-end of the parent and the subsidiary. In practice, when the fiscal period of the subsidiary differs from its parent's, the subsidiary will change its fiscal period to coincide with that of the parent. Another alternative is to adjust the financial statement data of the subsidiary each period to place the data on a basis consistent with the fiscal period of the parent.

Likewise, a difference in accounting methods between a parent and its subsidiary generally should have no effect on the decision to consolidate that subsidiary. In any event, adequate disclosure of the various accounting methods used must be given in the notes to the financial statements. Under US GAAP a parent and a subsidiary are permitted to have different accounting policies. This is most likely to occur when the subsidiary is following some specialized industry guide.

## 20.4    Consolidation Theories

With the issuance of FAS 141, the pooling of interests method was abolished and the purchase method became the preferred methodology of accounting for business combinations.

### 20.4.1    Parent Company Theory

The parent company theory assumes that consolidated financial statements are an extension of parent company statements and should be prepared from the viewpoint of the parent company stockholders. This theory is appropriate in situations where the parent company acquire the whole equity (100%) of the subsidiary and no minority non-controlling interest is at stake. Whenever a non-controlling interest exists, the FASB allows for non-controlling interest to be imputed from the price paid for the controlling interest.

### 20.4.2    Contemporary/Entity Theory

The entity theory, which was developed as attempts to mitigate the flaws of the parent company theory takes into account the total entity created by the parent company and the acquired subsidiary. This theory creates consolidated financial statements that will provide value to various groups including the parent company shareholders, non-controlling shareholders of the subsidiary, and creditors. No group holds preference over the others: the controlling shareholders, non-controlling shareholders, and consolidated entity are treated equally. All emphasis is given to the new group.

### 20.4.3    Traditional/Hybrid Theory

The traditional theory improves on the parent company theory's accounting for the non-controlling interest. Though it calculates consolidated net income using a similar process as in the parent company theory, it avoids reporting the non-controlling interest as an expense and a liability. Rather, the traditional theory reports non-controlling interest as a reduction of consolidated net income and an increase to equity that is essentially a wash to overall equity.[1] Indeed, the traditional hybrid theory is a mixed of both the parent company theory and the entity theory concerning the valuation of assets of the acquired subsidiary and the elimination of unrealized gains and losses from upstream sales.[2]

## 20.5   THE CONSOLIDATION PROCESS

Several items need to be given special attention to ensure that the consolidated financial statements appear as if they are the statements of a single company:

- Intercorporate stockholdings.
- Intercompany receivables and payables.
- Intercompany sales (i.e., unrealized profits)

The common stock of the parent is held by those outside the consolidated entity and is properly viewed as the common stock of the entire entity. In contrast, the common stock of the subsidiary is held entirely within the consolidated entity and is not stock outstanding from a consolidated viewpoint.

*Intercompany Receivables and Payables:* A single company cannot owe itself money, that is, a company cannot report (in its financial statements) a receivable to itself and a payable to itself. Thus, with respect to the consolidated balance sheet, the following entry is made to eliminate intercompany receivables and payables between the parent and the subsidiary.

*Intercompany Sales (Unrealized Profits):* A single company may not recognize a profit and write up its inventory simply because the inventory is transferred from one department or division to another (since no arm's length transaction has occurred to justify recognition of the profit). This also applies to intercompany sales within a consolidated entity. Since unrealized profits (in ending inventory) overstate ending inventory and understate cost of goods sold, consolidated net income as well as consolidated retained earnings are overstated.

---

[1] Catherine Baluch Gartner, et al., (2010): Consolidation Theories and Pushdown Accounting: Achieving Global Convergence, *Journal of Finance and Accountancy*, vol. 3, p. 5.

[2] Idem.

With respect to the consolidated balance sheet, the following elimination entry is required with respect to unrealized profits in ending inventory (e.g., $2000):

> (DR) Consolidated Retained Earnings $2000
> (CR) Consolidated Ending Inventory $2000

With the issuance of FAS 160 conveying the importance of reporting the non-controlling interest in a business combination, the entity theory of consolidation has become the standard for reporting business combinations under the acquisition method.

## 20.6    PUSHDOWN ACCOUNTING

Pushdown accounting is the practice of adjusting the stand-alone financial statements of an acquired entity to reflect the accounting basis of the investor rather than the acquired entity's historical costs. The "new basis" generally is the fair value of identifiable assets acquired and liabilities assumed and also may include the recognition of the debt and equity impact of the transaction. If the investor pays an amount in excess of fair value, the target carries the excess on its books as goodwill.[3]

The SEC requires pushdown accounting for SEC filings when a subsidiary is substantially wholly owned (approximately 97% or more ownership) with no publicly held debt or preferred stock outstanding.[4] However, because the SEC staff's guidance is applicable only to SEC registrants, diversity in practice exists with respect to the application of pushdown accounting among entities that are not SEC registrants. To clarify the issues, the FASB has issued on April 28, 2014, a proposed Accounting Standards Update (ASC Topic 805). Under the proposed ASU, the option to apply pushdown accounting would be

---

[3]Anne Coughlan (2014): New Pushdown Accounting Proposal Provides Clarity & Flexibility.

[4]Colley and Volkan (1988): Business Combinations: Goodwill and Push Down-Accounting, *The CPA Journal*, pp. 74–76.

evaluated and may be elected by the acquired entity for each individual change-in-control event in which an acquirer obtains control of the acquired entity.

If the acquired entity elects the option to apply pushdown accounting, it would reflect in its separate financial statements the new basis of accounting established by the acquirer for the individual assets and liabilities of the acquired entity by applying Topic 805, Business Combinations. On the reverse, if the acquirer did not establish a new basis of accounting for the individual assets and liabilities of the acquired entity because it was not required to apply Topic 805, the acquired entity would reflect in its separate financial statements the new basis of accounting that would have been established by the acquirer had the acquirer applied Topic 805. The acquired entity would recognize goodwill that arises due to the application of Topic 805 in its separate financial statements. However, if the application of Topic 805 results in a bargain purchase gain, the acquired entity would not recognize that gain in its income statement. In addition, any acquisition-related debt incurred by the acquirer would be recognized in the acquired entity's separate financial statements only if the acquired entity is required to recognize a liability for that debt in accordance with other applicable US GAAP.[5]

An acquired entity which elects the option to apply pushdown accounting in its separate financial statements is required to disclose information in the current reporting period that enables the users of financial statements to evaluate the effect of pushdown accounting on its financial statements. Conversely, an acquired entity which does not elect the option to apply pushdown accounting in its separate financial statements shall disclose in the current reporting period that the entity has (1) undergone a change-in-control event whereby an acquirer has obtained control of the entity during the reporting period and (2) elected to continue to prepare its financial statements using its historical basis that existed before the acquirer obtained control of the entity.[6]

---

[5] FASB (2014): Business Combinations (Topic 805)—Pushdown Accounting, p. 1.
[6] FASB (2014): Business Combinations (Topic 805)—Pushdown Accounting, p. 2.

## Example 1

Company A buys 100% of the voting stock of Company B from an unrelated third party for $500 million; the acquisition resulted in goodwill and not a bargain purchase. Company B's net book value was $40 million prior to acquisition, and Company B will continue to issue separate stand-alone financial statements after acquisition. If pushdown accounting is applied, Company B would establish a new basis for its net assets equal to $500 million in its own separate stand-alone financials.

## Example 2

On January 1, 2014, Danbury Corp. (Danbury) purchased a 100% interest in Holly's Fashion Accessories (HFA). Danbury issued 50,000 shares of common stock ($1 par value) that were trading at $30 on January 1 (the acquisition date).

The book value of HFA's net assets (including PP&E) was $750,000 on January 1. The balance in the PP&E account was $78,000. The balance in HFA's retained earnings account was $55,000. The fair value of net assets, exclusive of PP&E, was $1.0 million. HFA's PP&E is particularly hard to value as there is no active market. Consequently, the assessment of the fair value of this PP&E under IFRS) is $150,000, whereas the assessment of fair value under US GAAP is $200,000.

Question

## Exercise

Provide the necessary journal entries under both US GAAP and IFRS) to record pushdown accounting.

*Solution*

| | | |
|---|---|---|
| Net assets (excluding PP&E) | $328,000 | |
| PP&E | 122,000 | |
| Goodwill | 300,000 | |
| Retained earnings | 55,000 | |
| Additional paid-in capital | | $805,000 |

# CHAPTER 21

# Segment and Intermediary Financial Statements

## 21.1   GENERAL

Segment financial statements allow a business to show to the readers of the statements (i.e., investors) what parts of the business are performing better relative to the others. On the other hand, interim disclosures are required for the current quarter and year-to-date amounts. A public entity shall disclose all of the following about each reportable segment in condensed financial statements of interim periods.

## 21.2   SEGMENT STATEMENTS

Segment reporting refers to the reporting of the operating segments of a company in the disclosures accompanying its financial statements. Only publicly held entities are required to report segments. Privately held entities are not required. The purpose of the segment reporting is to provide information about the different types of business activities in which a public entity engages and the different economic environments in which it operates to help users of financial statements get a sound understanding of the entity. An operating segment is a component of a public entity that has all of the following characteristics: (i) It engages in business activities from which it may earn revenues and incur expenses (including revenues and expenses relating to transactions with other components of the same public entity), (ii) its operating results are regularly reviewed by the public entity's chief operating decision maker (CODM) to make

© The Author(s) 2018
F. I. Lessambo, *Financial Statements*,
https://doi.org/10.1007/978-3-319-99984-5_21

decisions about resources to be allocated to the segment and assess its performance, and (iii) its discrete financial information is available.

An operating segment may engage in business activities for which it has yet to earn revenues, for example, start-up operations may be operating segments before earning revenues. However, it shall be noticed that not every part of a public entity is necessarily an operating segment or part of an operating segment. A public entity's pension and other postretirement benefit plans are not considered operating segments. Entities shall report their segment information in the same manner management organizes the entity into units for internal decision-making and performance evaluation process.

### 21.2.1   Reportable Segments

An operating segment is a component of a public entity that has all of the following characteristics: (i) It engages in business activities from which it may earn revenues and incur expenses (including revenues and expenses relating to transactions with other components of the same public entity), (ii) its operating results are regularly reviewed by the public entity's CODM to make decisions about resources to be allocated to the segment and assess its performance, and (iii) its discrete financial information is available. A public entity shall report separately information about each operating segment that meets both of the aforementioned criteria. Entities report their segments using either the aggregation criteria or the quantitative thresholds.

1. The Aggregation Criteria

Two or more operating segments may be aggregated into a single operating segment if aggregation is consistent with the objectives of the CODM, the segments have similar economic characteristics, and the segments are similar in all of the following areas: (i) the nature of the products and services, (ii) the nature of the production processes, (iii) the type or class of customer for their products and services, (iv) the methods used to distribute their products or provide their services, and (v) if applicable, the nature of the regulatory environment, for example, banking, insurance, or public utilities.[1]

[1] ASC 280-50-11.

## Example: Asset Test

Chin Corp. has identified the following operating segments: A, B, C, and D.

Assuming that Chin Corp's CODM uses the total assets as the measure of segment assets. Compute the asset test for Chin Corp.'s operating segments.

|          | A | B | C  | D  | Combined | Consolidated |
|----------|---|---|----|----|----------|--------------|
| T.A. (M) | 5 | 8 | 12 | 30 | 55       | 55           |

Under the asset test, segments B, C, and D are reportable because the measure of total assets for each of these segments is at least $550,000, which is 10% of the combined segment total assets of $55 million.

## 2. The Quantitative Threshold

A public entity shall report separately information about an operating segment that meets any of the following quantitative thresholds[2]:

i. its reported revenue, including both sales to external customers and intersegment sales or transfers, is 10% or more of the combined revenue, internal and external, of all operating segments,

ii. the absolute amount of its reported profit or loss is 10% or more of the greater, in absolute amount, of either:
   a. the combined reported profit of all operating segments that did not report a loss, or
   b. the combined reported loss of all operating segments that did report a loss.

iii. its assets are 10% or more of the combined assets of all operating segments.

Operating segments that do not meet any of the quantitative thresholds may still be considered reportable, and separately disclosed, if the entity's

[2] ASC 280-50-12.

management believes that information about the segment would be useful to readers of the financial statements. An entity may combine information about operating segments that do not meet the quantitative thresholds with information about other operating segments that do not meet the quantitative thresholds to produce a reportable segment. However, to do so, the aggregation must be consistent with the objective and basic principles pertaining to the aggregation criteria.[3]

---

### Revenue Test Example

Yuco Inc. has identified four segments: A, B, C, D. Assuming that all category is attributable to operating segments which are insignificantly based upon a complete quantitative material assessment pursuant to ASC 280-10-50-12.

*Task*: Compute Yuco Inc. sales information. ($ amount in thousands)

|     | A | B | C | D | Others | Combined | Eliminations | Consoled |
|-----|------|------|------|--------|--------|----------|--------------|----------|
| *   | 3500 | 6000 | 7500 | 20,000 | 6500   | 43,500   | –            | 43,500   |
| **  | 2000 | 2000 | –    | 10,000 | –      | 14,000   | (14,000)     | –        |
| *** | 5000 | 8000 | 7500 | 30,000 | 6500   | 57,500   | (14,000)     | 43,500   |

Notice: *Represents the revenues from external customers; **represents intersegment revenue; and *** represents the total revenue

*Solution*: Segments B, C, and D are individually reportable under the revenue test as their revenues are at least $57,500 which is 10% of the combined revenue of the operating segments of $57,500,000. Segment A would not be reported individually under the revenue test.

---

### 21.2.2    Identification of Additional Segment

If total of external revenue reported by operating segments constitutes less than 75% of total consolidated revenue, additional operating segments shall be identified as reportable segments (even if they do not

---

[3] ASC 280-50-13.

meet the criteria in paragraph 280-10-50-12) until at least 75% of total consolidated revenue is included in reportable segments. If an operating segment is identified as a reportable segment in the current period due to the quantitative thresholds, prior period segment data presented for comparative purposes shall be restated to reflect the newly reportable segment as a separate segment even if that segment did not satisfy the criteria for reportability in the prior period unless it is impracticable to do so.[4] There may be a practical limit to the number of reportable segments that a public entity separately discloses beyond which segment information may become overly detailed. The GAAP do not prescribe any limit. As a matter of practice, anytime an entity has reported 10 segments, the public entity should consider whether a practical limit has been reached.

### The 75% of Consolidated Revenue Test Exercise

Yuco Inc. has identified five operating segments (A, B, C, D, E) which contribute the below mentioned percentages to its consolidated revenue. Assuming each of the operating segments that are below 10% of the consolidated revenue does not meet either the profit/loss or the asset quantitative threshold tests.

| Segments | Percentage of consolidated revenue (%) |
|----------|----------------------------------------|
| A        | 30                                     |
| B        | 40                                     |
| C        | 20                                     |
| D        | 6                                      |
| E        | 4                                      |
|          | 100                                    |

Solution: Yuco Inc. would have to separately report segments A, B, and C. If it happened that the percentage of consolidated revenue of segments A, B, and C were below the 75% threshold. Yuco Inc. could include segments D and E (the two with less than 10%) if they share similar economic characteristics in order to meet the 75% threshold, pursuant to ASC 280.

[4]ASC 280-50-17.

### 21.2.3    Disclosure Requirements

A public entity shall disclose all of the following for each period for which an income statement is presented:

a. The factors used to identify the public entity's reportable segments, including the basis of organization (e.g., whether management has chosen to organize the public entity around differences in products and services, geographic areas, regulatory environments, or a combination of factors and whether operating segments have been aggregated).
b. The types of products and services from which each reportable segment derives its revenues.

A public entity also shall disclose all of the following about each reportable segment if the specified amounts are included in the measure of segment profit or loss reviewed by the CODM or are otherwise regularly provided to the CODM, even if not included in that measure of segment profit or loss:

a. Revenues from external customers
b. Revenues from transactions with other operating segments of the same public entity
c. Interest revenue[5]
d. Interest expense
e. Depreciation, depletion, and amortization expense
f. Unusual items as described in paragraph 225-20-45-16
g. Equity in the net income of investees accounted for by the equity method
h. Income tax expense or benefit
i. Extraordinary items
j. Significant noncash items other than depreciation, depletion, and amortization expense.

---

[5]A public entity shall report interest revenue separately from interest expense for each reportable segment unless a majority of the segment's revenues are from interest and the CODM relies primarily on net interest revenue to assess the performance of the segment and make decisions about resources to be allocated to the segment. In that situation, a public entity may report that segment's interest revenue net of its interest expense and disclose that it has done so.

A public entity shall disclose both of the following about each reportable segment if the specified amounts are included in the determination of segment assets reviewed by the CODM or are otherwise regularly provided to the CODM, even if not included in the determination of segment assets:

a. The amount of investment in equity method investees
b. Total expenditures for additions to long-lived assets other than any of the following[6]:
   i. financial instruments
   ii. long-term customer relationships of a financial institution
   iii. mortgage and other servicing rights
   iv. deferred policy acquisition costs and deferred tax assets.

### 21.2.4   Measurement

The amount of each segment item reported shall be the measure reported to the CODM for purposes of making decisions about allocating resources to the segment and assessing its performance. Adjustments and eliminations made in preparing a public entity's general-purpose financial statements and allocations of revenues, expenses, and gains or losses shall be included in determining reported segment profit or loss only if they are included in the measure of the segment's profit or loss that are used by the CODM. Similarly, only those assets that are included in the measure of the segment's assets that is used by the CODM shall be reported for that segment. If amounts are allocated to reported segment profit or loss or assets, those amounts shall be allocated on a reasonable basis.[7]

If the CODM uses only one measure of a segment's profit or loss and only one measure of a segment's assets in assessing segment performance and deciding how to allocate resources, segment profit or loss and assets shall be reported at those measures. If the CODM uses more than one measure of a segment's profit or loss and more than one measure of a segment's assets, the reported measures shall be those that management believes are determined in accordance with the measurement

[6]ASC 280-50-25.
[7]ASC-280-50-27.

principles most consistent with those used in measuring the corresponding amounts in the public entity's consolidated financial statements.[8]

A public entity shall provide an explanation of the measurements of segment profit or loss and segment assets for each reportable segment. At a minimum, a public entity shall disclose all of the following:

a. The basis of accounting for any transactions between reportable segments.
b. The nature of any differences between the measurements of the reportable segments' profits or losses and the public entity's consolidated income before income taxes, extraordinary items, and discontinued operations. Those differences could include accounting policies and policies for allocation of centrally incurred costs that are necessary for an understanding of the reported segment information.
c. The nature of any differences between the measurements of the reportable segments' assets and the public entity's consolidated. Those differences could include accounting policies and policies for allocation of jointly used assets that are necessary for an understanding of the reported segment information.
d. The nature of any changes from prior periods in the measurement methods used to determine reported segment profit or loss and the effect, if any, of those changes on the measure of segment profit or loss.
e. The nature and effect of any asymmetrical allocations to segments. For example, a public entity might allocate depreciation expense to a segment without allocating the related depreciable assets to that segment.

### 21.2.4.1 Reconciliations

All significant reconciling items shall be separately identified and described. A public entity shall provide reconciliations of all of the following:

a. The total of the reportable segments' revenues to the public entity's consolidated revenues.

---

[8]ASC 28-50-28.

b. The total of the reportable segments' measures of profit or loss to the public entity's consolidated income before income taxes, extraordinary items, and discontinued operations. However, if a public entity allocates items such as income taxes and extraordinary items to segments, the public entity may choose to reconcile the total of the segments' measures of profit or loss to consolidated income after those items.

c. The total of the reportable segments' assets to the public entity's consolidated assets.

d. The total of the reportable segments' amounts for every other significant item of information disclosed to the corresponding consolidated amount. For example, a public entity may choose to disclose liabilities for its reportable segments, in which case the public entity would reconcile the total of reportable segments' liabilities for each segment to the public entity's consolidated liabilities if the segment liabilities are significant.

### 21.2.4.2 Interim Report

Interim disclosures are required for the current quarter and year-to-date amounts. A public entity shall disclose all of the following about each reportable segment in condensed financial statements of interim periods:

a. Revenues from external customers

b. Intersegment revenues

c. A measure of segment profit or loss

d. Total assets for which there has been a material change from the amount disclosed in the last annual report

e. A description of differences from the last annual report on the basis of segmentation or in the basis of measurement of segment profit or loss

f. A reconciliation of the total of the reportable segments' measures of profit or loss to the public entity's consolidated income before income taxes, extraordinary items, and discontinued operations. However, if a public entity allocates items such as income taxes and extraordinary items to segments, the public entity may choose to reconcile the total of the segments' measures of profit or loss to consolidated income after those items. Significant reconciling items shall be separately identified and described in that reconciliation.

### 21.2.4.3 Restatement of Previously Reported Information

If a public entity changes the structure of its internal organization in a manner that causes the composition of its reportable segments to change, the corresponding information for earlier periods, including interim periods, shall be restated unless it is impracticable to do so. Accordingly, a public entity shall restate those individual items of disclosure that it can practicably restate but need not restate those individual items, if any, that it cannot practicably restate. Following a change in the composition of its reportable segments, a public entity shall disclose whether it has restated the corresponding items of segment information for earlier periods.

## 21.2.5    Entity-Wide Information

Some public entities' business activities are not organized on the basis of differences in related products and services or differences in geographic areas of operations. That is, a public entity's segments may report revenues from a broad range of essentially different products and services, or more than one of its reportable segments may provide essentially the same products and services. Similarly, a public entity's segments may hold assets in different geographic areas and report revenues from customers in different geographic areas, or more than one of its segments may operate in the same geographic area.

### 21.2.5.1 Information About Products and Services

A public entity shall report the revenues from external customers for each product and service or each group of similar products and services unless it is impracticable to do so. The amounts of revenues reported shall be based on the financial information used to produce the public entity's general-purpose financial statements. If providing the information is impracticable, that fact shall be disclosed.[9]

### Example (Products and Services)

Yuco Inc. has determined its operating segments based on the below geographic areas: Northern USA; Southern USA; and

---

[9] ASC 280-50-40.

Mexico. Yuco Inc. is the business of manufacturing windows in each of the three areas. Additionally, Yuco Inc. trade on electrical engines in both the Northern and the Southern areas of the USA.

| Segments | Includes window sales | Includes electrical engines |
|---|---|---|
| Northern US | X | X |
| Southern US | X | X |
| Mexico | X | |

*Solution*: Yuco Inc. must disclose the amount of revenue attributable to its window and electrical engine product sales for the entity as a whole.

### 21.2.5.2 Information About Geographic Areas

A public entity shall report the following geographic information unless it is impracticable to do so:

a. Revenues from external customers attributed to the public entity's country of domicile and attributed to all foreign countries in total from which the public entity derives revenues. If revenues from external customers attributed to an individual foreign country are material, those revenues shall be disclosed separately. A public entity shall disclose the basis for attributing revenues from external customers to individual countries.
b. Long-lived assets other than financial instruments, long-term customer relationships of a financial institution, mortgage and other servicing rights, deferred policy acquisition costs, and deferred tax assets located in the public entity's country of domicile and located in all foreign countries in total in which the public entity holds assets. If assets in an individual foreign country are material, those assets shall be disclosed separately.

The amounts reported shall be based on the financial information that is used to produce the general-purpose financial statements. If providing the geographic information is impracticable, that fact shall be disclosed.

A public entity may wish to provide, in addition to the information required by the preceding paragraph, subtotals of geographic information about groups of countries.[10]

*21.2.5.3 Information About Major Customers*
A public entity shall provide information about the extent of its reliance on its major customers. If revenues from transactions with a single external customer amount to 10% or more of a public entity's revenues, the public entity shall disclose that fact, the total amount of revenues from each such customer, and the identity of the segment or segments reporting the revenues. The public entity need not disclose the identity of a major customer or the amount of revenues that each segment reports from that customer. For purposes of this Subtopic, a group of entities known to a reporting public entity to be under common control shall be considered as a single customer, and the federal government, a state government, a local government (e.g., a county or municipality), or a foreign government each shall be considered as a single customer.[11]

---

**Example: (Major Customers)**

Yuco Inc. sells its products to three subsidiaries of Zhifan LLC as follows:

- Subsidiary 1: 5% of the total revenue
- Subsidiary 2: 4% of the total revenue
- Subsidiary 3: 3% of the total revenue

*Solution*: When assessing whether more than 10% of Yuco Inc. sale derives from a single customer, Yuco Inc. is required to aggregate the sales to Subs 1, 2, and 3. Thus, Yuco Inc. would have to report Zhifan, LLC, as a major customer and disclose the total combined revenue of 12%.

---

[10]ASC 280-50-41.
[11]ASC 280-50-42.

## 21.2.6  Goodwill Considerations

Proper identification of operating segments affects more than just segment disclosures. It also affects the recognition and measurement of goodwill impairment. ASC 350 requires goodwill to be assessed for impairment at the reporting unit level, which is defined as an operating segment (i.e., before aggregation or combination), or one level below an operating segment (i.e., a component).[12]

# 21.3  INTERMEDIARY STATEMENTS

Interim financial information often is provided for each interim period or on a cumulative year-to-date basis, or both, and for the corresponding periods of the preceding year. The revenues of some entities fluctuate widely among interim periods because of seasonal factors, while in other entities heavy fixed costs incurred in one interim period may benefit other periods. In these situations, financial information for periods of less than a full year may be of limited usefulness.

## 21.3.1  Accounting Principles and Practices

In general, the results for each interim period shall be based on the accounting principles and practices used by an entity in the preparation of its latest annual financial statements unless a change in an accounting practice or policy has been adopted in the current year. However, certain accounting principles and practices followed for annual reporting purposes may require modification at interim reporting dates so that the reported results for the interim period may better relate to the results of operations for the annual period.

## 21.3.2  Revenue

Revenue from products sold or services rendered shall be recognized as earned during an interim period on the same basis as followed for the

---

[12]ASC 350-20-35-34 states, "A component of an operating segment is a reporting unit if the component constitutes a business for which discrete financial information is available and segment management, as that term is defined in paragraph 280-10-50-7, regularly reviews the operating results of that component."

full year. For example, revenues from long-term construction-type contracts accounted for under the percentage-of-completion method shall be recognized in interim periods on the same basis followed for the full year. Losses projected on such contracts shall be recognized in full during the interim period in which the existence of such losses becomes evident.

### 21.3.3    Costs and Expenses

Costs and expenses for interim reporting purposes may be classified as either of the following:

a. Costs associated with revenue—those costs that are associated directly with or allocated to the products sold or to the services rendered and that are charged against income in those interim periods in which the related revenue is recognized.
b. All other costs and expenses—those costs and expenses that are not allocated to the products sold or to the services rendered and that are charged against income in interim fiscal periods as incurred, or are allocated among interim periods based on an estimate of time expired, benefit received, or other activity associated with the periods.

### 21.3.4    Costs Associated with Revenue

Those costs and expenses that are associated directly with or allocated to the products sold or to the services rendered for annual reporting purposes (e.g., material costs, wages and salaries and related fringe benefits, manufacturing overhead, and warranties) shall be similarly treated for interim reporting purposes.

Practices vary in determining costs of inventory. For example, cost of goods produced may be determined based on standard or actual cost, while cost of inventory may be determined on an average, first-in, first-out (FIFO), or last-in, first-out (LIFO) cost basis. While entities shall generally use the same inventory pricing methods and make provisions for write-downs to market at interim dates on the same basis as used at annual inventory dates, the following exceptions are appropriate at interim reporting dates:

a. Some entities use estimated gross profit rates to determine the cost of goods sold during interim periods or use other methods different from those used at annual inventory dates. These entities shall disclose the method used at the interim date and any significant adjustments that result from reconciliations with the annual physical inventory.

b. Entities that use the LIFO method may encounter a liquidation of base period inventories at an interim date that is expected to be replaced by the end of the annual period. In such cases, the inventory at the interim reporting date shall not give effect to the LIFO liquidation, and cost of sales for the interim reporting period shall include the expected cost of replacement of the liquidated LIFO base.

c. Inventory losses from market declines shall not be deferred beyond the interim period in which the decline occurs. Recoveries of such losses on the same inventory in later interim periods of the same fiscal year through market price recoveries shall be recognized as gains in the later interim period. Such gains shall not exceed previously recognized losses. Some market declines at interim dates, however, can reasonably be expected to be restored in the fiscal year. Such temporary market declines need not be recognized at the interim date since no loss is expected to be incurred in the fiscal year.

d. Entities that use standard cost accounting systems for determining inventory and product costs should generally follow the same procedures in reporting purchase price, wage rate, usage, or efficiency variances from standard cost at the end of an interim period as followed at the end of a fiscal year. Purchase price variances or volume or capacity cost variances that are planned and expected to be absorbed by the end of the annual period should ordinarily be deferred at interim reporting dates. The effect of unplanned or unanticipated purchase price or volume variances, however, shall be reported at the end of an interim period following the same procedures used at the end of a fiscal year.

### 21.3.5   *All Other Costs and Expenses*

Charges are made to income for all other costs and expenses in annual reporting periods based upon any of the following:

a. Direct expenditures made in the period (salaries and wages)
b. Accruals for estimated expenditures to be made at a later date (vacation pay)
c. Amortization of expenditures that affect more than one annual period (such as insurance premiums, interest, and rents).

The objective in all cases is to achieve a fair measure of results of operations for the annual period and to present fairly the financial position at the end of the annual period. The following standards shall apply in accounting for costs and expenses other than product costs in interim periods:

a. Costs and expenses other than product costs shall be charged to income in interim periods as incurred or be allocated among interim periods based on an estimate of time expired, benefit received, or activity associated with the periods. Procedures adopted for assigning specific cost and expense items to an interim period shall be consistent with the bases followed by the entity in reporting results of operations at annual reporting dates. However, if a specific cost or expense item charged to expense for annual reporting purposes benefits more than one interim period, the cost or expense item may be allocated to those interim periods.
b. Some costs and expenses incurred in an interim period, however, cannot be readily identified with the activities or benefits of other interim periods and shall be charged to the interim period in which incurred. Disclosure shall be made as to the nature and amount of such costs unless items of a comparable nature are included in both the current interim period and the corresponding interim period of the preceding year.
c. Arbitrary assignment of the amount of such costs to an interim period shall not be made.
d. Gains and losses that arise in any interim period similar to those that would not be deferred at year end shall not be deferred to later interim periods within the same fiscal year.

### 21.3.6    Seasonal Revenue, Costs, or Expenses

Revenues of certain entities are subject to material seasonal variations. To avoid the possibility that interim results with material seasonal variations may be taken as fairly indicative of the estimated results for a full fiscal year, such entities shall disclose the seasonal nature of their activities and consider supplementing their interim reports with information for 12-month periods ended at the interim date for the current and preceding years.

### 21.3.7    Extraordinary Items, Unusual and Infrequent Items, and Disposals of Components

Effects of disposals of a component of an entity and unusual and infrequently occurring transactions and events that are material with respect to the operating results of the interim period but that are not designated as extraordinary items in the interim statements shall be reported separately. Extraordinary items, gains, or losses from disposal of a component of an entity, and unusual or infrequently occurring items shall not be prorated over the balance of the fiscal year.

### 21.3.8    Accounting Changes in Interim Periods

Each report of interim financial information shall indicate any change in accounting principles or practices from those applied in any of the following:

a. The comparable interim period of the prior annual period
b. The preceding interim periods in the current annual period
c. The prior annual report.

Changes in an interim or annual accounting practice or policy made in an interim period shall be reported in the period in which the change is made, in accordance with the provisions of Topic 250.

The effect of a change in an accounting estimate, including a change in the estimated effective annual tax rate, shall be accounted for in the period in which the change in estimate is made. No restatement of previously reported interim information shall be made for changes in estimates, but the effect on earnings of a change in estimate made in a current interim period shall be reported in the current and subsequent interim periods, if material in relation to any period presented and shall continue to be reported in the interim financial information of the subsequent year for as many periods as necessary to avoid misleading comparisons. Whenever possible, entities should adopt any accounting changes during the first interim period of a fiscal year. Changes in accounting principles and practices adopted after the first interim period in a fiscal year tend to obscure operating results and complicate disclosure of interim financial information.

### 21.3.9    Adjustments Related to Prior Interim Periods of the Current Fiscal Year

As indicated in paragraph 250-10-45-25, an adjustment related to prior interim periods of the current fiscal year is an adjustment or settlement of litigation or similar claims, of income taxes (except for the effects of retroactive tax legislation), of renegotiation proceedings, or of utility revenue under rate-making processes provided that the adjustment or settlement meets some specific criteria.

As indicated in paragraph 250-10-45-26, if an item of profit or loss occurs in other than the first interim period of the entity's fiscal year and all or a part of the item of profit or loss is an adjustment related to prior interim periods of the current fiscal year, as defined in the preceding paragraph, the item shall be reported as follows:

a. The portion of the item that is directly related to business activities of the entity during the current interim period, if any, shall be included in the determination of net income for that period.
b. Prior interim periods of the current fiscal year shall be restated to include the portion of the item that is directly related to business activities of the entity during each prior interim period in the determination of net income for that period.
c. The portion of the item that is directly related to business activities of the entity during prior fiscal years, if any, shall be included in the determination of net income of the first interim period of the current fiscal year.

### 21.3.10    Guidelines for Preparing Interim Statements

Many publicly traded companies report summarized financial information at periodic interim dates in considerably less detail than that provided in annual financial statements. While this information provides more timely information that would result if complete financial statements were issued at the end of each interim period, the timeliness of presentation may be partially offset by a reduction in detail in the information provided. As a result, certain guides as to minimum disclosure are desirable. (It should be recognized that the minimum disclosures of summarized interim financial data required of publicly traded companies do not constitute a fair presentation of financial position and results of operations in conformity with generally accepted accounting principles [GAAP].) If publicly traded companies report summarized financial information at interim dates (including reports on fourth quarters), the following data should be reported, as a minimum:

a. Sales or gross revenues, provision for income taxes, extraordinary items (including related income tax effects), net income, and comprehensive income
b. Basic and diluted earnings per share data for each period presented, determined in accordance with the provisions of Topic 260
c. Seasonal revenue, costs, or expenses
d. Significant changes in estimates or provisions for income taxes
e. Disposal of a component of an entity and extraordinary, unusual or infrequently occurring items
f. Contingent items
g. Changes in accounting principles or estimates
h. Significant changes in financial position
i. All of the following information about reportable operating segments determined according to the provisions of Topic 280, including provisions related to restatement of segment information in previously issued financial statements:
   i. Revenues from external customers
   ii. Intersegment revenues
   iii. A measure of segment profit or loss
   iv. Total assets for which there has been a material change from the amount disclosed in the last annual report
   v. A description of differences from the last annual report on the basis of segmentation or in the measurement of segment profit or loss
   vi. A reconciliation of the total of the reportable segments' measures of profit or loss to the entity's consolidated income before

income taxes, extraordinary items, and discontinued operations. However, if, for example, an entity allocates items such as income taxes and extraordinary items to segments, the entity may choose to reconcile the total of the segments' measures of profit or loss to consolidated income after those items. Significant reconciling items shall be separately identified and described in that reconciliation.

j. All of the following information about defined benefit pension plans and other defined benefit postretirement benefit plans disclosed for all periods presented pursuant to the provisions of Subtopic 715-20:

   i. The amount of net periodic benefit cost recognized, for each period for which a statement of income is presented, showing separately the service cost component, the interest cost component, the expected return on plan assets for the period, the gain or loss component, the prior service cost or credit component, the transition asset or obligation component, and the gain or loss recognized due to a settlement or curtailment

   ii. The total amount of the employer's contributions paid, and expected to be paid, during the current fiscal year, if significantly different from amounts previously disclosed pursuant to paragraph 715-20-50-1. Estimated contributions may be presented in the aggregate combining all of the following:

   1. Contributions required by funding regulations or laws
   2. Discretionary contributions
   3. Noncash contributions.

k. The information about the use of fair value to measure assets and liabilities recognized in the statement of financial position pursuant to paragraphs 820-10-50-1 through 50-6

l. The information about derivative instruments as required by Section 815-10-50, 815-20-50, 815-25-50, 815-30-50, and 815-35-50

m. The information about fair value of financial instruments as required by Sections 825-10-50

n. The information about certain investments in debt and equity securities as required by Sections 320-10-50 and 942-320-50

o. The information about other-than-temporary impairments as required by Sections 320-10-50, 325-20-50, and 958-320-50.

### 21.3.11   SEC Materials: Regulation S-X Rule 10-01, Interim Financial Statements

The SEC requires that interim financial statement be prepared in accordance with the GAAP and filed on Form 10-Q within 45 days following the close of the quarter. In practice, the fourth quarter is not required, but SEC Rule 14a-3 requires that selected data relating to the fourth quarter be included in the annual report to the shareholders. It should be noticed that 10-Q Forms are not audited—a simple review by the external auditor suffices. Part 1 of the Q-10 Form provides the following information:

a. Item 1: Consolidated balance sheet
   i. Consolidated statement of income
   ii. Consolidated statement of cash flows
   iii. Notes to consolidated financial statements
b. Item 2: Management' discussion of financial condition and results of operations.

# CHAPTER 22

# IFRS and GAAP

## 22.1 GENERAL

Foreign public firms are now permitted to file using the International Financial Reporting Standards (IFRS) without reconciliation to US GAAP as previously required. This move has created a mandate to converge IFRS and US GAAP and financial statement requirements. By 2017, 126 jurisdictions required the use of IFRS Standards for all or most publicly listed companies, with a further 13 permitting their use. During 2017, we welcomed the announcement that 17 West and Central African jurisdictions, coordinated by the Organization for the Harmonization of Business Law in Africa, will require the use of IFRS Standards from 2019. Adding Papua New Guinea, the total number of jurisdictions requiring the use of IFRS Standards is now 144.

IFRS Standards provides a high quality, internationally recognized set of accounting standards that bring transparency, accountability, and efficiency to financial markets around the world.

- Transparency

IFRS Standards bring transparency by enhancing the international comparability and quality of financial information, enabling investors and other market participants to make informed economic decisions.

© The Author(s) 2018
F. I. Lessambo, *Financial Statements*,
https://doi.org/10.1007/978-3-319-99984-5_22

• Accountability

IFRS Standards strengthen accountability by reducing the information gap between the providers of capital and the people to whom they have entrusted their money. Our standards provide information that is needed to hold management to account. As a source of globally comparable information, IFRS Standards are also of vital importance to regulators around the world.

• Efficiency

And IFRS Standards contribute to economic efficiency by helping investors to identify opportunities and risks across the world, thus improving capital allocation. For businesses, the use of a single, trusted accounting language lowers the cost of capital and reduces international reporting costs.

## 22.2   PRINCIPLES-BASED VS RULES-BASED

One of the major differences lies in the conceptual approach: US GAAP is rule-based, whereas IFRS is principle-based. The inherent characteristic of a principles-based framework is the potential of different interpretations for similar transactions. This situation implies second-guessing and creates uncertainty and requires extensive disclosures in the financial statements.

In a principle-based accounting system, the areas of interpretation or discussion can be clarified by the standards-setting board and provide fewer exceptions than a rules-based system. However, IFRS include positions and guidance that can easily be considered as sets of rules instead of sets of principles. At the time of the IFRS adoption, this led English observers to comment that international standards were really rule-based compared to UK GAAP that were much more principle-based.

The difference between these two approaches is on the methodology to assess an accounting treatment. Under US GAAP, the research is more focused on the literature whereas, under IFRS, the review of the facts pattern is more thorough.

However, the professional judgment is not a new concept in the US environment. The SEC is addressing this topic in order to find the right balance between the "educated" professional judgment, that is acceptable, and the "guessed" professional judgment.

## 22.3    SELECTED INTERNATIONAL ACCOUNTING STANDARDS

### 22.3.1    IAS 1—Presentation of Financial Statement

IAS 1, issued in September 2007, applies to annual periods beginning on or after January 1, 2009. IAS 1 prescribes the basis for presentation of general purpose financial statements to ensure comparability both with the entity's financial statements of previous periods and with the financial statements of other entities. It sets out overall requirements for the presentation of financial statements, guidelines for their structure, and minimum requirements for their content. IAS 1 applies to all general purpose financial statements that are prepared and presented in accordance with IFRS. The objective of financial statements is to provide information about the financial position, financial performance, and cash flows of an entity that is useful to a wide range of users in making economic decisions. Financial statements also show the results of the management's stewardship of the resources entrusted to it.

#### 22.3.1.1 Complete Set of Financial Statements
An entity shall present with equal prominence all of the financial statements in a complete set of financial statements. A complete set of financial statements comprises:

a. A statement of financial position as at the end of the period;
b. A statement of comprehensive income for the period;
c. A statement of changes in equity for the period;
d. A statement of cash flows for the period;
e. Notes, comprising a summary of significant accounting policies and other explanatory information; and
f. A statement of financial position as at the beginning of the earliest comparative period when an entity applies an accounting policy retrospectively or makes a retrospective restatement of items in its financial statements, or when it reclassifies items in its financial statements.

#### 22.3.1.2 Core Principles
IAS core principles include: (i) fair presentation and compliance with IFRSs, (ii) going concern, (iii) accrual basis of accounting, (iv) materiality and aggregation, (v) offsetting, (vi) frequency of reporting, (vii) comparative information, and (viii) consistency of presentation.

### 22.3.1.3 Financial Statements: Structure and Content

An entity shall clearly identify the financial statements and distinguish them from other information in the same published document. More, an entity shall clearly identify each financial statement and the notes. In addition, an entity shall display the following information prominently and repeat it when necessary for the information presented to be understandable.

- The statement of financial position must differentiate between current and non-current assets and liabilities.
- The comprehensive statement of income: an entity shall present all items of income and expense recognized in a period: (a) in a single statement of comprehensive income, or (b) in two statements: a statement displaying components of profit or loss (separate statement of comprehensive income) and a second statement beginning with profit or loss and displaying components of other comprehensive income (statement of comprehensive income). An entity shall not present any items of income or expense as extraordinary items, in the statement of comprehensive income or the separate statement of comprehensive income (if presented), or in the notes.
- Statement of changes in equity

IAS 1.106 provides a list of items to be presented on the face of the statement of changes in equity. Entities may present the required reconciliations for each component of other comprehensive income either (1) in the statement of changes in equity or (2) in the notes to the financial statements (IAS 1.106(d) (ii) and IAS 1.106A).

- Statement of cash flows

The statement of cash flows must clearly provide for the four components of cash flows: (i) cash; (ii) cash flow from operations; (iii) cash flow from financing activities; and (iv) cash flows from investing activities.

- Notes

An entity may present notes providing: (i) information about the basis of preparation of the financial statements and specific accounting policies as a separate section of the financial statements, (ii) sources of estimation uncertainty, (iii) and other disclosures.

## 22.3.2    IAS 2—Inventories

IAS 2 Inventories requires inventories to be measured at the lower of cost and net realizable value (NRV) and outlines acceptable methods of determining cost, including specific identification (in some cases), first-in, first-out (FIFO), and weighted average cost. Certain inventories are excluded from the scope of IAS 2. These include:

- work in process arising under construction contracts;
- financial instruments; and
- biological assets related to agricultural activity and agricultural produce at the point of harvest.

Measurement of inventories cost should include all (i) costs of purchase (including taxes, transport, and handling) net of trade discounts received; (ii) costs of conversion (including fixed and variable manufacturing overheads) and; (iii) other costs incurred in bringing the inventories to their present location and condition. However, inventory cost should not include: abnormal waste, storage costs, administrative overheads unrelated to production, selling costs, foreign exchange differences arising directly on the recent acquisition of inventories invoiced in a foreign currency interest cost when inventories are purchased with deferred settlement terms. For items that are interchangeable, IAS 2 allows the FIFO or weighted average cost formulas.

Any write-down to NRV should be recognized as an expense in the period in which the write-down occurs. Any reversal should be recognized in the income statement in the period in which the reversal occurs.

## 22.3.3    IAS 5—Non-Current Assets Held for Sale and Discontinued Operations

IFRS 5 achieves substantial convergence with the requirements of US SFAS 144 Accounting for the impairment or disposal of long-lived assets with respect to the timing of the classification of operations as discontinued operations and the presentation of such operations. Under IAS 5, the following conditions must be met for an asset (or "disposal group") to be classified as held for sale:

- management is committed to a plan to sell;
- the asset is available for immediate sale;

- an active program to locate a buyer is initiated;
- the sale is highly probable, within 12 months of classification as held for sale;
- the asset is being actively marketed for sale at a sales price reasonable in relation to its fair value; and
- actions required to complete the plan indicate that it is unlikely that plan will be significantly changed or withdrawn.

The assets need to be disposed of through sale. Therefore, operations that are expected to be wound down or abandoned would not meet the definition (but may be classified as discontinued once abandoned). The classification, presentation, and measurement requirements of IFRS 5 also apply to a non-current asset (or disposal group) that is classified as held for distribution to owners. To that end, the entity must be committed to the distribution, the assets must be available for immediate distribution and the distribution must be highly probable.

Measurement: Immediately before the initial classification of the asset as held for sale, the carrying amount of the asset will be measured in accordance with applicable IFRSs. Resulting adjustments are also recognized in accordance with applicable IFRSs. Impairment, if any, must be considered both at the time of classification as held for sale and subsequently. Likewise, a gain for any subsequent increase in fair value less costs to sell of an asset can be recognized in the profit or loss to the extent that it is not in excess of the cumulative impairment loss that has been recognized in accordance with IFRS 5 or previously in accordance with IAS 36.

Non-current assets or disposal groups that are classified as held for sale are not depreciated.

Presentation: Assets classified as held for sale, and the assets and liabilities included within a disposal group classified as held for sale, must be presented separately on the face of the statement of financial position.

### 22.3.4    IAS 7-Statements of Cash Flows

IAS 7 was reissued in December 1992, retitled in 2007, and is operative for financial statements covering periods beginning on or after January 1, 2004. Cash flows are inflows and outflows of cash and cash equivalents. Cash flow information is useful in assessing the ability of the entity to generate cash and cash equivalents and enables users to develop models to assess and compare the present value of the future cash flows of different entities. It also enhances the comparability of the reporting of operating performance by different entities because it eliminates the effects of using different accounting treatments for the same transactions and events. Cash flows exclude movements between items that constitute cash or cash equivalents because these components are part of the cash management of an entity rather than part of its operating, investing, and financing activities. Finally, investing and financing transactions that do not require the use of cash or cash equivalents are excluded from a statement of cash flow. Such transactions are disclosed elsewhere in the financial statements in a way that provides all the relevant information about these investing and financing activities.

### 22.3.4.1 Statements of Cash Flows: Presentation
The statement of cash flow shall report cash flows during the period classified by operating, investing, and financing activities.

*Operating Cash Flow*
Cash flows from operating activities are primarily derived from the principal revenue-producing activities of the entity. They generally result from the transactions and other events that enter into the determination of profit or loss. Examples of cash flows from operating activities include:

- cash receipts from the sale of goods and the rendering of services;
- cash receipts from royalties, fees, commissions, and other revenue;
- cash payments to suppliers for goods and services;
- cash payments to and on behalf of employees;
- cash receipts and cash payments of an insurance entity for premiums and claims, annuities, and other policy benefits;
- cash payments or refunds of income taxes unless they can be specifically identified with financing and investing activities; and
- cash receipts and payments from contracts held for dealing or trading purposes.

The amount of cash flows arising from operating activities is a key indicator of the extent to which the operations of the entity have generated sufficient cash flows to repay loans, maintain the operating capability of the entity, pay dividends, and make new investments without recourse to external sources of financing.

## Investing Cash Flow

Investing activities are the acquisition and disposal of long-term assets, and other investments not included in cash equivalents. Only expenditures that result in a recognized asset in the statement of financial position are eligible for classification as investing activities. Examples of cash flows arising from investing activities include:

- cash payments to acquire property, plant, and equipment, intangibles and other long-term assets, including payments relating to capitalized development costs and self-constructed property, plant, and equipment;
- cash receipts from sales of property, plant, and equipment, intangibles, and other long-term assets;
- cash payments to acquire equity or debt instruments of other entities and interests in joint ventures (other than payments for those instruments considered to be cash equivalents or those held for dealing or trading purposes);
- cash receipts from sales of equity or debt instruments of other entities and interests in joint ventures (other than receipts for those instruments considered to be cash equivalents and those held for dealing or trading purposes);
- cash advances and loans made to other parties (other than advances and loans made by a financial institution);
- cash receipts from the repayment of advances and loans made to other parties (other than advances and loans of a financial institution);
- cash payments for futures contracts, forward contracts, option contracts, and swap contracts except when the contracts are held for dealing or trading purposes, or the payments are classified as financing activities; and
- cash receipts from futures contracts, forward contracts, option contracts, and swap contracts except when the contracts are held for dealing or trading purposes, or the receipts are classified as financing activities.

## Financing Cash Flow

Financing activities are activities that result in changes in the size and composition of the contributed equity and borrowings of the entity. Cash flows arising from financing activities are important because it is useful in predicting claims on future cash flows by providers of capital to the entity. Examples of cash flows arising from financing activities include:

- cash proceeds from issuing shares or other equity instruments;
- cash payments to owners to acquire or redeem the entity's shares;
- cash proceeds from issuing debentures, loans, notes, bonds, mortgages, and other short- or long-term borrowings;
- cash repayments of amounts borrowed; and
- cash payments by a lessee for the reduction of the outstanding liability relating to a finance lease.

### 22.3.4.2 Reporting Cash Flow from Operating Activities

An entity shall report cash flows from operating activities using either: (a) the direct method, whereby major classes of gross cash receipts and gross cash payments are disclosed; or (b) the indirect method, whereby profit or loss is adjusted for the effects of transactions of a non-cash nature, any deferrals or accruals of past or future operating cash receipts or payments, and items of income or expense associated with investing or financing cash flows.

### 22.3.4.3 Foreign Currency Cash Flows

Cash flows arising from transactions in a foreign currency shall be recorded in an entity's functional currency by applying to the foreign currency amount the exchange rate between the functional currency and the foreign currency at the date of the cash flow. The cash flows of a foreign subsidiary shall be translated at the exchange rates between the functional currency and the foreign currency at the dates of the cash flows.

### 22.3.5    IAS16—Leases

*Effective for annual reporting periods beginning on or after January 1, 2019, with earlier application permitted (as long as IFRS 15 is also applied)*, IFRS 16 introduces a single lessee accounting model and requires a lessee to recognize assets and liabilities for all leases with a term of more than 12 months, unless the underlying asset is of low value. A lessee is required to recognize a right-of-use asset representing its right to use the underlying leased asset and a lease liability representing its obligation to make lease payments.

A lessee measures right-of-use assets similarly to other non-financial assets (such as property, plant, and equipment) and lease liabilities similarly to other financial liabilities. As a consequence, a lessee recognizes depreciation of the right-of-use asset and interest on the lease liability. The depreciation is usually on a straight-line basis. In the statement of cash flows, a lessee separates the total amount of cash paid into principal (presented within financing activities) and interest (presented within either operating or financing activities) in accordance with IAS 7.

Assets and liabilities arising from a lease are initially measured on a present value basis. The measurement includes non-cancelable lease payments (including inflation-linked payments) and also includes payments to be made in optional periods if the lessee is reasonably certain to exercise an option to extend the lease, or not to exercise an option to terminate the lease. The initial lease asset equals the lease liability in most cases.

The lease asset is the right to use the underlying asset and is presented in the statement of financial position either as part of property, plant, and equipment or as its own line item.

IFRS 16 substantially carries forward the lessor accounting requirements in IAS 17. Accordingly, a lessor continues to classify its leases as operating leases or finance leases, and to account for those two types of leases differently.

IFRS 16 replaces IAS 17 effective January 1, 2019, with earlier application permitted. IFRS 16 has the following transition provisions:

- Existing finance leases: continue to be treated as finance leases.
- Existing operating leases: option for full or limited retrospective restatement to reflect the requirements of IFRS 16.

### 22.3.5.1 Sale and Leaseback Transactions
A sale and leaseback transaction involves the sale of an asset and the leasing back of the same asset. The lease payment and the sale price are usually interdependent because they are negotiated as a package. The accounting treatment of a sale and leaseback transaction depends upon the type of lease involved.

### 22.3.5.2 A Sale and Leaseback Results in Finance Lease
If a sale and leaseback transaction results in a finance lease, any excess of sales proceeds over the carrying amount shall not be immediately recognized as income by a seller–lessee. Instead, it shall be deferred and amortized over the lease term.

### 22.3.5.3  A Sale and Leaseback Results in Operating Lease

If a sale and leaseback transaction results in an operating lease, and it is clear that the transaction is established at fair value, any profit or loss shall be recognized immediately. If the sale price is below fair value, any profit or loss shall be recognized immediately except that, if the loss is compensated for by future lease payments at below market price, it shall be deferred and amortized in proportion to the lease payments over the period for which the asset is expected to be used. If the sale price is above fair value, the excess over fair value shall be deferred and amortized over the period for which the asset is expected to be used.

## 22.3.6    IAS 24 Related Disclosures

IAS 24 was reissued in November 2009 and applies to annual periods beginning on or after January 1, 2011. IAS 24 defines various classes of entities and people as related parties and sets out the disclosures required in respect of those parties, including the compensation of key management personnel. Related party relationships are a normal feature of commerce and business. Such relationships could have an effect on the profit or loss and financial position of an entity. Thus, the profit or loss and financial position of an entity may be affected by a related party relationship even if related party transactions do not occur. The mere existence of the relationship may be sufficient to affect the transactions of the entity with other parties.

### 22.3.6.1  Disclosures

An entity shall disclose the relationship between a parent and its subsidiaries, information related to key management personnel compensation, and all related party transactions during the periods covered by the financial statements.

- Relationships between a parent and its subsidiaries shall be disclosed irrespective of whether there have been transactions between them. An entity shall disclose the name of its parent and, if different, the ultimate controlling party. If neither the entity's parent nor the ultimate controlling party produces consolidated financial statements available for public use, the name of the next most senior parent that does so shall also be disclosed.

- An entity shall disclose key management personnel compensation in total and for each of the following categories: (a) short-term employee benefits; (b) post-employment benefits; (c) other long-term benefits; (d) termination benefits; and (e) share-based payment.
- If an entity has had related party transactions during the periods covered by the financial statements, it shall disclose the nature of the related party relationship as well as information about those transactions and outstanding balances, including commitments, necessary for users to understand the potential effect of the relationship on the financial statements. At a minimum, disclosures shall include:
  a. The amount of the transactions;
  b. The amount of outstanding balances, including commitments, and:
    i. their terms and conditions, including whether they are secured, and the nature of the consideration to be provided in settlement; and
    ii. details of any guarantees given or received;
  c. Provisions for doubtful debts related to the amount of outstanding balances; and
  d. the expense recognized during the period in respect of bad or doubtful debts due from related parties.

These disclosures shall be made separately for each of the following categories: (a) the parent; (b) entities with joint control or significant influence over the entity; (c) subsidiaries; (d) associates; (e) joint ventures in which the entity is a venturer; (f) key management personnel of the entity or its parent; and (g) other related parties.

### 22.3.6.2 Exemption to Disclosures Rules: Government-Related Entities

A reporting entity is exempt from the disclosure requirements of paragraph 18 in relation to related party transactions and outstanding balances, including commitments, with: (a) a government that has control, joint control, or significant influence over the reporting entity and (b) another entity that is a related party because the same government has control, joint control, or significant influence over both the reporting entity and the other entity.

A reporting entity exempts from the disclosure shall disclose the following about the transactions and related outstanding balances:

a. The name of the government and the nature of its relationship with the reporting entity (i.e., control, joint control, or significant influence);
b. The following information in sufficient detail to enable users of the entity's financial statements to understand the effect of related party transactions on its financial statements:
    i. The nature and amount of each individually significant transaction and
    ii. For other transactions that are collectively, but not individually, significant, a qualitative or quantitative indication of their extent.

### 22.3.7   IAS 27—Consolidated Financial Statements

IAS 27, reissued in January 2008, applies to annual periods beginning on or after July 1, 2009. IAS 27 is superseded by IAS 27—Separate Financial Statements and IFRS 10—Consolidated Financial Statements with effect from annual periods beginning on or after January 1, 2013.

#### 22.3.7.1 Presentation of Consolidated Financial Statements
IAS 27 shall be applied in the preparation and presentation of consolidated financial statements for a group of entities under the control of a parent.[1] It also applies in accounting for investments in subsidiaries, jointly controlled entities, and associates when an entity elects, or is required by local regulations, to present separate financial statements.

A parent shall present consolidated financial statements in which it consolidates its investments in subsidiaries in accordance with IAS 27. However, a parent need not present consolidated financial statements if and only if:

a. the parent is itself a wholly-owned subsidiary, or is a partially owned subsidiary of another entity and its other owners, including those not otherwise entitled to vote, have been informed about,

---

[1] This Standard does not deal with methods of accounting for business combinations and their effects on consolidation, including goodwill arising on a business combination.

and do not object to, the parent not presenting consolidated financial statements;

b. the parent's debt or equity instruments are not traded in a public market (a domestic or foreign stock exchange or an over-the-counter market, including local and regional markets);

c. the parent did not file, nor is it in the process of filing, its financial statements with a securities commission or other regulatory organization for the purpose of issuing any class of instruments in a public market; and

d. the ultimate or any intermediate parent of the parent produces consolidated financial statements available for public use that comply with International Financial Reporting Standards.

### 22.3.7.2 Scope of Consolidated Financial Statements

Consolidated financial statements shall include all subsidiaries of the parent. Control is presumed to exist when the parent owns, directly or indirectly through subsidiaries, more than half of the voting power of an entity unless, in exceptional circumstances, it can be clearly demonstrated that such ownership does not constitute control. In assessing whether potential voting rights contribute to control, the entity examines all facts and circumstances (including the terms of exercise of the potential voting rights and any other contractual arrangements whether considered individually or in combination) that affect potential voting rights, except the intention of management and the financial ability to exercise or convert such rights.

### 22.3.7.3 Consolidation Procedures

Intragroup balances, transactions, income, and expenses shall be eliminated in full. Intragroup losses may indicate an impairment that requires recognition in the consolidated financial statements. In order that the consolidated financial statements present financial information about the group as that of a single economic entity, the following steps are then taken:

a. the carrying amount of the parent's investment in each subsidiary and the parent's portion of equity of each subsidiary are eliminated;

b. non-controlling interests in the profit or loss of consolidated subsidiaries for the reporting period are identified; and

c. non-controlling interests in the net assets of consolidated subsidiaries are identified separately from the parent's ownership interests in them. Non-controlling interests in the net assets consist of:

i. the amount of those non-controlling interests at the date of the original combination calculated in accordance with IFRS 3; and

ii. the non-controlling interests' share of changes in equity since the date of the combination.

Consolidated financial statements shall be prepared using uniform accounting policies for like transactions and other events in similar circumstances. If a member of the group uses accounting policies other than those adopted in the consolidated financial statements for like transactions and events in similar circumstances, appropriate adjustments are made to its financial statements in preparing the consolidated financial statements.

Non-controlling interests shall be presented in the consolidated statement of financial position within equity, separately from the equity of the owners of the parent. Changes in a parent's ownership interest in a subsidiary that do not result in a loss of control are accounted for as equity transactions (i.e., transactions with owners in their capacity as owners).

### 22.3.7.4 Loss of Control

A parent can lose control of a subsidiary with or without a change in absolute or relative ownership levels. A parent that loses control of a subsidiary must:

a. de-recognize the assets (including any goodwill) and liabilities of the subsidiary at their carrying amounts at the date when control is lost;

b. de-recognize the carrying amount of any non-controlling interests in the former subsidiary at the date when control is lost (including any components of other comprehensive income attributable to them);

c. recognize: (i) the fair value of the consideration received, if any, from the transaction, event, or circumstances that resulted in the loss of control and (ii) if the transaction that resulted in the loss of control involves a distribution of shares of the subsidiary to owners in their capacity as owners, that distribution;

d. recognize any investment retained in the former subsidiary at its fair value at the date when control is lost;

e. reclassify to profit or loss, or transfers directly to retained earnings if required in accordance with other IFRSs, the amounts identified in paragraph 35; and

f. recognize any resulting difference as a gain or loss in profit or loss attributable to the parent.

On the loss of control of a subsidiary, any investment retained in the former subsidiary and any amounts owed by or to the former subsidiary shall be accounted for in accordance with other IFRSs from the date when control is lost.

### 22.3.7.5 Accounting for Investments in Subsidiaries, Jointly Controlled Entities and Associates in Separate Financial Statements

When an entity prepares separate financial statements, it shall account for investments in subsidiaries, jointly controlled entities and associates: (a) at cost, or (b) in accordance with IAS 39.

The entity shall apply the same accounting for each category of investments. Investments accounted for at cost shall be accounted for in accordance with IFRS 5 Non-current Assets Held for Sale and Discontinued Operations when they are classified as held for sale (or included in a disposal group that is classified as held for sale) in accordance with IFRS 5. The measurement of investments accounted for in accordance with IAS 39 is not changed in such circumstances. An entity shall recognize a dividend from a subsidiary, jointly controlled entity or associate in profit or loss in its separate financial statements when its right to receive the dividend is established. Investments in jointly controlled entities and associates that are accounted for in accordance with IAS 39 in the consolidated financial statements shall be accounted for in the same way in the investor's separate financial statements.

### 22.3.7.6 Disclosure

The following disclosures shall be made in consolidated financial statements:

a. the nature of the relationship between the parent and a subsidiary when the parent does not own, directly or indirectly through subsidiaries, more than half of the voting power;

b. the reasons why the ownership, directly or indirectly through subsidiaries, of more than half of the voting or potential voting power of an investee does not constitute control;

c. the end of the reporting period of the financial statements of a subsidiary when such financial statements are used to prepare consolidated financial statements and are as of a date or for a period that is different from that of the parent's financial statements and the reason for using a different date or period;

d. the nature and extent of any significant restrictions (e.g., resulting from borrowing arrangements or regulatory requirements) on the ability of subsidiaries to transfer funds to the parent in the form of cash dividends or to repay loans or advances;

e. a schedule that shows the effects of any changes in a parent's ownership interest in a subsidiary that do not result in a loss of control on the equity attributable to owners of the parent; and

f. if control of a subsidiary is lost, the parent shall disclose the gain or loss, if any, and:

 i. the portion of that gain or loss attributable to recognizing any investment retained in the former subsidiary at its fair value at the date when control is lost; and

 ii. the line item(s) in the statement of comprehensive income in which the gain or loss is recognized (if not presented separately in the statement of comprehensive income).

When separate financial statements are prepared for a parent that, elects not to prepare consolidated financial statements, those separate financial statements shall disclose:

a. the fact that the financial statements are separate financial statements; that the exemption from consolidation has been used; the name and country of incorporation or residence of the entity whose consolidated financial statements that comply with International Financial Reporting Standards have been produced for public use; and the address where those consolidated financial statements are obtainable;

b. a list of significant investments in subsidiaries, jointly controlled entities and associates, including the name, country of incorporation or residence, proportion of ownership interest and, if different, proportion of voting power held; and

c. a description of the method used to account for the investments listed under (b).

When a parent (other than a parent aforementioned), venturer with an interest in a jointly controlled entity or an investor in an associate prepares separate financial statements, those separate financial statements shall disclose:

  a. the fact that the statements are separate financial statements and the reasons why those statements are prepared if not required by law;
  b. a list of significant investments in subsidiaries, jointly controlled entities and associates, including the name, country of incorporation or residence, proportion of ownership interest and, if different, proportion of voting power held; and
  c. a description of the method used to account for the investments listed under (b);

and shall identify the financial statements prepared in accordance with the aforementioned presentation rules or IAS 28 and IAS 31 to which they relate.

### 22.3.8    IAS 32, Financial Instrument—Presentation

IAS 32 was reissued in December 2003 and applies to annual periods beginning on or after January 1, 2005. It aims to establish principles for presenting financial instruments as liabilities or equity and for offsetting financial assets and liabilities.[2] IAS 32 applies to those contracts to buy or sell a non-financial item that can be settled net in cash or another financial instrument, except for contracts that were entered into and continue to be held for the purpose of the receipt or delivery of a non-financial item in accordance with the entity's expected purchase, sale, or usage requirements.[3]

*Classification as Liability or Equity*
The fundamental principle of IAS 32 is that a financial instrument should be classified as either a financial liability or an equity instrument according to the substance of the contract, not its legal form, and the definitions of financial liability and equity instrument. Two exceptions from

[2] IAS 32.1.
[3] IAS 32.8.

this principle are certain puttable instruments meeting specific criteria and certain obligations arising on liquidation (see below). The entity must make the decision at the time the instrument is initially recognized. The classification is not subsequently changed based on changed circumstances.[4]

A financial instrument is an equity instrument only if (a) the instrument includes no contractual obligation to deliver cash or another financial asset to another entity and (b) if the instrument will or may be settled in the issuer's own equity instruments, it is either: (i) a non-derivative that includes no contractual obligation for the issuer to deliver a variable number of its own equity instruments; or (ii) a derivative that will be settled only by the issuer exchanging a fixed amount of cash or another financial asset for a fixed number of its own equity instruments.[5]

*Puttable Instruments*
Puttable financial instruments and obligations arising only on liquidation that currently meet the definition of a financial liability will be classified as equity because they represent the residual interest in the net assets of the entity.[6]

*Classifications of Right Issues*
Right issues offered for a fixed amount of foreign currency current practice appear to require such issues to be accounted for as derivative liabilities. The amendment states that if such rights are issued pro rata to an entity's all existing shareholders in the same class for a fixed amount of currency, they should be classified as equity regardless of the currency in which the exercise price is denominated.

*Compound Financial Instruments*
Some financial instruments—sometimes called compound instruments—have both a liability and an equity component from the issuer's perspective. In that case, IAS 32 requires that the component parts be accounted for and presented separately according to their substance based on the definitions

---

[4]IAS 32.15.
[5]IAS 32.16.
[6]IAS 32.16A-D.

of liability and equity. The split is made at issuance and not revised for subsequent changes in market interest rates, share prices, or other event that changes the likelihood that the conversion option will be exercised.[7]

*Treasury Shares*

The cost of an entity's own equity instruments that it has reacquired ("treasury shares") is deducted from equity. Gain or loss is not recognized on the purchase, sale, issue, or cancelation of treasury shares. Treasury shares may be acquired and held by the entity or by other members of the consolidated group. Consideration paid or received is recognized directly in equity.[8]

*Offsetting*

IAS 32 also prescribes rules for the offsetting of financial assets and financial liabilities. It specifies that a financial asset and a financial liability should be offset and the net amount reported when, and only when, an entity.[9] (a) has a legally enforceable right to set off the amounts and (b) intends either to settle on a net basis, or to realize the asset and settle the liability simultaneously.[10]

*Cost of Issuing or Reacquiring Equity Instruments*

Costs of issuing or reacquiring equity instruments (other than in a business combination) are accounted for as a deduction from equity, net of any related income tax benefit[11] (IAS 32.35).

### 22.3.9    IAS 33—Earnings Per Shares

IAS 33 was reissued in December 2003 and applies to annual periods beginning on or after January 1, 2005. IAS 33 applies to entities whose securities are publicly traded or that are in the process of issuing securities to the public.[12] Other entities that choose to present EPS information

---

[7] IAS 32.29–30.
[8] IAS 32.33.
[9] IAS 32.42.
[10] IAS 32.48.
[11] IAS 32.35.
[12] IAS 33.2.

must also comply with IAS 33.[13] An entity whose securities are publicly traded (or that is in process of public issuance) must present, on the face of the statement of comprehensive income, basic and diluted EPS for.[14] Basic and diluted EPS must be presented even if the amounts are negative (loss per share).[15] An entity that reports a discontinued operation must disclose the basic and diluted amounts per share for the discontinued operation either on the face of the comprehensive income (or separate income statement if presented) or in the notes to the financial statements.[16]

*Basic EPS*

Basic EPS is calculated by dividing profit or loss attributable to ordinary equity holders of the parent entity (the numerator) by the weighted average number of ordinary shares outstanding (the denominator) during the period. The earnings numerators used for the computation is a net amount that is obtained after deducting all expenses including taxes, minority interests, and preference dividends. The denominator (number of shares) is computed by adjusting the shares in issue at the beginning of the period by the number of shares bought back or issued during the period, multiplied by a time-weighting factor. It should also be noted that contingently issuable shares are included in the basic EPS denominator when the contingency has been met.[17]

*Diluted EPS*

Diluted EPS is calculated by adjusting the earnings and number of shares for the effects of dilutive options and other dilutive potential ordinary shares.[18] The effects of anti-dilutive potential ordinary shares are ignored in calculating diluted EPS.[19]

[13]IAS 33.3.
[14]IAS 33.66.
[15]IAS 33.69.
[16]IAS 33.68 and 68A.
[17]IAS 33.24.
[18]IAS 33.31.
[19]IAS 33.41.

*Retrospective Adjustments*

When the number of ordinary or potential ordinary shares outstanding increases as a result of a capitalization, bonus issue, or share split, or decreases as a result of a reverse share split, the computation of the basic and diluted EPS for all periods presented shall be adjusted retrospectively. In such situations, the EPS calculations for those and any prior period financial statements presented are based on the new number of shares. Disclosure is required.[20] Likewise, basic and diluted EPS shall also be adjusted for the effects of errors and adjustments resulting from changes in accounting policies, accounted for retrospectively.[21]

### 22.3.10    IAS 34—Interim Financial Reporting

IAS 34 was issued in June 1998 and is operative for periods beginning on or after January 1, 1999. It aims to provide the minimum content of an interim financial report and to prescribe the principles for recognition and measurement in complete or condensed financial statements for an interim period. IAS 34 does not mandate which entities should publish interim financial reports, how frequently, or how soon after the end of an interim period. IAS 34 encourages publicly traded entities to provide interim financial reports that conform to the recognition, measurement, and disclosure principles set out in IAS 34, at least as of the end of the first half of their financial year, such reports to be made available not later than 60 days after the end of the interim period.

*Minimum Content of the Interim Financial Reporting*

The minimum components specified for an interim financial report are[22]:

- a condensed balance sheet (statement of financial position);
- either (a) a condensed statement of comprehensive income or (b) a condensed statement of comprehensive income and a condensed income statement;
- a condensed statement of changes in equity;
- a condensed statement of cash flows;
- selected explanatory notes.

---

[20] IAS 33.64.
[21] IAS 33.64.
[22] IAS 34.8.

If an entity publishes a complete set of financial statements in its interim financial report, the form and content of those statements shall conform to the requirements of IAS 1 for a complete set of financial statements. Likewise, if an entity publishes a set of condensed financial statements in its interim financial report, those condensed statements shall include, at a minimum, each of the headings and subtotals that were included in its most recent annual financial statements and the selected explanatory notes as required by this Standard. Additional line items or notes shall be included if their omission would make the condensed interim financial statements misleading.

*The Periods to Be Covered*
The periods to be covered by the interim financial statements are as follows[23]:

- balance sheet (statement of financial position) as of the end of the current interim period and a comparative balance sheet as of the end of the immediately preceding financial year
- statement of comprehensive income (and income statement, if presented) for the current interim period and cumulatively for the current financial year to date, with comparative statements for the comparable interim periods (current and year to date) of the immediately preceding financial year
- statement of changes in equity cumulatively for the current financial year to date, with a comparative statement for the comparable year-to-date period of the immediately preceding financial year
- statement of cash flows cumulatively for the current financial year to date, with a comparative statement for the comparable year-to-date period of the immediately preceding financial year

*Significant Events and Transactions*
An entity shall include in its interim financial report an explanation of events and transactions that are significant to an understanding of the changes in financial position and performance of the entity since the end of the last annual reporting period. A user of an entity's interim financial report will have access to the most recent annual financial report of that entity.

---

[23] IAS 34.20.

Therefore, it is unnecessary for the notes to an interim financial report to provide relatively insignificant updates to the information that was reported in the notes in the most recent annual financial report. The following is a non-exhaustive list of events and transactions for which disclosures would be required if they are significant:

a. the write-down of inventories to net realizable value and the reversal of such a write-down;
b. recognition of a loss from the impairment of financial assets, property, plant, and equipment, intangible assets, or other assets, and the reversal of such an impairment loss;
c. the reversal of any provisions for the costs of restructuring;
d. acquisitions and disposals of items of property, plant, and equipment;
e. commitments for the purchase of property, plant, and equipment;
f. litigation settlements;
g. corrections of prior period errors;
h. changes in the business or economic circumstances that affect the fair value of the entity's financial assets and financial liabilities, whether those assets or liabilities are recognized at fair value or amortized cost;
i. any loan default or breach of a loan agreement that has not been remedied on or before the end of the reporting period; and
j. related party transactions;
k. transfers between levels of the fair value hierarchy used in measuring the fair value of financial instruments;
l. changes in the classification of financial assets as a result of a change in the purpose or use of those assets; and
m. changes in contingent liabilities or contingent assets.

*Accounting Policies, Measurement, and Materiality*
An entity shall apply the same accounting policies in its interim financial statements as are applied in its annual financial statements, except for accounting policy changes made after the date of the most recent annual financial statements that are to be reflected in the next annual financial statements. However, the frequency of an entity's reporting (annual, half-yearly, or quarterly) shall not affect the measurement of its annual results. To achieve that objective, measurements for interim reporting purposes shall be made on a year-to-date basis.

Measurements for interim reporting purposes should be made on a year-to-date basis, so that the frequency of the entity's reporting does not affect the measurement of its annual results.[24] Important measurement points include:

- Revenues that are received seasonally, cyclically, or occasionally within a financial year should not be anticipated or deferred as of the interim date, if anticipation or deferral would not be appropriate at the end of the financial year.[25]
- Costs that are incurred unevenly during a financial year should be anticipated or deferred for interim reporting purposes if, and only if, it is also appropriate to anticipate or defer that type of cost at the end of the financial year.[26]
- Income tax expense should be recognized based on the best estimate of the weighted average annual effective income tax rate expected for the full financial year.

The measurement procedures to be followed in an interim financial report shall be designed to ensure that the resulting information is reliable and that all material financial information that is relevant to an understanding of the financial position or performance of the entity is appropriately disclosed.

While measurements in both annual and interim financial reports are often based on reasonable estimates, the preparation of interim financial reports generally will require a greater use of estimation methods than annual financial reports.

In deciding how to recognize, measure, classify, or disclose an item for interim financial reporting purposes, materiality is to be assessed in relation to the interim period financial data, not forecast annual data.[27]

If an estimate of an amount reported in an interim period is changed significantly during the financial interim period in the financial year but a separate financial report is not published for that period, the nature and amount of that change must be disclosed in the notes to the annual financial statements.[28]

[24] IAS 34.28.
[25] IAS 34.37.
[26] IAS 34.39.
[27] IAS 34.23.
[28] IAS 34.26.

*Restatement of Previously Reported Interim Periods*

A change in accounting policy, other than one for which the transition is specified by a new IFRS, shall be reflected by:

a. restating the financial statements of prior interim periods of the current financial year and the comparable interim periods of any prior financial years that will be restated in the annual financial statements in accordance with IAS 8; or

b. when it is impracticable to determine the cumulative effect at the beginning of the financial year of applying a new accounting policy to all prior periods, adjusting the financial statements of prior interim periods of the current financial year, and comparable interim periods of prior financial years to apply the new accounting policy prospectively from the earliest date practicable.

# PART VI

# Case Study

Financial statement analysis involves analyzing the firm's financial statements to extract information susceptible to provide relevant information to a large audience of financial statements' readers. For instance, an analysis of the financial statement would reveal whether the firm is able to meet its long-term debt commitment, whether the firm is financially distressed, whether the company is using its physical assets efficiently, whether the firm is generating adequate return for its shareholders, whether the firm can sustain its competitive advantage, etc. While the information provided and analyzed is historical, the intent is clear to arrive at a bunch of relevant information (or recommendations) that meets the expectations of all readers.

Financial analysis is performed by both internal management and external groups. Management would like to assess or evaluate the overall current performance, identify problem/opportunity areas, develop budgets, and implement strategies for the future. External groups (such as investors, regulators, lenders, suppliers, customers) also perform financial analysis in deciding whether to invest in a particular firm, whether to extend credit, etc. There are several rating agencies (such as Moody's, Standard & Poors) that routinely perform financial analysis of firms in order to arrive at a composite rating.

In the following chapter, which is aimed to introduce readers to the practice of financial statement analysis, I chose to start with the industry analysis, including the Porter's *Five Forces*. Since its introduction in 1979, Michael Porter's *Five Forces* has become the de facto framework for industry analysis. The five forces measure the competitiveness of the market deriving its attractiveness. The analyst uses conclusions derived from the analysis to determine the company's risk from its industry (current or potential). The five forces are (i) threat of new entrants, (ii) threat of substitute products or services, (iii) bargaining power of buyers, (iv) bargaining power of suppliers, and (v) competitive rivalry among existing firms. For each selected corporation, I attach the consolidated statement of income, the consolidated balance sheet (for some the statement of shareholders' equity), and the consolidated statement of cash flows. There is specific information analysts look after in each one of these reported statements. For instance, to get the consolidated statement of income, one has to respond to the following questions: (i) Has the size of the company changed? (ii) Have the operations or the nature of the operations changed? (iii) Are there unusual items? and (iv) What is the quality of the reported earnings? The analysis would be complete with both the vertical and horizontal comparisons, as well as the ratio analysis shows overall industry trends and the particular performances of the chosen companies.

• Financial Statement Analysis

The three commonly used tools available for any financial statement analysis are: (i) the horizontal analysis, (ii) the vertical analysis, and (iii) the ratio analysis.

*Horizontal analysis* evaluates a series of financial statement data over a period of time. According to the FASB, for any FY, a company should present an income statement, which represents the current two years and the two previous FY. The balance sheet for any given FY includes the statements of the previous years. Finally, the statements of cash flows for any given FY reproduce the statement of cash flows for the previous FY. Horizontal analysis allows quick comparison in terms of increase or decrease within the reported financial statements.

Horizontal analysis looks at amounts on the financial statements over the past years.

### Example

The amount of cash reported on the balance sheet at December 31 2012, 2013, 2014 will be expressed as a percentage of the December 31, 2012, amount. Instead of dollar amounts, the horizontal analysis shows a percentage increase number from FY 2012 up to 2014.

The same analysis is conducted for each item on the balance sheet and for each item on the income statement. This allows readers of the financial statements to see how each item has changed in relationship to the changes in other items. Horizontal analysis is also referred to as trend analysis.

*Vertical analysis*, also known as "common-size analysis," expresses each item of the reported financial statements (statement of income, statement of position, and statement of cash flows) as a percentage of a base amount (i.e., total assets or net sales). For instance, the vertical analysis of the balance sheet means every amount on the balance sheet is restated to be a percentage of total assets.

## Example

If inventory is $50,000 and total assets are $500,000, then inventory is presented as 10 ($50,000 divided by $500,000). If cash is $20,000, then it will be presented as 25 ($20,000 divided by $500,000), and so on. The total of the assets will now add up to 100. The restated amounts from the vertical analysis of the balance sheet will be presented as a common-size balance sheet. A common-size balance sheet allows you to compare your company's balance sheet to another company's balance sheet or to the average for its industry.

Vertical analysis of an income statement results in every item of the income statement amount being presented as a percentage of sales.

## Example

If sales were $2,000,000, they would be restated to be 100 ($2,000,000 divided by $2,000,000). If the cost of goods sold is $500,000, it will be presented as 50 ($500,000 divided by sales of $1,000,000). If interest expense is $25,000, it will be presented as 4 ($25,000 divided by $1,000,000). The restated amounts are known as a common-size income statement.

As for the common-size balance sheet, the common-size income statement allows a comparison of one company's income statement to another company's or to the industry average.

*Ratio analysis* expresses quick financial measurements based on selected items from the financial statements. Ratio analysis is a form of financial statement analysis that is used to obtain a quick indication of a firm's financial performance in several key areas. Ratios are key to financial analysis, as they provide input for evaluating and comparing a company to its peers or to an industry benchmark.

It should be noted that a comprehensive financial statement analysis also provides key information concerning the company's earning power and irregular items, as well as the quality of the earnings.

- Earning Power and Irregular items

Earning power is used to analyze stocks to assess whether the underlying company is worthy of investment. Possessing greater long-term earnings, power is one indication that a stock may be a good investment. Several metrics, such as the company's return on assets (ROA), the company's return on equity (ROE), are used to determine a company's earnings power. The higher the BEP ratio, the more effective a company is at generating income from its assets.

---

### Example

Jackson Inc. earnings before interest and taxes for the financial year ended December 31, 2014 are $15 million, while its total assets as of December 31, 2014 are $90 million. Jackson Inc.net income for the same period is $5 million.
Compute Jackson Inc. basic earning power ratio and its return on assets.

$$\text{Basic Earning Power (BEP) Ratio} = \frac{\text{EBIT}}{\text{Total assets}} = \frac{\$15 \text{ million}}{\$90 \text{ million}} = 6\%$$

$$\text{Return On Assets (ROA) Ratio} = \frac{\text{Net income}}{\text{Total assets}} = \frac{\$5 \text{ million}}{\$90 \text{ million}} = 5.55\%$$

• Quality of Earning

A quality of earnings report provides a detailed analysis of all the components of a company's revenue and expenses. The primary objective of a quality of earnings report is to assess the sustainability and accuracy of historical earnings as well as the achievability of future projections. The measure of quality is the degree to which earnings are generated from internally developed initiatives, as opposed to external forces. If a company has increased earnings year over year from improved cost efficiencies or sales generated from a marketing campaign, that company has a high quality of earnings. If a company's earnings are attributed to outside source such as increasing commodity prices, this is seen as low quality of earnings.

Quality of earnings analysis includes[1]:

(a) Breakdown of revenue by appropriate components, such as customers and product/service lines;

(b) Analysis of historic revenue trends;

(c) Determination of one-time expenses versus recurring expenses;

(d) Determination of fixed versus variable costs;

(e) Analysis of impact on both revenue and expenses due to management changes;

(f) Analysis of assumptions used in cash flow projections and scenario analysis.

The below selected companies are illustrative and aim to introduce students to financial analyst world.

---

[1] John Carvalho (2015): divestopedia.

# CHAPTER 23

# Apple and Microsoft Case Study

## 23.1    INDUSTRY ANALYSIS

i. *Threat of New Entrants:* The threat of new entrants for Microsoft is very low. In fact, Microsoft has practically been a monopoly company. It held over 90% of the market share with their operating system and browser. Competitors have a hard time accessing the market due to economic, technological, or legal barriers.

ii. *Bargaining Power of Suppliers:* The main suppliers for the industry are hardware device suppliers and software tool suppliers. Principle hardware components are mainly obtained from a sole supplier (Intel). The power of suppliers is strong because of high importance of inputs.

iii. *Bargaining Power of Buyers:* The main buyers in the industry are corporations, individual consumers, as well as government bodies. These buyers could be divided into two segments: (1) lower end buyers who are small businesses that serve local or regional firms and (2) upper end buyers that include large corporations and customers for whom a name reputation carries importance. The buying power of these customers is limited because there are few alternatives. Microsoft's reputation in the industry helps gain a competitive advantage.

iv. *Threat of Substitute Products:* Threat of substitutes always exists. Apple is one of its most important threats. Microsoft's profitability suffered when better Apple software came into the market.

© The Author(s) 2018
F. I. Lessambo, *Financial Statements*,
https://doi.org/10.1007/978-3-319-99984-5_23

Microsoft has always positioned itself at a lower price than Apple to retain their position in the software market.

v. *Rivalry Among Competing Firms:* Competition among existing rivals is forcing to new product development, discounting, advertisement, and service improvements. The dominant players like Microsoft continue to intensify competition in the high-end market from the diversification and other fields. The low switching and high exit barriers also add to the rivalry. Thus, there is moderate competition in the industry.

## 23.2    APPLE

### 23.2.1    Overview

Apple Inc. is a US Company. Founded by Steve Jobs and Steve Wozniak nearly four decades ago in a residential garage, Apple has become the world's most valuable high tech company. Its success results from a simple priority: Apple strives to make the best products on Earth through a singular focus on its customers. Apple has introduced new products, new categories, and even new markets that have profoundly improved people's lives around the world. True to its California roots, Apple remains headquartered in Cupertino, and it is now building a large new campus in that community to accommodate its substantial growth over the past decade.

Apple designs, manufactures, and markets a range of personal computers, mobile communication and media devices, and portable digital music players. The Company also provides consumers a variety of related software and services, including access to third-party digital content and applications. Apple sells its products worldwide through retail stores, online stores, its direct sales force, third-party cellular network carriers, wholesalers, retailers, and value-added resellers. The hallmarks for which Apple is best known creativity, innovation and design-drive its development activities, almost all of which take place on Apple's main campus in Cupertino.

Apple launched the personal computer revolution in 1976 with the Apple I, followed by the highly successful Apple II. In 1984, Apple reignited that revolution when it introduced its first category-defining product, the Macintosh. With innovations such as the graphical user interface and mouse, the Macintosh made computing accessible to consumers and set the standard for all personal computers that followed.

In 1998, Apple introduced the iMac, a groundbreaking new computer for the consumer market. In 2001, the Company introduced the iPod, another category-defining product that marked Apple's expansion beyond personal computing into the digital marketplace.

Two years later, Apple launched the iTunes online music store, changing forever the way consumers legally acquired digital content. The innovative design and customer-focused engineering evident in these products laid the foundation for the Company's explosive growth over the next decade.

In 2007, Apple introduced the iPhone, which quickly set the standard for smartphones. In 2010, Apple introduced the iPad, which established a new market for tablet computers. The iPhone and the iPad illustrate Apple's emphasis on delivering an unmatched user experience and superior technical performance. These products generated unprecedented commercial success and growth for the Company and created extraordinary value for its shareholders.

In 2008, following the introduction of the iPhone, Apple launched the App Store, which has fundamentally transformed how customers acquire and use software. Today, Apple customers can choose from among 850,000 applications in the App Store. Customers currently download approximately 800 apps per second. Just days ago, the fifty billion app was downloaded—about seven downloaded apps for every person on Earth.

The Company sells its products worldwide through its retail stores, online stores, and direct sales force, as well as through third-party cellular network carriers, wholesalers, retailers, and value-added resellers. In addition, the Apple sells a variety of third-party iPhone, iPad, Mac and iPod compatible products, including application software, and various accessories, through its online and retail stores. The Company sells to consumers; small and mid-sized businesses; and education, enterprise, and government customers.

### 23.2.2   *Business Strategy*

The Company is committed to bringing the best user experience to its customers through its innovative hardware, software, and services. The Company's business strategy leverages its unique ability to design and develop its own operating systems, hardware, application software, and services to provide its customers new products and solutions with superior ease-of-use, seamless integration, and innovative design. The Company believes continual investment in research and development, marketing, and advertising is critical to the development and sale of innovative products and technologies. As part of its strategy, the Company continues to expand its platform for the discovery and delivery of third-party digital content and applications through the iTunes Store. As part of the iTunes Store, the Company's App Store and iBooks Store allow customers to discover and download applications and books through either a Mac or Windows-based computer or through "iOS devices," namely iPhone, iPad, and iPod touch ®. The Company's Mac App Store allows customers to easily discover, download, and install Mac applications. The Company also supports a community for the development of third-party software and hardware products and digital content that complement the Company's offerings. The Company believes a high-quality buying experience with knowledgeable salespersons who can convey the value of the Company's products and services greatly enhances its ability to attract and retain customers. Therefore, the Company's strategy also includes enhancing and expanding its own retail and online stores and its third-party distribution network to effectively reach more customers and provide them with a high-quality sales and post-sales support experience.

### 23.2.3    Financial Statements

#### 23.2.3.1  Apple—Consolidated Statement of Income
See Table 23.1.

#### 23.2.3.2  Apple—Consolidated Balance Sheet
The amount of the net sales has increased consistently from 2012 to 2014, with a significant increase in 2013. Likewise, the COGS shows the same trend, that is, an increase from 2012 to 2014. However, as to the net income, it has declined from 2012 to 2013 with a little improvement in 2014 (Table 23.2).

The amount of the total assets has increased from $207,000 (2013) to $231,839 (2014) with a big change in the long-term marketable securities. The amount of the total liabilities has also increased from $207,000 (2013) to $231,839 (2014).

## Table 23.1  Apple—Consolidated statement of income

**CONSOLIDATED STATEMENTS OF OPERATIONS**
(In millions, except number of shares which are reflected in thousands and per share amounts)

|  | Years ended | | |
|---|---|---|---|
|  | September 27, | September 28, | September 29, |
|  | 2014 | 2013 | 2012 |
| Net sales | $ 182,795 | $ 170,910 | $ 156,508 |
| Cost of sales | 112,258 | 106,606 | 87,846 |
| Gross margin | 70,537 | 64,304 | 68,662 |
| Operating expenses: |  |  |  |
| Research and development | 6,041 | 4,475 | 3,381 |
| Selling, general and administrative | 11,993 | 10,830 | 10,040 |
| Total operating expenses | 18,034 | 15,305 | 13,421 |
| Operating income | 52,503 | 48,999 | 55,241 |
| Other income/(expense), net | 980 | 1,156 | 522 |
| Income before provision for income taxes | 53,483 | 50,155 | 55,763 |
| Provision for income taxes | 13,973 | 13,118 | 14,030 |
| Net income | $ 39,510 | $ 37,037 | $ 41,733 |
| |  |  |  |
| Earnings per share: |  |  |  |
| Basic | $ 6.49 | $ 5.72 | $ 6.38 |
| Diluted | $ 6.45 | $ 5.68 | $ 6.31 |
| |  |  |  |
| Shares used in computing earnings per share: |  |  |  |
| Basic | 6,085,572 | 6,477,320 | 6,543,726 |
| Diluted | 6,122,663 | 6,521,634 | 6,617,483 |
| |  |  |  |
| Cash dividends declared per common share | $ 1.82 | $ 1.64 | $ 0.38 |

See accompanying Notes to Consolidated Financial Statements.

Apple Inc. | 2014 Form 10-K | 45

## Table 23.2  Apple—Consolidated balance sheet

**CONSOLIDATED BALANCE SHEETS**
(In millions, except number of shares which are reflected in thousands and par value)

|  | September 27, | September 28, |
|---|---|---|
|  | 2014 | 2013 |
| **ASSETS:** |  |  |
| Current assets: |  |  |
| Cash and cash equivalents | $ 13,844 | $ 14,259 |
| Short-term marketable securities | 11,233 | 26,287 |
| Accounts receivable, less allowances of $86 and $99, respectively | 17,460 | 13,102 |
| Inventories | 2,111 | 1,764 |
| Deferred tax assets | 4,318 | 3,453 |
| Vendor non-trade receivables | 9,759 | 7,539 |
| Other current assets | 9,806 | 6,882 |
| Total current assets | 68,531 | 73,286 |
| Long-term marketable securities | 130,162 | 106,215 |
| Property, plant and equipment, net | 20,624 | 16,597 |
| Goodwill | 4,616 | 1,577 |
| Acquired intangible assets, net | 4,142 | 4,179 |
| Other assets | 3,764 | 5,146 |
| Total assets | $ 231,839 | $ 207,000 |
| **LIABILITIES AND SHAREHOLDERS' EQUITY:** |  |  |
| Current liabilities: |  |  |
| Accounts payable | $ 30,196 | $ 22,367 |
| Accrued expenses | 18,453 | 13,856 |
| Deferred revenue | 8,491 | 7,435 |
| Commercial paper | 6,308 | 0 |
| Total current liabilities | 63,448 | 43,658 |
| Deferred revenue – non-current | 3,031 | 2,625 |
| Long-term debt | 28,987 | 16,960 |
| Other non-current liabilities | 24,826 | 20,208 |
| Total liabilities | 120,292 | 83,451 |
| Commitments and contingencies |  |  |
| Shareholders' equity: |  |  |
| Common stock and additional paid-in capital, $0.00001 par value; 12,600,000 shares authorized; |  |  |
| 5,866,161 and 6,294,494 shares issued and outstanding, respectively | 23,313 | 19,764 |
| Retained earnings | 87,152 | 104,256 |
| Accumulated other comprehensive income/(loss) | 1,082 | (471) |
| Total shareholders' equity | 111,547 | 123,549 |
| Total liabilities and shareholders' equity | $ 231,839 | $ 207,000 |

*Source* SEC—Apple, Form 10-K

### 23.2.3.3 Apple—Consolidated Statement of Shareholders' Equity

The balance amount of the total shareholders' equity has increased from 2011 to 2013. Fiscal year 2014 shows a decrease from the previous year: $123,549 (2013) to $111,547 (2014) (Table 23.3).

### 23.2.3.4 Apple—Consolidated Statement of Cash Flows

A constant increase of the operating activities: $50,856 (2012) to $53,666 (2013) to $59,713 (2014). However, the firm has significantly decreased its investing activities from the same period of time: $48,227 (2012) to $33,774 (2013) to $22,579 (2014). The financing activities seem to be constant with a little increase from $10,746 (2012) to $14,259 (2013) (Table 23.4).

**Table 23.3**   Apple—Consolidated statement of shareholders' equity

CONSOLIDATED STATEMENTS OF SHAREHOLDERS' EQUITY
(In millions, except number of shares which are reflected in thousands)

| | Common Stock and Additional Paid-In Capital | | Retained Earnings | Accumulated Other Comprehensive Income/(Loss) | Total Shareholders' Equity |
| --- | --- | --- | --- | --- | --- |
| | Shares | Amount | | | |
| Balances as of September 24, 2011 | 6,504,937 | $  13,331 | $  62,841 | $  443 | $  76,615 |
| Net income | 0 | 0 | 41,733 | 0 | 41,733 |
| Other comprehensive income/(loss) | 0 | 0 | 0 | 56 | 56 |
| Dividends and dividend equivalents declared | 0 | 0 | (2,523) | 0 | (2,523) |
| Share-based compensation | 0 | 1,740 | 0 | 0 | 1,740 |
| Common stock issued, net of shares withheld for employee taxes | 69,521 | 200 | (762) | 0 | (562) |
| Tax benefit from equity awards, including transfer pricing adjustments | 0 | 1,151 | 0 | 0 | 1,151 |
| Balances as of September 29, 2012 | 6,574,458 | 16,422 | 101,289 | 499 | 118,210 |
| Net income | 0 | 0 | 37,037 | 0 | 37,037 |
| Other comprehensive income/(loss) | 0 | 0 | 0 | (970) | (970) |
| Dividends and dividend equivalents declared | 0 | 0 | (10,676) | 0 | (10,676) |
| Repurchase of common stock | (328,837) | 0 | (22,950) | 0 | (22,950) |
| Share-based compensation | 0 | 2,253 | 0 | 0 | 2,253 |
| Common stock issued, net of shares withheld for employee taxes | 48,873 | (143) | (444) | 0 | (587) |
| Tax benefit from equity awards, including transfer pricing adjustments | 0 | 1,232 | 0 | 0 | 1,232 |
| Balances as of September 28, 2013 | 6,294,494 | 19,764 | 104,256 | (471) | 123,549 |
| Net income | 0 | 0 | 39,510 | 0 | 39,510 |
| Other comprehensive income/(loss) | 0 | 0 | 0 | 1,553 | 1,553 |
| Dividends and dividend equivalents declared | 0 | 0 | (11,215) | 0 | (11,215) |
| Repurchase of common stock | (488,677) | 0 | (45,000) | 0 | (45,000) |
| Share-based compensation | 0 | 2,863 | 0 | 0 | 2,863 |
| Common stock issued, net of shares withheld for employee taxes | 60,344 | (49) | (399) | 0 | (448) |
| Tax benefit from equity awards, including transfer pricing adjustments | 0 | 735 | 0 | 0 | 735 |
| Balances as of September 27, 2014 | 5,866,161 | $  23,313 | $  87,152 | $  1,082 | $  111,547 |

Source SEC—Apple, Form 10-K

## Table 23.4 Apple—Consolidated statement of cash flows

CONSOLIDATED STATEMENTS OF CASH FLOWS
(In millions)

| | September 27, 2014 | September 28, 2013 | September 29, 2012 |
|---|---|---|---|
| Cash and cash equivalents, beginning of the year | $ 14,259 | $ 10,746 | $ 9,815 |
| Operating activities: | | | |
| Net income | 39,510 | 37,037 | 41,733 |
| Adjustments to reconcile net income to cash generated by operating activities: | | | |
| Depreciation and amortization | 7,946 | 6,757 | 3,277 |
| Share-based compensation expense | 2,863 | 2,253 | 1,740 |
| Deferred income tax expense | 2,347 | 1,141 | 4,405 |
| Changes in operating assets and liabilities: | | | |
| Accounts receivable, net | (4,232) | (2,172) | (5,551) |
| Inventories | (76) | (973) | (15) |
| Vendor non-trade receivables | (2,220) | 223 | (1,414) |
| Other current and non-current assets | 167 | 1,080 | (3,162) |
| Accounts payable | 5,938 | 2,340 | 4,467 |
| Deferred revenue | 1,460 | 1,459 | 2,824 |
| Other current and non-current liabilities | 6,010 | 4,521 | 2,552 |
| Cash generated by operating activities | 59,713 | 53,666 | 50,856 |
| Investing activities: | | | |
| Purchases of marketable securities | (217,128) | (148,489) | (151,232) |
| Proceeds from maturities of marketable securities | 18,810 | 20,317 | 13,035 |
| Proceeds from sales of marketable securities | 189,301 | 104,130 | 99,770 |
| Payments made in connection with business acquisitions, net | (3,765) | (496) | (350) |
| Payments for acquisition of property, plant and equipment | (9,571) | (8,165) | (8,295) |
| Payments for acquisition of intangible assets | (242) | (911) | (1,107) |
| Other | 16 | (160) | (48) |
| Cash used in investing activities | (22,579) | (33,774) | (48,227) |
| Financing activities: | | | |
| Proceeds from issuance of common stock | 730 | 530 | 665 |
| Excess tax benefits from equity awards | 739 | 701 | 1,351 |
| Taxes paid related to net share settlement of equity awards | (1,158) | (1,082) | (1,226) |
| Dividends and dividend equivalents paid | (11,126) | (10,564) | (2,488) |
| Repurchase of common stock | (45,000) | (22,860) | 0 |
| Proceeds from issuance of long-term debt, net | 11,960 | 16,896 | 0 |
| Proceeds from issuance of commercial paper, net | 6,306 | 0 | 0 |
| Cash used in financing activities | (37,549) | (16,379) | (1,698) |
| Increase/(decrease) in cash and cash equivalents | (415) | 3,513 | 931 |
| Cash and cash equivalents, end of the year | $ 13,844 | $ 14,259 | $ 10,746 |
| Supplemental cash flow disclosure: | | | |
| Cash paid for income taxes, net | $ 10,026 | $ 9,128 | $ 7,682 |
| Cash paid for interest | $ 339 | $ 0 | $ 0 |

*Source* SEC—Apple, Form 10-K

# 23.3 MICROSOFT

## 23.3.1 Overview

Microsoft was founded in 1975. Its mission is to enable people and organizations throughout the world to do more and achieve more by creating technology that transforms the way people learn, work, play, and communicate. Microsoft develops and markets software, services, and devices that deliver new opportunities, greater convenience, and enhanced value to people's lives. Microsoft does business worldwide and has offices in more than 100 countries.

Microsoft generates revenue by developing, licensing, and supporting a wide range of software products and services, by designing, manufacturing, and selling devices, and by delivering relevant online advertising to a global customer audience. In addition to selling individual products and services, Microsoft offers suites of products and services.

Microsoft products include operating systems for computing devices, servers, phones, and other intelligent devices; server applications for distributed computing environments; productivity applications; business solution applications; desktop and server management tools; software development tools; video games; and online advertising. Microsoft also designs and sells hardware including PCs, tablets, gaming and entertainment consoles, phones, other intelligent devices, and related accessories.

Microsoft offers cloud-based solutions that provide customers with software, services, and content over the Internet by way of shared computing resources located in centralized data centers. Examples of cloud-based computing services include Bing, Microsoft Azure, Microsoft Dynamics CRM Online, Microsoft Office 365, OneDrive, Skype, Xbox Live, and Yammer. Cloud revenue is earned primarily from usage fees, advertising, and subscriptions. We also provide consulting and product and solution support services, and we train and certify computer system integrators and developers.

Microsoft conducts research and develops advanced technologies for future software, devices, and services. The company believes that we will continue to grow and meet our customers' needs as the productivity and platform company for the mobile-first and cloud-first world. That it will continue to create new opportunities for partners, increase customer satisfaction, and improve our service excellence, business efficacy, and internal processes.

*Operating Segments*
During the first quarter of fiscal year 2014, Microsoft has changed its organizational structure as part of our transformation to a devices and services company. As a result, information that our chief operating decision maker regularly reviews for the purposes of allocating resources and assessing performance changed. Therefore, beginning in fiscal year 2014, Microsoft reported its financial performance based on its new segments:

- Devices and Consumer ("D&C") Licensing,
- D&C Hardware, and
- D&C Other, Commercial Licensing, and Commercial Other.

On April 25, 2014, Microsoft acquired substantially all of Nokia Corporation's ("Nokia") Devices and Services Business ("NDS"). Microsoft reports the financial performance of NDS in its new Phone Hardware segment. Prior to the acquisition of NDS, financial results associated with Microsoft joint strategic initiatives with Nokia were reflected in our D&C Licensing segment. The contractual relationship with Nokia related to those initiatives terminated in conjunction with the acquisition. With the creation of the new Phone Hardware segment, the D&C Hardware segment was renamed Computing and Gaming Hardware in the fourth quarter of fiscal year 2014.

Microsoft segments provide management with a comprehensive financial view of our key businesses. The segments enable the alignment of strategies and objectives across the development, sales, marketing, and services organizations, and they provide a framework for timely and rational allocation of development, sales, marketing, and services resources within businesses. Additional information on our operating segments and geographic and product information is contained in Note 21—Segment Information and Geographic Data of the Notes to Financial Statements.

*Competition*

The Windows operating system faces competition from various software products and from alternative platforms and devices, mainly from Apple and Google. We believe Windows competes effectively by giving customers choice, value, flexibility, security, an easy-to-use interface, compatibility with a broad range of hardware and software applications, including those that enable productivity, and the largest support network for any operating system.

Competitors to the versions of Office included in D&C Licensing include global application vendors such as Apple and Google, numerous web-based competitors, and local application developers in Asia and Europe. Apple distributes versions of its preinstalled application software, such as email, note taking, and calendar products, through its PCs, tablets, and phones. Google provides a hosted messaging and productivity suite and distributes its productivity services through the Android and Chrome operating systems. Web-based offerings competing with individual applications can also position themselves as alternatives to our products. We believe our products compete effectively based on our strategy of providing powerful, flexible, secure, and easy-to-use solutions that work across a variety of devices.

Windows Phone operating system faces competition from iOS, Android, and Blackberry operating systems. Windows Phone competes based on differentiated user interface, personalized applications, compatibility with Windows PCs and tablets, and other unique capabilities.

### 23.3.2    Business Strategy

Accessibility, as part of overall usability, is a fundamental consideration for Microsoft during product design, development, evaluation, and release. Microsoft endeavors to integrate accessibility into planning, design, research, development, testing, and documentation. Microsoft addresses accessibility by:

- Continuing our long-standing commitment and leadership in developing innovative accessibility solutions;
- Making the computer easier to see, hear, and use by building accessibility into Microsoft products and services;
- Promoting innovation of accessibility in the development community and working with industry organizations to encourage innovation; and
- Building collaborative relationships with a wide range of organizations to raise awareness of the importance of accessibility in meeting the technology needs of people with disabilities.

### 23.3.3    Microsoft Financial Statements

*23.3.3.1 Microsoft—Consolidated Statement of Income*
The increase in the revenue is line up with the increase in the COGS from 2012 to 2014. The net income is also growing within the same reported period: $16,978 (2012) to $21,863 (2013) to $22,074 (2014) (Table 23.5).

*23.3.3.2 Microsoft—Consolidated Balance Sheet*
The amount of the total assets has increased from $142,431 to $172,384. The liabilities' increase seems to be triggered by the current liabilities within the same reported periods (Table 23.6).

**Table 23.5** Microsoft—Consolidated statement of income

# INCOME STATEMENTS

(In millions, except per share amounts)

| Year Ended June 30, | | 2014 | | 2013 | | 2012 |
|---|---|---|---|---|---|---|
| Revenue | $ | 86,833 | $ | 77,849 | $ | 73,723 |
| Cost of revenue | | 26,934 | | 20,249 | | 17,530 |
| Gross margin | | 59,899 | | 57,600 | | 56,193 |
| Research and development | | 11,381 | | 10,411 | | 9,811 |
| Sales and marketing | | 15,811 | | 15,276 | | 13,857 |
| General and administrative | | 4,821 | | 5,149 | | 4,569 |
| Goodwill impairment | | 0 | | 0 | | 6,193 |
| Integration and restructuring | | 127 | | 0 | | 0 |
| Operating income | | 27,759 | | 26,764 | | 21,763 |
| Other income, net | | 61 | | 288 | | 504 |
| Income before income taxes | | 27,820 | | 27,052 | | 22,267 |
| Provision for income taxes | | 5,746 | | 5,189 | | 5,289 |
| Net income | $ | 22,074 | $ | 21,863 | $ | 16,978 |
| Earnings per share: | | | | | | |
| Basic | $ | 2.66 | $ | 2.61 | $ | 2.02 |
| Diluted | $ | 2.63 | $ | 2.58 | $ | 2.00 |
| Weighted average shares outstanding: | | | | | | |
| Basic | | 8,299 | | 8,375 | | 8,396 |
| Diluted | | 8,399 | | 8,470 | | 8,506 |
| Cash dividends declared per common share | $ | 1.12 | $ | 0.92 | $ | 0.80 |

*Source* SEC—Microsoft, Form 10-K

### 23.3.3.3 Microsoft—Consolidated Statement of Shareholders' Equity

The amount of the total shareholders' equity has increased consistently from $66,363 (2012) to $78,944 (2013) to $89,784 (2014) (Table 23.7).

### 23.3.3.4 Microsoft—Consolidated Statement of Cash Flows

The net cash from operations has increased from $28,833 (2013) to $32,231 (2014) after a small decline in 2013. The net cash used in financing has increased from $8148 (2013) to $8394 (2014) after a decline in 2013. The same can be said concerning the net cash used in investing (Table 23.8).

**Table 23.6**   Microsoft—Consolidated balance sheet

**Assets**

| | | |
|---|---:|---:|
| Current assets: | | |
| Cash and cash equivalents | $   8,669 | $    3,804 |
| Short-term investments (including securities loaned of **$541** and $579) | 77,040 | 73,218 |
| Total cash, cash equivalents, and short-term investments | 85,709 | 77,022 |
| Accounts receivable, net of allowance for doubtful accounts of **$301** and $336 | 19,544 | 17,486 |
| Inventories | 2,660 | 1,938 |
| Deferred income taxes | 1,941 | 1,632 |
| Other | 4,392 | 3,388 |
| Total current assets | 114,246 | 101,466 |
| Property and equipment, net of accumulated depreciation of **$14,793** and $12,513 | 13,011 | 9,991 |
| Equity and other investments | 14,597 | 10,844 |
| Goodwill | 20,127 | 14,655 |
| Intangible assets, net | 6,981 | 3,083 |
| Other long-term assets | 3,422 | 2,392 |
| Total assets | $ 172,384 | $ 142,431 |
| **Liabilities and stockholders' equity** | | |
| Current liabilities: | | |
| Accounts payable | $   7,432 | $    4,828 |
| Short-term debt | 2,000 | 0 |
| Current portion of long-term debt | 0 | 2,999 |
| Accrued compensation | 4,797 | 4,117 |
| Income taxes | 782 | 592 |
| Short-term unearned revenue | 23,150 | 20,639 |
| Securities lending payable | 558 | 645 |
| Other | 6,906 | 3,597 |
| Total current liabilities | 45,625 | 37,417 |
| Long-term debt | 20,645 | 12,601 |
| Long-term unearned revenue | 2,008 | 1,760 |
| Deferred income taxes | 2,728 | 1,709 |
| Other long-term liabilities | 11,594 | 10,000 |
| Total liabilities | 82,600 | 63,487 |
| Commitments and contingencies | | |
| Stockholders' equity: | | |
| Common stock and paid-in capital – shares authorized 24,000; outstanding **8,239** and 8,328 | 68,366 | 67,306 |
| Retained earnings | 17,710 | 9,895 |
| Accumulated other comprehensive income | 3,708 | 1,743 |
| Total stockholders' equity | 89,784 | 78,944 |
| Total liabilities and stockholders' equity | $ 172,384 | $ 142,431 |

*Source* SEC—Microsoft, Form 10-K

## 23.4   FINANCIAL ANALYSIS

### 23.4.1   Common-Size Income Statement Analysis

Common-size income statement is an income statement in which states every line item on the income statement as a percentage of the value of sales. Common-size analysis is an excellent tool to compare companies of different sizes or to compare different years of data for the same company. There are two reasons to use common-size analysis: (1) to evaluate

**Table 23.7**  Microsoft—Consolidated statement of shareholders' equity

STOCKHOLDERS' EQUITY STATEMENTS

(In millions)

| Year Ended June 30, | 2014 | 2013 | 2012 |
|---|---|---|---|
| **Common stock and paid-in capital** | | | |
| Balance, beginning of period | $ 67,306 | $ 65,797 | $ 63,415 |
| Common stock issued | 607 | 920 | 1,924 |
| Common stock repurchased | (2,328) | (2,014) | (1,714) |
| Stock-based compensation expense | 2,446 | 2,406 | 2,244 |
| Stock-based compensation income tax benefits (deficiencies) | 272 | 190 | (75) |
| Other, net | 63 | 7 | 3 |
| Balance, end of period | 68,366 | 67,306 | 65,797 |
| **Retained earnings (deficit)** | | | |
| Balance, beginning of period | 9,895 | (856) | (8,195) |
| Net income | 22,074 | 21,863 | 16,978 |
| Common stock cash dividends | (9,271) | (7,694) | (6,721) |
| Common stock repurchased | (4,988) | (3,418) | (2,918) |
| Balance, end of period | 17,710 | 9,895 | (856) |
| **Accumulated other comprehensive income** | | | |
| Balance, beginning of period | 1,743 | 1,422 | 1,863 |
| Other comprehensive income (loss) | 1,965 | 321 | (441) |
| Balance, end of period | 3,708 | 1,743 | 1,422 |
| Total stockholders' equity | $ 89,784 | $ 78,944 | $ 66,363 |

See accompanying notes.

*Source* SEC—Microsoft, Form 10-K

information from one period to the next within a company and (2) to evaluate a company relative to its competitors.

- Apple

The increase in the net sales from $156,508 (2012) to $170,910 (2013) to $182,795 (2014) is not reflected in the net income from the same period. The trends in the net income are a bit hard to comprehend. However, the amount of cash dividends declared per common share has significantly increased within the same period (Table 23.9).

- Microsoft

The increase in the amount of the revenue from $73,723 (2012) to $77,849 (2013) to $86,833 is reflected in the increase of the net income from the same period. The cash dividends declared per common share has also increase within that period (Table 23.10).

## Table 23.8   Microsoft—Consolidated statement of cash flows

**CASH FLOWS STATEMENTS**

(In millions)

| Year Ended June 30, | 2014 | 2013 | 2012 |
|---|---|---|---|
| **Operations** | | | |
| Net income | $ 22,074 | $ 21,863 | $ 16,978 |
| Adjustments to reconcile net income to net cash from operations: | | | |
| Goodwill impairment | 0 | 0 | 6,193 |
| Depreciation, amortization, and other | 5,212 | 3,755 | 2,967 |
| Stock-based compensation expense | 2,446 | 2,406 | 2,244 |
| Net recognized losses (gains) on investments and derivatives | (109) | 80 | (200) |
| Excess tax benefits from stock-based compensation | (271) | (209) | (93) |
| Deferred income taxes | (331) | (19) | 954 |
| Deferral of unearned revenue | 44,325 | 44,253 | 36,104 |
| Recognition of unearned revenue | (41,739) | (41,921) | (33,347) |
| Changes in operating assets and liabilities: | | | |
| Accounts receivable | (1,120) | (1,807) | (1,156) |
| Inventories | (161) | (802) | 184 |
| Other current assets | (29) | (129) | 493 |
| Other long-term assets | (628) | (478) | (248) |
| Accounts payable | 473 | 537 | (31) |
| Other current liabilities | 1,075 | 146 | 410 |
| Other long-term liabilities | 1,014 | 1,158 | 174 |
| Net cash from operations | 32,231 | 28,833 | 31,626 |
| **Financing** | | | |
| Proceeds from issuance of short-term debt, maturities of 90 days or less, net | 500 | 0 | 0 |
| Proceeds from issuance of debt | 10,350 | 4,883 | 0 |
| Repayments of debt | (3,888) | (1,346) | 0 |
| Common stock issued | 607 | 931 | 1,913 |
| Common stock repurchased | (7,316) | (5,360) | (5,029) |
| Common stock cash dividends paid | (8,879) | (7,455) | (6,385) |
| Excess tax benefits from stock-based compensation | 271 | 209 | 93 |
| Other | (39) | (10) | 0 |
| Net cash used in financing | (8,394) | (8,148) | (9,408) |
| **Investing** | | | |
| Additions to property and equipment | (5,485) | (4,257) | (2,305) |
| Acquisition of companies, net of cash acquired, and purchases of intangible and other assets | (5,937) | (1,584) | (10,112) |
| Purchases of investments | (72,690) | (75,396) | (57,250) |
| Maturities of investments | 5,272 | 5,130 | 15,575 |
| Sales of investments | 60,094 | 52,464 | 29,700 |
| Securities lending payable | (87) | (168) | (394) |
| Net cash used in investing | (18,833) | (23,811) | (24,786) |
| Effect of exchange rates on cash and cash equivalents | (139) | (8) | (104) |
| Net change in cash and cash equivalents | 4,865 | (3,134) | (2,672) |
| Cash and cash equivalents, beginning of period | 3,804 | 6,938 | 9,610 |
| Cash and cash equivalents, end of period | $ 8,669 | $ 3,804 | $ 6,938 |

See accompanying notes.

**Table 23.9** Apple—Common-sized income statement

CONSOLIDATED STATEMENTS OF OPERATIONS
(In millions, except number of shares which are reflected in thousands and per share amounts)

| | Years ended | | | | | |
|---|---|---|---|---|---|---|
| | September 27,2014 | % | September 28,2013 | % | September 29,2012 | % |
| Net Sales | $182,795 | 100 | 170,910 | 100 | 156,508 | 100 |
| Cost of Sales | 112,258 | 61 | 106,606 | 62 | 87,846 | 56 |
| Gross Margin | $70,537 | 39 | $64,304 | 38 | $68,662 | 44 |
| Operating expenses: | | | | | | |
| Research and development | 6,041 | 3 | 4,475 | 3 | 3,381 | 2 |
| Selling, general & administrative | 11,993 | 7 | 10,830 | 6 | 10,040 | 6 |
| Total Operating expenses | 18,034 | 10 | 15,305 | 9 | 13,421 | 9 |
| Operating Income | 52,503 | 29 | 48,999 | 29 | 55,241 | 35 |
| Other income(expenses),net | 980 | 1 | 1,156 | 1 | 522 | 0 |
| Income before provision for income tax | 53,483 | 29 | 50,155 | 29 | 55,763 | 36 |
| Provision for income tax | 13,973 | 8 | 13,118 | 8 | 14,030 | 9 |
| Net Income | 39,510 | 22 | 37,037 | 22 | 41,733 | 27 |
| Earning per share: | | | | | | |
| Basic | 6.49 | | 5.72 | | 6.38 | |
| Diluted | 6.45 | | 5.68 | | 6.31 | |
| Shares used in computing earning per share: | | | | | | |
| Basic | 6,085,572 | | 6,477,320 | | 6,543,726 | |
| Diluted | 6,122,663 | | 6,521,634 | | 6,617,483 | |
| Cash dividends declared per common share | 1.82 | | 1.64 | | 0.38 | |

**Table 23.10** Microsoft—Common-sized income statement

INCOME STATEMENTS
(in millions except per share amounts)

| Year Ended June,30 | 2014 | % | 2013 | % | 2012 | % |
|---|---|---|---|---|---|---|
| | $ | | $ | | $ | |
| Revenue | 86,833 | 100 | 77,849 | 100 | 73,723 | 100 |
| Cost of revenue | 26,934 | 31 | 20,249 | 26 | 17,530 | 24 |
| Gross margin | 59,899 | 69 | 57,600 | 74 | 56,193 | 76 |
| Research and development | 11,381 | 13 | 10,411 | 13 | 9,811 | 13 |
| Sales and marketing | 15,811 | 18 | 15,276 | 20 | 13,857 | 19 |
| General and administrative | 4,821 | 6 | 5,149 | 7 | 4,569 | 6 |
| Goodwill impairment | 0 | 0 | 0 | 0 | 6,193 | 8 |
| Integration and restructuring | 127 | 0 | 0 | 0 | 0 | 0 |
| Operating Income | 27,759 | 32 | 26,764 | 34 | 21,763 | 30 |
| Other income net | 61 | 0 | 288 | 0 | 504 | 1 |
| Income before income taxes | 27,820 | 32 | 27,052 | 35 | 22,267 | 30 |
| Provision for income taxes | 5,746 | 7 | 5,189 | 7 | 5,289 | 7 |
| Net income | 22,074 | 25 | 21,863 | 28 | 16,978 | 23 |
| Earning per share: | | | | | | |
| Basic | 2.66 | | 2.61 | | 2.02 | |
| Diluted | 2.63 | | 2.58 | | 2 | |
| Weighted average shares outstanding: | | | | | | |
| Basic | 8,299 | | 8,375 | | 8,396 | |
| Diluted | 8,399 | | 8,470 | | 8,506 | |
| Cash dividends declared per common share | 1.12 | | 0.92 | | 0.8 | |

### 23.4.2 Common-Size Balance Sheet Analysis

A common-size balance sheet is a balance sheet that displays both the numeric value and relative percentage for total assets, total liabilities, and equity accounts. Each single asset line item is compared to the value of total assets, and each single liability line item is compared to the value of total liabilities, and any equity account is compared to the value of total equity.

- Apple

The amount of the account receivables seems to increase at a lower rate 8% (2014) than the amount of the account payables, 13% (2014). Also, we can notice a significant increase in the amount of the long-term marketable securities (Table 23.11).

- Microsoft

The change in the amount of the account receivables from 12% (2013) to 11% (2014) seems to line up with the change in the decrease of the amount of the account payables, 3% (2013) to 4% (2014). The short-term investment has decreased within the two years (Table 23.12).

**Table 23.11**  Apple—Common-sized balance sheet

| | September 27,2014 | % | September 28,2013 | % |
|---|---|---|---|---|
| **CONSOLIDATED BALANCE SHEETS** | | | | |
| (in millions, except number of shares which are reflected in thousands and per share value) | | | | |
| ASSETS: | | | | |
| Current assets: | | | | |
| Cash and cash equivalents | 13,844 | 6 | 14,259 | 7 |
| Short term marketable securities | 11,233 | 5 | 26,287 | 13 |
| Account Receivable,less allowances of $86 and $99,respectively | 17,460 | 8 | 13,102 | 6 |
| Inventories | 2,111 | 1 | 1,764 | 1 |
| Deferred tax assets | 4,318 | 2 | 3,453 | 2 |
| Vendor non-trade receivables | 9,759 | 4 | 7,539 | 4 |
| other current assets | 9,806 | 4 | 6,882 | 3 |
| Total current assets | 68,531 | 30 | 73,286 | 35 |
| Long term marketable securities | 130,162 | 56 | 106,215 | 51 |
| Property,plant and equipment, net | 20,624 | 9 | 16,597 | 8 |
| Goodwill | 4,616 | 2 | 1,577 | 1 |
| Acquired intangible assets, net | 4,142 | 2 | 4,179 | 2 |
| Other assets | 3,764 | 2 | 5,146 | 2 |
| Total Assets | 231,839 | 100 | 207,000 | 100 |
| **LIABILITIES AND SHAREHOLDERS' EQUITY:** | | | | |
| Current Liabilities: | | | | |
| Accounts payable | 30,196 | 13 | 22,367 | 11 |
| Accrued expenses | 18,453 | 8 | 13,856 | 7 |
| Deferred revenue | 8,491 | 4 | 7,435 | 4 |
| Commercial paper | 6,308 | 3 | 0 | 0 |
| Total current liabilities | 63,448 | 27 | 43,658 | 21 |
| Deferred revenue-non current | 3,031 | 1 | 2,625 | 1 |
| Long term debt | 28,987 | 13 | 16,960 | 8 |
| Other non-current liabilities | 24,826 | 11 | 20,208 | 10 |
| Total liabilities | 120,292 | 52 | 83,451 | 40 |
| Commitments and contingencies | | | | |
| Shareholders' equity: | | | | |
| Common stock and additional paid-in capital, $0.00001 par value; 12,600,000 shares authorized; 5,866,161 and 6,294,494 shares issued and outstanding, respectively | 23,313 | 10 | 19,764 | 9.50 |
| Retained earnings | 87,152 | 38 | 104,256 | 50 |
| Accumulated other comprehensive income (loss) | 1,082 | 0.47 | -471 | -0.23 |
| Total shareholders' equity | 111,547 | 48 | 123,549 | 60 |
| Total liabilities and shareholders' equity | 231,839 | 100 | 207,000 | 100 |

**Table 23.12**   Microsoft—Common-sized balance sheet

| ASSETS | | % | | % |
|---|---|---|---|---|
| Current assets: | | | | |
| Cash and cash equivalents | 8,669 | 5 | 3,804 | 3 |
| Short term investments(including securities loaned $541 and $579 | 77,040 | 45 | 73,218 | 51 |
| Total cash and cash equivalents and short term investments | 85,709 | 50 | 77,022 | 54 |
| Account Receivable,less allowances for doubtful accounts $301 and $336 | 19,544 | 11 | 17,486 | 12 |
| Inventories | 2,660 | 2 | 1,938 | 1 |
| Deferred income taxes | 1,941 | 1 | 1,632 | 1 |
| Other | 4,392 | 3 | 3,388 | 2 |
| Total current assets | 114,246 | 66 | 101,466 | 71 |
| Property and equipment,net of accumulated depreciation of $14,793 and $12,513 | 13,011 | 8 | 9,991 | 7 |
| Equity and other investments | 14,597 | 8 | 10,844 | 8 |
| Goodwill | 20,127 | 12 | 14,655 | 10 |
| Intangible assets, net | 6,981 | 4 | 3,083 | 2 |
| Other long-term assets | 3,422 | 2 | 2,392 | 2 |
| Total Assets | 172,384 | 100 | 142,431 | 100 |

| LIABILITIES AND SHAREHOLDERS' EQUITY: | | | | |
|---|---|---|---|---|
| Current Liabilities: | | | | |
| Accounts payable | 7,432 | 4 | 4,828 | 3 |
| Short-term debt | 2,000 | 1 | 0 | 0 |
| Current portion of long-term debt | 0 | 0 | 2,999 | 2 |
| Accrued compensation | 4,797 | 3 | 4,117 | 3 |
| Income taxes | 782 | 0 | 592 | 0 |
| Short-term unearned revenue | 23,150 | 13 | 20,639 | 14 |
| Securities lending payable | 558 | 0 | 645 | 0 |
| Other | 6,906 | 4 | 3,597 | 3 |
| Total current liabilities | 45,625 | 26 | 37,417 | 26 |
| Long term debt | 20,645 | 12 | 12,601 | 9 |
| long-term unearned revenue | 2,008 | 1 | 1,760 | 1 |
| Deferred income taxes | 2,728 | 2 | 1,709 | 1 |
| Other long term liabilities | 11,594 | 7 | 10,000 | 7 |
| Total liabilities | 82,600 | 48 | 63,487 | 45 |
| Commitments and contingencies | | | | |
| Stockholders' equity: | | | | |
| Common stock and additional paid-in capital-shares authorized 24,000 outstanding 8,239 and 8,328 | 68,366 | 40 | 67,306 | 47 |
| Retained earnings | 17,710 | 10 | 9,895 | 7 |
| Accumulated other comprehensive income | 3,708 | 2 | 1,743 | 1 |
| Total stockholders' equity | 89,784 | 52 | 78,944 | 55 |
| Total liabilities and stockholders' equity | 172,384 | 100 | 142,431 | 100 |

### 23.4.3    Comparative Common-Size Analysis

Common-size analysis is also an effective way of comparing two companies with different levels of revenues and assets within the same industry.

### 23.4.4    Financial Ratio Analysis

Financial ratios analysis is the most common and widespread tools used to analyze a business financial performance over a period of time, with key competitors and within its overall industry. The trend of these ratios over time is studied to check whether the financial status of a firm is improving or deteriorating, outperforming or underperforming. For the sake of this illustration, I selected the following ratios: three liquidity ratios (current ratio, quick ratio, and cash ratio); three solvency ratios (debt-to-assets ratio, debt-to-equity ratio, and financial leverage); and three profitability ratio margins (gross profit margin, operating profit margin, and net profit margin). Very often, analysts would also calculate market-to-book and value-to-book ratios, which are beyond the scope of this illustration.

### Liquidity Ratios

$$(i)\, \text{Current ratio} = \frac{\text{Total current assets}}{\text{Total current liabilities}}$$

Apple

**2013**   $\frac{73,286}{43,658} = 1.68$        **2014**   $\frac{68,531}{63,448} = 1.08$

Microsoft

**2013**   $\frac{101,466}{37,417} = 2.71$        **2014**   $\frac{114,246}{45,625} = 2.50$

$$(ii)\, \text{Quick ratio} = \frac{\begin{array}{c}(\text{Cash} + \text{Cash equivalents} \\ + \text{Marketable securities} + \text{Receivables})\end{array}}{\text{Total current liabilities}}$$

Apple

**2013**   $\frac{14,259 + 26,287 + 13,102}{43,658} = 1.23$   **2014**   $\frac{13,844 + 11,233 + 17,460}{63,448} = 0.67$

Microsoft

**2013**   $\frac{3804 + 73,218 + 17,486}{37,417} = 2.53$   **2014**   $\frac{8669 + 77,040 + 19,544}{45,625} = 2.31$

$$(iii)\, \text{Cash ratio} = \frac{(\text{Cash} + \text{Cash equivalents})}{\text{Total current liabilities}}$$

Apple

**2013** $\frac{14,259}{43,658} = 0.33$     **2014** $\frac{13,844}{63,448} = 0.22$

Microsoft

**2013** $\frac{3804}{37,417} = 0.10$     **2014** $\frac{8669}{45,625} = 0.19$

### Solvency Ratios

$$\text{(i) Debt-to-assets ratio} = \frac{\text{Total debt}}{\text{Total assets}}$$

Apple

**2013** $\frac{16,960}{207,000} = 0.08$     **2014** $\frac{28,987}{231,839} = 0.12$

Microsoft

**2013** $\frac{12,601}{142,431} = 0.09$     **2014** $\frac{20,645}{172,384} = 0.12$

$$\text{(ii) Debt-to-equity ratio} = \frac{\text{Total debt}}{\text{Total equity}}$$

Apple

**2013** $\frac{16,960}{123,549} = 0.14$     **2014** $\frac{28,987}{111,547} = 0.26$

Microsoft

**2013** $\frac{12,601}{78,944} = 0.16$     **2014** $\frac{20,645}{89,744} = 0.23$

$$\text{(iii) Financial leverage ratio} = \frac{\text{Total liabilities}}{\text{Total assets}}$$

Apple

**2013** $\frac{83,451}{207,000} = 0.40$     **2014** $\frac{120,292}{231,839} = 0.52$

Microsoft

**2013**        $\frac{63,487}{142,431} = 0.45$        **2014**        $\frac{82,600}{172,384} = 0.48$

## Profitability Ratio Margins

$$\text{(i) Gross profit margin} = \frac{(\text{Net Sales} - \text{COGS})}{\text{Net sales}}$$

Apple

**2013**        $\frac{170,910 - 106,606}{170,910} = 0.38$        **2014**        $\frac{182,795 - 112,258}{182,795} = 0.39$

Microsoft

**2013**        $\frac{77,849 - 20,249}{77,849} = 0.74$        **2014**        $\frac{86,833 - 26,934}{86,833} = 0.69$

$$\text{(ii) Operating profit margin} = \frac{\text{Operating income}}{\text{Net sales}}$$

Apple

**2013**        $\frac{48,999}{170,910} = 0.29$        **2014**        $\frac{52,503}{182,795} = 0.29$

Microsoft

**2013**        $\frac{26,764}{77,849} = 0.34$        **2014**        $\frac{27,759}{86,833} = 0.32$

$$\text{(iii) Net profit margin} = \frac{\text{Net income}}{\text{Net Sales}}$$

Apple

**2013**        $\frac{37,037}{170,910} = 0.22$        **2014**        $\frac{39,510}{182,795} = 0.22$

Microsoft

**2013**        $\frac{21,863}{77,849} = 0.28$        **2014**        $\frac{22,074}{86,833} = 0.25$

### 23.4.5   Comparative Financial Ratio Analysis

Comparative financial ratio analysis compares one company's performance to another business. Such a comparison allows managers and executives to determine the financial standing of the company relative to its key competitors under the same economic conditions. Comparative ratio analysis tends to strip away any accounting policies that change or alter a company's earnings, allowing for a one-tone review on financial performance. An effective comparative ratios analysis would require besides the industry information that the analyst look for each one of the companies used in the comparison its line of business (major products, major suppliers) as well as its major factors or influences.

# GLOSSARY

## A

*Accelerated depreciation*: Method that records greater depreciation than straight-line depreciation in the early years and less depreciation than straight-line in the later years of an asset's holding period.

*Accounting*: Recording and reporting of financial transactions, including the origination of the transaction, its recognition, processing, and summarization in the financial statements.

*Accounting cycle*: The sequence of steps followed in the accounting process to measure business transactions and transform the measurements into financial statements for a specific period.

*Accrual accounting*: The attempt to record the financial effects of transactions and other events in the periods in which those transactions or events occur rather than only in the periods in which cash is received or paid by the business, using all the techniques developed by accountants to apply the matching principle.

*Adjusted trial balance*: A trial balance prepared after all adjusting entries have been recorded and posted to the accounts. Should have equal credit and debit totals.

*Adjusting event*: An event after the reporting period that provides further evidence of conditions that existed at the end of the reporting period, including an event that indicates that the going concern

© The Editor(s) (if applicable) and The Author(s), under exclusive license to Springer Nature Switzerland AG, part of Springer Nature 2018
F. I. Lessambo, *Financial Statements*,
https://doi.org/10.1007/978-3-319-99984-5

assumption in relation to the whole or part of the enterprise is not appropriate.

*Amortization*: Gradual and periodic reduction of any amount, such as the periodic write-down of a bond premium, the cost of an intangible asset or periodic payment of mortgages or other debt.

*Asset*: An economic resource that is expected to be of benefit in the future. Probable future economic benefits obtained as a result of past transactions or events.

# B

*Balance sheet*: Is a statement of a company's financial position at a particular moment in time. It shows the two sides of a company's financial situation: what it owns and what it owes.

# C

*Carrying value*: Amount, net or contra account balances, that an asset or liability shows on the balance sheet of a company.

*Cash basis*: Method of bookkeeping by which revenues and expenditures are recorded when they are received and paid.

*Cost of goods sold*: Figure representing the cost of buying raw materials and producing finished goods.

*Current asset*: Asset that one can reasonably expect to convert into cash, sell, or consume in operations within a single operating cycle, or within a year if more than one cycle is completed each year.

*Current liability*: Obligation whose liquidation is expected to require the use of existing resources classified as current assets, or the creation of other current liabilities.

# D

*Deferred income taxes*: Assets or liabilities that arise from timing or measurement differences between tax and accounting principles.

*Dilution*: a reduction in earnings per share or an increase in loss per share resulting from the assumption that convertible instruments are converted, that options or warrants are exercised, or that ordinary shares are issued upon the satisfaction of specified conditions.

*Dividends*: Distribution of earnings to owners of a corporation in cash, other assets of the corporation, or the corporation's capital stock.

*Double-Declining-Balance Depreciation Method (DDB)*: Method of accelerated depreciation, approved by the Internal Revenue Service permitting twice the rate of annual depreciation as the straight-line depreciation method.

**E**

*Ending inventory*: Merchandise on hand at the end of an accounting period.

*Equity account*: Account in the equity section of the balance sheet. Includes capital stock, additional paid-in-capital, and retained earnings.

*Equity instrument*: Any contract that evidences a residual interest in the assets of an entity after deducting all of its liabilities.

*Event after the reporting period*: An event, which could be favorable or unfavorable, that occurs between the end of the reporting period and the date that the financial statements are authorized for issue.

*Expense*: Something spent on a specific item or for a particular purpose.

*Extraordinary items*: Events and transactions distinguished by their unusual nature and by the infrequency of their occurrence. Extraordinary items are reported separately, less applicable income taxes, in the entity's statement of income or operations.

**F**

*Factoring*: Selling a receivable at a discounted value to a third party for cash.

*Fair value*: the amount for which an asset is exchanged, or a liability settled, between knowledgeable, willing parties in an arm's length transaction.

*Financial Accounting Standards Board (FASB)*: Independent, private, non-governmental authority for the establishment of accounting principles in the United States.

*Financial instrument*: A contract that gives rise to a financial asset of one entity and a financial liability or equity instrument of another entity.

*Financial statements*: Presentation of financial data including balance sheets, income statements, and statements of cash flow, or any supporting statement that is intended to communicate an entity's financial position at a point in time and its results of operations for a period then ended.

*Foreign currency*: A currency other than the functional currency of the entity being referred to (for example, the dollar could be a foreign currency for a foreign entity). Composites of currencies, such as the Special Drawing Rights, used to set prices or denominate amounts of loans, and so forth, have the characteristics of foreign currency.

*Foreign currency statements*: Financial statements that employ as the unit of measure a functional currency that is not the reporting currency of the reporting entity.

*Foreign currency translation*: The process of expressing in the reporting currency of the reporting entity those amounts that are denominated or measured in a different currency.

*Functional currency*: An entity's functional currency is the currency of the primary economic environment in which the entity operates; normally, that is the currency of the environment in which an entity primarily generates and expends cash.

*Full disclosure*: Requirement to disclose all material facts relevant to a transaction.

## G

*General ledger*: Collection of all asset, liability, owners' equity, revenue, and expense accounts.

*Goodwill*: Premium paid in the acquisition of an entity over the fair value of its identifiable tangible and intangible assets less liabilities assumed.

## H

*Held-to-maturity security*: A debt security that management intends to hold to its maturity or payment date and whose cash value is not needed until that date.

*HistoricalCost*: Original cost of an asset to an entity.

## I

*Impairment*: An accounting principle that describes a permanent reduction in the value of a company's asset, normally a fixed asset.

*Income statement*: Summary of the effect of revenues and expenses over a period of time.

*Intangible asset*: Asset having no physical existence such as trademarks and patents.

*Interim financial statements*: Financial statements that report the operations of an entity for less than one year.

*Interim period:* a financial reporting period shorter than a full financial year (most typically a quarter or half-year).

*Inventory:* Tangible property held for sale, or materials used in a production process to make a product.

*Investment securities:* Generally, an instrument that provides an ownership position in a corporation (a stock), a creditor relationship with a corporation or governmental body (a bond), rights to contractual cash flows backed by pools of financial assets or rights to ownership such as those represented by options, subscription rights and subscription warrants.

## J

*Journal:* Any book containing original entries of daily financial transactions.

*Journal entry:* A notation in the general journal. It records a single transaction.

## L

*Lease:* Conveyance of land, buildings, equipment or other assets from one person (lessor) to another (lessee) for a specific period of time for monetary or other consideration, usually in the form of rent.

*Liability:* Debts or obligations owed by one entity to another entity payable in money, goods, or services.

*LIFO liquidation:* The reduction of inventory levels at year's end below beginning-of-the-year levels for businesses using the LIFO inventory method.

## M

*Mark-to-market:* Method of valuing assets that results in adjustment of an asset's carrying amount to its market value.

*MD&A:* SEC requirement in financial reporting for an explanation by management of significant changes in operations, assets, and liquidity.

## N

*Net interest margin:* A measure of the yield on interest earning assets relative to total interest expense. It is the amount of interest income less interest expense, divided by average interest earning assets.

*Net operating income:* Represents operating income less operating expenses for owned real estate properties.

*Non-adjusting event:* An event after the reporting period that is indicative of a condition that arose after the end of the reporting period.

*Non-controlling interest:* Portion of shareowners' equity in a subsidiary that is not attributable a parent company.

## O

*Operating cycle:* Period of time between the acquisition of goods and services involved in the manufacturing process and the final cash realization resulting from sales and subsequent collections.

*Operating expense:* An expense other than COGS that is incurred in running a business.

*Operating profit (or loss):* The difference between the revenues of a business and the related costs and expenses, excluding income derived from a sources other than its regular activities and before income deductions.

*Other comprehensive income:* Changes in assets and liabilities that do not result from transactions with shareowners and are not included in net income but are recognized in a separate component of shareowners' equity. Other comprehensive income includes the Investment securities; currency translation adjustments; cash flow hedges; recognized assets, liabilities or forecasted transactions that are attributable to a specific risk; benefit plans.

## P

*Periodic inventory system:* A system for determining inventory on hand by a physical count that is taken at the end of an accounting period.

*Perpetual inventory system:* A system that requires a continuous record of all receipts and withdrawals of each item of inventory.

*Pro forma:* Presentation of financial information that gives effect to an assumed event.

*Puttable instrument:* a financial instrument that gives the holder the right to put the instrument back to the issuer for cash or another financial asset or is automatically put back to the issuer on occurrence of an uncertain future event or the death or retirement of the instrument holder.

## R

*Receivables:* Amounts of money due from customers or other debtors.

*Re-measurement:* is a process to measure financial statement amounts that are denominated or stated in another currency into the functional currency of the reporting entity. Re-measurement affects earnings.

*Reporting currency*: The currency in which a reporting entity prepares its financial statements.

*Reporting entity*: An entity or group whose financial statements are being referred to.

*Retained earnings*: Accumulated undistributed earnings of a company retained for future needs or for future distribution to its owners.

*Revenues*: Sales of products, merchandise, and services; and earnings from interest, dividend, rent, etc.

## S

*Salvage value*: Selling price assigned to retired fixed assets or merchandise unsalable through usual channels.

*Securitization*: A process whereby loans or other receivables are packaged, underwritten and sold to investors. In a typical transaction, assets are sold to a special purpose entity, which purchases the assets with cash raised through issuance of beneficial interests (usually debt instruments) to third-party investors. Whether or not credit risk associated with the securitized assets is retained by the seller depends on the structure of the securitization.

*Statement of cash flows*: One of the basic financial statements that is required as part of a complete set of financial statements prepared in conformity with GAAP. It categorizes net cash provided or used during a period as operating, investing and financing activities, and reconciles beginning and ending cash and cash equivalents.

*Straight-line depreciation*: Account method that reflects an equal amount of wear and tear during each period of an asset's useful life.

## T

*Taxable income*: Taxable income is generally equal to a taxpayer's adjusted gross income during the tax year less any allowable exemptions and deductions.

*Transaction*: The act of transacting, especially a business agreement or exchange; event or condition recognized by an entry in the book account.

*Translation*: is the process used for expressing the financial results of a separate entity so that it may be included in the parent entity's consolidated financial statements when the separate entity's functional currency is different from the parent's. Translation affects equity.

## U

*Unearned income*: Payments received for services which have not yet been performed.

## V

*Valuation*: The process of determining the present value of a bond based on the current market interest rate.

*Variable Interest Entity (VIE)*: An entity that must be consolidated by its primary beneficiary, the party that holds a controlling financial interest. A variable interest entity has one or both of the following characteristics: (1) its equity at risk is not sufficient to permit the entity to finance its activities without additional subordinated financial support from other parties, or (2) as a group, the equity investors lack one or more of the following characteristics: (a) the power to direct the activities that most significantly affect the economic performance of the entity, (b) obligation to absorb expected losses, or (c) right to receive expected residual returns.

## W

*Weighted-average-cost method*: An average-cost method procedure for determining the cost of ending inventory under the periodic inventory system.

*Work in progress*: Inventory account consisting of partially completed goods awaiting completion and transfer to finished inventory.

*Working capital*: Excess of current assets over current liabilities.

*Write-offs*: Describes a reduction in recognized value. In accounting terminology, it refers to recognition of the reduced or zero value of an asset.

## Y

*Yield to maturity*: Rate of return on a security to its maturity, giving effect to the stated interest rate, accrual of discount, or amortization of premium.

# BIBLIOGRAPHY

ARB 43: Restatement and Revision of Accounting Research Bulletins—Chapter 3.

ASC 205-20-45-1B.

ASC 280-50-12.

ASC 280-50-13.

ASC 280-50-17.

ASC 350.

ASC 470-20-05—Liabilities.

ASC 480-10-25-4—Distinguishing Liabilities from Equity Provides That a Mandatorily Redeemable Financial Instrument Is Classified as a Liability Unless the Redemption is Required to Occur Only Upon the Liquidation or Termination of the Reporting Entity.

ASC 815-20-25.

ASC 815-20-25-3—Derivatives and Hedging.

ASC 825—Financial Instruments.

Baluch, Gartner et al. (2010): Consolidation Theories and Push-Down Accounting: Achieving Global Convergence. *Journal of Finance and Accounting* 3: 5.

Carvalho, John (2015): Divestopedia.

Colley and Volkan (1988): Accounting for Goodwill, Accounting Horizons, Sarasota, 2 (1): 35.

Coughlan, Anne (2014): New Pushdown Accounting Proposal Provides Clarity & Flexibility.

© The Editor(s) (if applicable) and The Author(s), under exclusive license to Springer Nature Switzerland AG, part of Springer Nature 2018
F. I. Lessambo, *Financial Statements*,
https://doi.org/10.1007/978-3-319-99984-5

FASB Emerging Issues Task Force, Income Tax Consequences of Issuing Convertible Debt with a Beneficial Conversion Feature (Issue No. 5–8), August 29, 2005 and FASB Staff Position APB 14-1, Accounting for Convertible Debt Instruments That May Be Settled in Cash Upon Conversion (Including Partial Cash Settlement), May 9, 2008.

FASB (2014): Business Combinations (Topic 805)—Pushdown Accounting.

Grahame, Steven (2006): Financial Management, September 2006, Papers P1, P2, and P3.

IAS 32.1.

IAS 32.8.

IAS 32.15.

IAS 32.16.

IAS 32.16A-D.

IAS 32.29-30.

IAS 32.33.

IAS 32.42.

IAS 32.48.

IAS 32.35.

IAS 33.2.

IAS 33.3.

IAS 33.66.

IAS 33.69.

IAS 33.68 and 68A.

IAS 33.24.

IAS 33.31.

IAS 33.41.

IAS 33.64.

IAS 33.64.

IAS 34.8.

IAS 34.20.

IAS 34.28.

IAS 34.37.

IAS 34.39.

IAS 34.23.

IAS 34.26.

IAS 36.

Lessambo, Felix (2016): *International Aspects of US Taxation System, Chapter 2.* New York: Palgrave Macmillan.

Saunders, Anthony and Marcia M. Cornett (2009): *Financial Markets & Institutions*, p. 224. Irwin: McGraw-Hill.

SFAS 157: Fair Value Measurements.

SFAS 159: The Fair Value Option for Financial Liabilities.

McCarthy, P. D. (2004): Unnecessary Complexity in Accounting Principles. *The CPA Journal* 74 (3): 18–19.

US Congress (2011): Present Law and Issues Related to the Taxation of Financial Instrument and Products—A Report to the Joint Committee on Taxation, p. 49.

United States Senate—Permanent Subcommittee on Investigations (April 1, 2014): Caterpillar's Offshore Tax Strategy, p. 9.

# INDEX

**A**

Accounting, 4–16, 18, 19, 21, 25, 30–
33, 35, 37, 38, 41, 43–45, 48,
51, 54–56, 65, 66, 69, 70, 72,
75, 76, 84–87, 95, 99, 100, 103,
105, 110, 113, 118, 122, 128,
130, 135, 136, 138, 140, 143,
151, 155, 161, 165, 166, 168,
175, 177–182, 187, 189, 201,
229, 243, 247, 264, 270–272,
274–276, 284, 289, 291–295,
299–303, 305, 307, 308, 311,
313, 314, 320, 322, 324
    Standard Board of Australia, 13
    Standard Board of Japan, 11
    Standard Board of New Zealand, 15
Account payable, 346
Account receivable, 57, 62, 223, 346
    assignment, 58, 59, 62, 292
    factoring, 58, 60–62, 236
    securitization, 63–66
Amortization, 24, 85–87, 95, 96, 102,
103, 109, 114, 122–124, 153,
178, 202, 237, 265, 282, 292

Assets
    current, 23, 24, 69, 71, 73, 75,
77–79, 86, 102, 104, 106, 117,
118, 121, 123, 126, 138, 141,
155, 163, 167, 172, 188, 189,
191, 202, 207–214, 222, 224,
225, 229, 230, 234, 236, 244,
246, 257, 264–268, 271, 275,
281, 285, 292–294, 296, 302,
317, 321, 324
    intangible, 10, 23, 24, 82, 95, 96,
99, 103, 105, 306, 322
    long-term, 21, 23, 33, 73, 77, 82,
96, 105, 117, 123, 188, 196–
198, 206–208, 211, 214, 222,
227–229, 242, 244, 253–255,
257, 287, 290, 306, 307, 310,
334, 346
    other current, 73, 75, 77, 79, 207,
210
    tangible, 82, 96
Assignment
    of receivables, 62

© The Editor(s) (if applicable) and The Author(s), under exclusive
license to Springer Nature Switzerland AG, part of Springer Nature 2018
F. I. Lessambo, *Financial Statements*,
https://doi.org/10.1007/978-3-319-99984-5

**B**

Bad debt, 55–57, 60, 179
    accounting for, 56, 179
Balance sheet, 10, 16, 18, 23, 24, 28,
    38, 53, 57, 65, 66, 69, 71, 73,
    75, 77, 96, 103, 114, 120, 121,
    125, 126, 128, 129, 131, 132,
    155, 156, 175, 181, 183, 189,
    191, 210, 213, 215–217, 227,
    235, 239, 244, 245, 253, 254,
    256, 257, 268, 273, 274, 320,
    321, 335, 345–347
Bank overdraft, 27, 28
Bank reconciliation, 25, 27
Bankruptcy ratios, 244


**C**

Capital, 3–5, 13, 23, 25, 75, 78, 79,
    81, 97, 107, 109, 128–132,
    135–139, 142, 153, 160, 161,
    171, 181, 185, 198, 205, 206,
    213, 219, 222–225, 227, 228,
    233, 237–239, 244, 270, 276,
    300, 307
    authorized, 130, 131
    issued, 4, 130–132, 135, 160, 181
    outstanding, 130, 131, 138, 139,
        171
Cash, 17, 23–34, 36–39, 47, 48, 54,
    60, 61, 63, 65, 66, 71, 73, 76,
    79, 81–83, 92, 96, 97, 100, 107,
    108, 111, 113–115, 118, 127,
    129, 131–138, 142, 153, 159,
    188, 189, 195–205, 207–213,
    223, 224, 229, 232–234, 237,
    238, 244, 253, 255–258, 261,
    262, 265, 268, 297, 301, 302,
    304–308, 315–317, 320, 341,
    343
    equivalent, 25, 82, 196
    petty, 25, 29, 31

Cash flow
    direct, 197, 200, 201, 256, 257,
        307
    financing, 27, 28, 65, 114, 195–
        198, 200, 202, 205, 256, 302,
        305–307
    indicator ratios, 232
    indirect, 197, 200–203, 256, 257,
        307
    investing, 32, 195–200, 202, 204,
        205, 302, 305–307
    operations, 81, 82, 114, 196, 201,
        202, 229, 302, 305
Common stock, 128–139, 141–143,
    170, 205, 206, 221, 255, 270,
    271, 273, 276
Computer software, 101–103
Consolidation, 16, 261, 264, 269–
    271, 274, 315
    methods, 264, 271, 311
Cost, 13, 14, 24, 30, 32, 33, 36–38,
    41–48, 55, 70, 71, 82–87, 90–92,
    95–97, 100, 107, 109, 111, 119,
    122–126, 129, 135, 136, 151–
    155, 159, 178, 185, 225, 226,
    231, 232, 242, 243, 252, 265,
    266, 268, 269, 273, 290–292,
    296, 300, 303, 314, 322, 332
    of building, 84, 152
    of equipment, 84, 152


**D**

Debt ratios, 227
Depletion, 24, 85, 202, 282
Depreciation, 24, 81, 82, 85–92, 99,
    112, 114, 128, 150, 151, 153,
    178, 182, 202, 203, 237, 252,
    282, 284, 308
    methods, 85, 284
Derivatives, 35, 36, 65, 104
    accounting for, 35

Differed taxes, 181
Disclosures, 162, 189, 195, 205, 277,
    285, 295, 300, 302, 309, 310,
    314, 322
Disposition of PPE, 91
Due process, 7, 11, 12

**E**
Earnings, 17, 21, 30, 33, 34, 37–39,
    48, 72, 97, 123, 127, 138, 143,
    153, 155, 176, 184, 186–189,
    191, 203, 214, 222, 229, 234,
    236, 237, 239, 245, 252, 293,
    319, 351
    changes in retained, 175, 177
    computation, 169, 171, 176
    EBIT, 152, 153, 222, 223, 229,
        245, 256
    EBITDA, 237, 256, 257
    per share, 34, 138, 139, 141, 142,
        169–173, 234, 235, 295, 318,
        319
    retained, 24, 128, 129, 136–139,
        143, 161, 168, 175–180, 234,
        238, 245, 253, 254, 265, 273,
        276, 314
Efficiency ratios, 217, 223
Entity theory, 272–274
Equity
    holding, 155
    method, 128, 265, 266, 270, 272,
        282, 283
Event, 18–20, 30, 33, 38, 60, 63, 97,
    98, 128, 177, 181, 187, 190,
    196, 227, 234, 271, 275, 293,
    305, 313, 318, 321, 322
    adjusting, 18, 19
    subsequent, 18, 318
Expenses, 23, 25, 29, 34, 69–71,
    79, 103, 118, 119, 123, 124,
    149–152, 154, 156, 182, 183,

    185, 191, 201, 213, 217, 218,
    220, 228, 232, 237, 244, 251,
    252, 255, 258, 265, 277, 278,
    283, 290–292, 295, 312, 319
    pre-paid, 23, 69

**F**
FASB, 4–9, 31, 95, 105, 127, 140,
    149, 151, 161, 165, 189, 271,
    272, 274, 275
    mission, 6
    oversight, 5, 6, 8
    standard-setter, 9
Financial, 3–11, 13–21, 24, 31–33,
    35–37, 48, 51, 63, 65–67, 76,
    78, 81, 82, 86, 93, 97, 107, 113,
    115, 119, 120, 127–129, 149,
    153, 155, 160–162, 166–169,
    172, 175, 179, 181–183, 185,
    187–189, 192, 195, 201, 204,
    207, 214–216, 219, 221, 222,
    227–229, 232, 234, 238, 239,
    241, 242, 245–247, 252, 255,
    257, 261, 264–266, 268–275,
    278, 280, 283, 285–287, 289,
    292, 293, 295, 296, 299–302,
    304, 305, 308, 309, 311–318
    reporting, 3–11, 13, 15, 16, 128,
        289, 322, 323
    standard-setter, 9
Financial Reporting Council (FRC),
    9, 13
First-in, First-out (FIFO), 46, 47,
    49–51, 178, 290, 303
Forecasting
    balance sheet, 252, 256, 257, 265
    cash flows, 255
    expenses, 252, 255
    income statement, 252–254, 256
    sales, 251–253, 255–257
Foreign currency

accounting, 161, 252, 257, 258,
261, 268
functional, 261, 262, 264, 266, 307
hedging, 39, 268
re-measurement, 267

**G**
Goodwill, 23, 82, 95–101, 178, 182,
202, 274–276, 289, 311, 313
impairment, 96–101, 178, 289

**H**
Hedging, 37–39, 268
accounting for, 37
fair value, 37–39
net investment, 37, 39
Highly inflationary, 261, 267, 268
Hybrid theory, 273

**I**
Income, 10, 16, 17, 21–23, 26, 27,
34, 37, 41, 46, 47, 51, 65, 69,
71, 72, 77, 79, 81, 91, 92, 103,
109, 114, 121, 123, 124, 126–
129, 140, 142, 143, 149–154,
156, 157, 160, 163–169, 174–
177, 179, 181–189, 191, 195,
196, 198, 200–205, 213, 214,
217–222, 226, 239, 251–254,
256, 264–268, 270, 272, 273,
275, 282, 284, 285, 290–292,
294–297, 301–303, 307, 308,
312, 315, 318–321, 323, 334,
340, 342, 343
unearned, 72
Income statement, 149–153, 164,
165, 175, 202, 268, 319, 321,
342
multiple-step, 149
single-step, 149, 150

Intangibles, 23, 306
International Financial Reporting
Standards (IFRS), 4, 5, 11,
13–16, 18, 28, 51, 100, 101,
204, 205, 270, 276, 299–301,
303, 304, 307, 308, 311, 313,
314, 324
core principles, 301
disclosures, 18, 54, 55
presentation, 167, 301, 303
Inventories, 24, 41, 42, 47, 79, 182,
252, 256, 291, 303, 322
periodic method, 49
perpetual method, 42, 43, 49, 152
valuation, 41, 46, 47
Investment valuation ratios, 234

**L**
Last-in, First-out (LIFO), 46–49, 51,
178, 290, 291
reserve, 47, 48
restrictions, 51
Lease
finance, 107, 109, 110, 114, 308
operating, 107, 109, 111, 114, 115
sale-leaseback, 111, 112
short-term, 113–115
Liabilities, 18–20, 23–25, 28, 31, 35,
65, 66, 75–79, 96, 99, 113, 114,
127, 128, 155, 156, 178, 181,
182, 189, 191, 205–211, 213,
215–217, 222, 224, 225, 227,
233, 235, 237, 244, 246, 252,
254, 262, 264–266, 274, 275,
285, 296, 302, 304, 307, 308,
313, 316–318, 322, 340, 345
current, 23, 24, 65, 69, 71, 73, 75,
77, 78, 189, 202, 207–211,
213, 222, 224, 225, 244,
264–266, 268, 302, 317, 321,
340

long-term, 23, 77, 207, 222, 227,
  228, 246, 254, 334
postretirement, 296
Losses, 20, 30, 32–34, 38, 39, 45, 54,
  55, 65, 82, 92, 119, 122, 123,
  149, 151, 152, 155, 159, 164,
  191, 202, 244, 251, 267, 268,
  273, 283, 284, 290–293, 312
net operating, 185

**M**
Management Discussion & Analysis
  (MD&A), 17
Marketable securities, 23–25, 32, 33,
  79, 208–210, 213, 224, 244,
  267, 334, 346

**O**
Other comprehensive income, 128,
  129, 159–161, 165–167, 302,
  313
accumulated, 128, 129, 160, 161,
  165–168
reclassification, 166, 167

**P**
Parent company, 186, 188, 261, 264,
  270, 272, 273
theory, 272, 273
Payable, 21, 23, 31, 59, 75, 76, 79,
  113, 117, 187, 197, 202, 203,
  212, 231, 232, 234, 253, 254,
  256, 257, 267, 268, 273, 346
accounts, 23, 43, 44, 59, 75, 76,
  79, 113, 197, 203, 211, 231,
  232, 244, 253, 256, 257
notes, 59, 76, 79, 197, 198, 244,
  254

Pension, 23, 117–126, 159, 278
Pension plans, 118–122, 124, 296
assets, 119, 120, 122–124, 159
defined benefits, 117, 120–122,
  124, 125, 296
defined contribution, 117–120
Preferred stock, 24, 78, 128, 131,
  132, 134, 170, 171, 255, 274
Proxy statement, 17

**R**
Ratios
bankruptcy, 229, 244–246
cash flows indicator, 232
debt, 33, 34, 56, 60, 62, 63, 65, 66,
  76, 77, 111, 127, 128, 159,
  202, 204–206, 210, 213–217,
  224, 227–229, 233, 237, 238,
  244–246, 251, 253, 348
efficiency, 208, 217, 220, 223, 225,
  226, 233, 239, 291, 299
financial, 3, 149, 161, 162, 182,
  183, 207, 215, 216, 221, 222,
  226–229, 233, 234, 238–242,
  245–247, 264, 269–272
investment valuation, 234
liquidity, 207–209, 213–215, 224,
  242, 244, 254, 348
operating performance, 229
profitability, 21, 149, 153, 217,
  219, 221–223, 239, 331, 348
solvency, 21, 214–217, 227, 348
strategic, 13, 162, 238, 339
Receivables, 53–58, 60–62, 66, 202,
  209, 210, 212, 223, 224, 244,
  247, 256, 268, 273, 346
aging method, 57
factoring trouble debt restructuring,
  54, 66

**S**

Securities, 4–6, 13, 16, 17, 23–25,
30–35, 55, 63, 66, 78, 130, 152,
155, 159, 160, 196, 207–209,
213, 224, 267, 296, 312, 318,
319, 334, 346
available-for-sale, 30, 32, 34, 35,
39, 155, 159, 191
held-to-maturity, 30, 32, 34, 37,
159
trading, 30, 32–34, 155, 207, 209
Segment
disclosure, 277, 289
identification, 280
reportable, 277, 278, 280, 282–
286, 295
statement, 277
Stock
common, 24, 46, 51, 77, 128–139,
141–143, 160, 170, 172, 174,
205, 221, 246, 255, 269–271,
273

dividends, 128, 129, 138, 139, 141,
143, 155, 156, 170, 171, 198,
205
employee, 139, 140, 142, 269, 310
preferred, 24, 78, 128, 129, 131,
132, 134, 135, 140, 170, 171,
246, 255, 274
split, 127, 138, 142, 143
treasury, 128, 129, 131, 135–137,
198, 205

**T**

Tangible, 82, 96
Taxable income, 21, 47, 183, 184

**W**

Working capital, 75, 77–79, 213, 224,
225, 239, 244
determinants, 78
financing, 78

Printed by Printforce, the Netherlands